T0339679

GODS, HEROES AND TYRANTS

GODS, HEROES AND TYRANTS

GREEK CHRONOLOGY IN CHAOS

Emmet Sweeney

Algora Publishing
New York

Library of Congress Cataloging-in-Publication Data —

Sweeney, Emmet John.
  Gods, heroes and tyrants: Greek chronology in chaos / Emmet Sweeney.
    p. cm.
  Includes bibliographical references and index.
    ISBN 978-0-87586-681-9 (trade paper: alk. paper) — ISBN 978-0-87586-682-6 (hard
cover: alk. paper) — ISBN 978-0-87586-683-3 (ebook) 1. Greece—History—To 146
B.C.—Chronology. I. Title. II. Title: Greek chronology in chaos.

  DF217.S94 2009
  938'.01—dc22

                        2008048531

Front Cover: An Attic Red-Figure Kylix Attributed to Colmar Painter © Christie's
Images/CORBIS. Date Created: ca. 490-480 B.C.

Printed in the United States

TABLE OF CONTENTS

Introduction

In the book that follows I shall be arguing that early Greek history as found in the textbooks is seriously misdated. I am not the first to make such a proposal. That honor goes to Immanuel Velikovsky, whose series *Ages in Chaos* (1952) held that the whole of ancient Near Eastern history before the classical age was a fabrication. Velikovsky identified Egyptian chronology as the source of the problem; and indeed the chronology of early Greek history, during the so-called "Mycenaean" period, was constructed along the lines demanded by Egyptian history. Thus when it became clear, towards the end of the nineteenth century, that the great flowering of "Mycenaean" culture coincided with the Egyptian New Kingdom, especially the Eighteenth Dynasty, it was decreed that the Mycenaean Age belonged in the fifteenth and fourteenth centuries BC, where Egyptologists had already placed the Eighteenth Dynasty. There were many dissenting voices at the time, most notably from the ranks of the classicists, and that great curmudgeon Cecil Torr fought a prolonged and very public battle with Flinders Petrie over the issue. In a thousand ways, claimed Torr, the Mycenaean Age showed itself to belong in the eighth or even seventh century BC. With what justification then did Petrie and the Egyptologists force their timescales into the world of the Aegean? Still, such doubts were ultimately laid to rest. The Egyptologists, who by this time were claiming a scientific foundation for their chronology, stressed the numerous connections disclosed by archaeology between the Mycenaean Age and the Eighteenth Dynasty and thereby compelled a second millennium date for the former.

Many of the objections raised by Torr were later resurrected by Velikovsky. Echoing his predecessor, Velikovsky demonstrated that Mycenaean art and culture seemed to find its closest parallels in art and culture of the eighth and seventh centuries BC. Furthermore, it was found that Mycenaean material occurred at no great depth beneath that of the classical period, whilst in many places it was apparently associated with Archaic ware of the seventh and even sixth centuries. This, for example, was the case at various sites throughout the Peloponnese and southern Greece and most especially on Crete and Cyprus. And, in a multitude of ways, legend and tradition agreed. So, for example, Homer's *Iliad* is full of references to the Phrygians, who were evidently close allies of the Trojans. Indeed, so intimate is the connection that we might suspect the Trojans themselves of being a branch of the Phrygian nation. Yet Phrygia, it is known, did not exist until the eighth century BC, when the Moschians, or Bryges, a Thracian people, migrated across the Bosporus and settled in Asia Minor. Greek tradition is explicit that Priam, king of Troy during the famous siege, was a contemporary of Gordius, the first Phrygian king and founder of the capital city Gordion.

All of this was highlighted by Velikovsky, as it had earlier been by Torr. Velikovsky also questioned Egyptian chronology itself, as Torr had done. Yet, whereas Torr had been content to argue his case in one short booklet, Velikovsky launched a major assault on the whole basis of ancient chronology, an assault published in a series of books named "Ages in Chaos." Yes, he said, the high point of the Mycenaean Age was contemporary with the Eighteenth Dynasty; but the Eighteenth Dynasty did not belong in the fifteenth and fourteenth centuries BC; it belonged in the tenth and ninth centuries.

Incredibly, in the debate which had raged at the end of the nineteenth century, no one (with the single exception of Torr) had thought to question the Egyptologists' dates. Revealing these to be flawed changed everything: Now the affinities between Mycenaean material and that of the seventh and eighth centuries, affinities demonstrated again and again, could be re-examined. According to Velikovsky, the Eighteenth Dynasty commenced near the beginning of the tenth century and ended in the last quarter of the ninth. This meant, in effect, that the most splendid epoch of Mycenae's history, during which numerous artifacts of mid-Eighteenth Dynasty origin were imported into Greece, must have occurred in the early ninth century BC. The gold-rich burials discovered by Schliemann in the Shaft Graves at Mycenae, which contained objects contemporaneous with the early Eighteenth Dynasty, must then have belonged to the early tenth or late eleventh century BC.

It was along these lines that Velikovsky worked. In fact, he died before *The Dark Ages of Greece* could see the light of day. Whether he could have completed the book remains a moot point, but one thing is certain: He would have encountered a serious problem. We have seen that following his revised Egyptian system he wanted to locate the flowering of Mycenaean culture in the ninth century. Yet examination of Mycenaean culture revealed to him, as to Torr and others, that that culture best fitted the world of the latter eighth and seventh centuries BC. Even Velikovsky admitted that the most famous event of the Mycenaean Age, the Trojan War, could not be placed earlier than the end of the eighth century. Thus, for Velikovsky, there was a long gap between the high point of Mycenaean civilization and the Trojan War. Now, Greek legend seemed to imply that the campaign against Troy had occurred at the very zenith of Mycenae's power and influence. This is the unmistakable impression gained by the prominence of the story in Hellenic tradition. Why then the centuries-long gap? What happened at Mycenae in the three centuries between the interments in the Shaft Graves and the reign of Agamemnon? According to the archaeology, these were the years of Mycenae's power.

Strangely, Velikovsky thus found himself in accord with conventional academics, for they too dated the fall of Troy long after Mycenae's high point. Cross-referencing with Egypt, they agreed that the flowering of Mycenaean culture be placed at the time of the Eighteenth Dynasty (fourteenth and fifteenth centuries), but that Troy fell around the start of the twelfth century. (Here, strikingly, they followed the date of 1184 BC supplied by Eratosthenes: a date arrived at by use of the Spartan King Lists of Herodotus. These lists were treated as a table of generations, each of which was accorded forty years.)

Thus both orthodox academics and Velikovsky suggested an uncomfortable gap of well over a century between the zenith of Mycenae's power and the most important event of the city's history — the campaign against Troy. The followers of orthodoxy got their gap from Egypt; Velikovsky got his from the Bible. In both cases, it has caused major embarrassment and confusion; one instance of which was the question of the Shaft Graves at Mycenae. Heinrich Schliemann, following a tradition reported by Pausanias that Agamemnon and his entourage were buried in a series of pits just within the walls of Mycenae's citadel, excavated in that very spot and uncovered the fabulously wealthy Shaft Graves. Understandably, Schliemann was convinced that these were the burials of Agamemnon and his followers. Had he not found them by trusting tradition? Were the burials not those of a powerful war-leader and his retainers? Did the contents of the pits not accord precisely with how tradition reported those burials, even down to the number of people interred and their sex? Yet soon it was pointed out that material from the Shaft Graves made them contemporaneous with the rise of the Eighteenth Dynasty, therefore sometime in the late sixteenth century BC. How then could they represent the final resting place of Agamemnon in 1184 BC?

After some initial resistance even Schliemann came to accept what appeared to be the inevitable: These were not the burials of Agamemnon and his followers, but the burials of some unknown autocrats who had lived over three centuries earlier!

Velikovsky's chronology did not solve this problem; it merely moved it down the timescale. For him too, the Shaft Graves contained the remains of an unknown lord and his retainers who lived and died three centuries before Agamemnon.

It will be obvious, of course, that Egyptian chronology is the key. The spoiling of Greek history has, as Velikovsky rightly believed, its source in the application of Egyptian timescales. Greek tradition said that Agamemnon was the most powerful ruler of Mycenae. It insisted that he was buried in the Shaft Graves within the citadel walls; and evidence of all kinds seemed to link the Mycenaean period and the Trojan War to the late eighth and seventh centuries BC. What then if the Eighteenth Dynasty actually began not in the sixteenth century BC (as the textbooks say) or the late eleventh century (as Velikovsky said), but the late eighth century?

If that was the case, everything would fit together in a logical and satisfying way. But who says the Eighteenth Dynasty began in the late eighth century? Gunnar Heinsohn says it.

I do not at this point wish to enter into a prolonged explanation of Heinsohn's system. Suffice to say that by the late 1980s he became aware that the mighty kingdom of Mita (or Mitanni), which arose in the Middle East simultaneously with the Eighteenth Dynasty, was none other than the empire of the "Mighty Medes" who, according to the ancient historians, had crushed the empire of Assyria sometime in the seventh century BC. (*Die Sumerer gab es nicht*, 1988) (The Mitanni too boasted of having conquered and plundered the cities of the "Old Assyrians," whose most famous kings were named Sargon and Naram-Sin). If the Mitanni were the Medes, then they belonged in the seventh century BC, and the Eighteenth Dynasty, with whom they interacted, belonged in the same epoch.

This of course represented a realignment of history much more dramatic than anything even Velikovsky had envisaged. It is a realignment which both Heinsohn and the present author have defended in detail over the past decade and a half. The implications for the histories of Egypt and Mesopotamia, as for the land of Israel, are far-reaching. From the point of view of Greek history, it means that the very high point of the Mycenaean Age belongs in the seventh century; and this means that the Shaft Graves in the Mycenaean citadel, which are contemporary with the start of the Eighteenth Dynasty, belong in the last quarter of the eighth century: precisely where a host of evidence would place the fall of Troy.

The book that follows then is a reconstruction of this early period of Greek history upon the new chronological lines. Right at the beginning the reader will find how, following Schliemann's discoveries at Troy, Mycenae and Tiryns, classical scholars were involved in a prolonged and rancorous debate about how these remains should be dated. The majority of classicists and Hellenic scholars were convinced that they belonged primarily in the eighth century BC. This was suggested by the evidence cited above, of which classical scholars were well aware. The Egyptologists however won out, and the Mycenaean period was placed firmly in the second millennium. The immediate consequence of this, we shall find, was the insertion of a "Dark Age" into the Greek past: for little or no material remains existed which could fill the gap of many centuries between the time of the Eighteenth Dynasty and the beginning of Greek history in the eighth and seventh centuries.

We shall then proceed to examine how the adoption of Egyptian dating caused problems in every area of Greek history. One of the most pressing of these related to the nature and interpretation of pottery sequences. Along with "Mycenaean" pottery, the early excavators found large quantities of a type they named "Geometric." It was clear right from the beginning that Geometric culture was the direct ancestor of that of the Greeks of the Classical Age, and the sequence from Late Geometric to Archaic art in the seventh century could be easily traced. Yet everywhere, in almost every site of southern Greece, Geometric pottery was found inextricably mixed with Mycenaean. Indeed, on occasion it was found underneath Mycenaean ware. This fact caused immense problems and not a few heated debates in the 1920s and 30s. Some scholars insisted the evidence demanded a down-dating of the Mycenaean Age to the eighth and seventh centuries, and one — Dörpfeld — insisting it required a back-dating of the Geometric Age into in the second millennium, where it would again be contemporary with the Mycenaean. In the end, neither option was accepted, and instead an impossibility was put in its place: Namely that Geometric art somehow evolved out of Mycenaean after the decline of Mycenaean civilization in the twelfth century. Such a "solution" required historians to ignore the results of excavation, and to try to find some form of relationship or connection between two types of pottery which seemed to be utterly alien to each other. Indeed, it was discovered, and even admitted, that the true ancestor of Geometric culture was that of the Middle Helladic Age, an epoch which saw the production of simple pottery incised with basic geometric patterns. But the Middle Helladic Age predated the Mycenaean (also known as Late Helladic), and accepting a link between Middle Helladic and Geometric would mean, in effect, an admission that Geometric art had come before Mycenaean.

But the full consequences of these facts were never assimilated or worked out; and the myth of a Geometric art evolving out of Mycenaean found its way into the textbooks, where it exists and causes all kinds of problems to this day.

Another enigma produced by Egyptian dating concerned literature and language. Homer, it emerged, had possessed a detailed knowledge of Mycenaean life and geography. Discovery after discovery revealed an intimate acquaintance on the part of the poet with the art, customs, dress, and language of the Mycenaean Age. Yet here again chronology caused an insurmountable problem. How could the epic poet, working in the seventh century, or the eighth at the earliest, have acquired such knowledge of a world that died four or five centuries earlier, a world from which he was moreover separated by a Dark Age of ignorance, barbarism and almost total depopulation? Again, the Linear B script of Mycenaean times, which early scholars could not believe was Greek, proved to be just that: and not only Greek, but a late form of Greek, more advanced in many ways than the language of Homer and Hesiod. Also, the Linear tablets revealed a culture and geography strikingly in line with that described by Homer, which raised, once again, the question of how Homer, composing his poems four or five centuries later, could have gained such knowledge.

This question, like that of art and pottery, has remained unresolved and unresolvable in the course of a century of debate.

Another enigma, which we explore in the fourth chapter, concerns the strange echoes of the Mycenaean Age which occur in the archaeology of lands far removed from Greece; yet these echoes, these cultural parallels, are found in material of the sixth, fifth and even fourth centuries BC. Thus for example *tholos* tombs in Thrace, of the fifth and fourth centuries BC, are constructed precisely like those of southern Greece and the Peloponnese, where they are however dated between the sixteenth and thirteenth centuries BC. In the past five years, a gold face mask belonging to a Thracian king, which looks astonishingly like the face masks of the Mycenaean Shaft Graves, has come to light. Yet the Thracian mask is dated to the end of the fourth century — supposedly over a thousand years after the Mycenaean masks. In Italy too, in Tuscany and Sicily, archaeologists have found strange echoes of Mycenaean custom and style which however date from the sixth and fifth centuries. The same is true of Cyprus, where a version of the Mycenaean Linear Script was used as late as the fourth century BC, and the art and material culture of the island displays a thousand parallels with Greece of the Mycenaean period (though in Cyprus these features are dated to the sixth, fifth and fourth centuries BC).

In Chapter 5 we look at the question of historical texts from the Near Eastern world and their relationship to the great events of Mycenaean history. There are some dramatic revelations. We find, for example, that Greek warriors fresh from the sack of Ilion took part in Egypt's war of liberation against the Assyrians, whilst Agamemnon and his lieutenant Mopsus, as well as their warlike activities, both occur in Hittite documents recovered from Boghaz-koi.

The final two chapters attempt a reconstruction of Greece's internal and international history from the earliest events that might reasonably be regarded as reliable — events surrounding a great natural catastrophe which marked the founding of the Olympiads — through the internal struggles within the country prior to the Trojan War, especially the various conflicts with the city of Thebes, and leading on eventually to the Dorian Invasion and the rise of the tyrannies in the seventh and sixth centuries. We will find that, with the abandonment of the false Egyptian chronology, Greek history shows a natural and logical progression, with, far from a Dark Age, a great abundance of source material and documentation of every kind. Indeed, we shall find that Hellenic history of the eight, seventh and sixth centuries is the most thoroughly documented and best known of all ancient histories.

The sources I have used have naturally been diverse. The work of the historian, like that of the detective, demands that nothing be overlooked, no matter how apparently mundane or insignificant. This is particularly the case in an endeavor such as this, where we have tried to reconstruct a history that has, essentially, been lost for over two thousand years. The evidence of pottery and bronze-making has been called to the witness-stand, along with that of the linguist, the epigraphist and the critic of literature. Ancient legend and ancient history have been quoted side by side, and the mute testimony of stones and pottery quoted alongside the poets.

I am in debt to all of the scholars who have gone before me: particularly to the archaeologists and excavators whose Herculean endeavors brought again to the light of day the fabulous and colorful world of Homer's heroes. It is however to Immanuel Velikovsky that the present work owes most. Whilst differing from him on certain issues, I make no apology in stating that I have delved freely into his ideas in the preparation of this volume. Without his insights on Egyptian history, would the false edifice of "Mycenaean History" ever have been challenged? It is extremely unlikely. And I would be remiss if I failed to mention others of the "Velikovskian" school. When it came to the reconstruction of Greek history, Velikovsky was, in his latter years, given invaluable assistance by Eddie Schorr and Jan Sammer; and their work, which forms two Appendices to Velikovsky's *Dark Ages of Greece*, has provided me, too, with much important information and insights.

It goes without saying that what is to follow is not the definitive and final word. Errors have undoubtedly been made, as is only to be expected in a pioneering venture. Nevertheless, I feel that the outline presented here will stand the test of time, and am convinced that, had the history and chronology of Egypt not entered the debate in the latter years of the nineteenth century, then the history that follows is essentially the one that would now be found in the textbooks.

CHAPTER 1. AN AGE OF HEROES

WHERE DOES GREEK HISTORY BEGIN?

The Greeks of classical times regarded the foundation of the Olympic Games as the starting-point of their history. Everything that came before was held to be *mythikon*, the "age of myths;" everything after was *historikon*, the age of history. The traditional date for the first Olympiad is fixed at 776 BC, and to this day classicists are content to cite this as an important dividing line in the Hellenic past. Strange to relate however, some of the important characters and events of what we now regard as Greek myth appear to come *after* the foundation of the Olympiads. Indeed a very strong tradition linked Heracles, the son of Zeus, to the establishment of the festival.[1]

The world of Greek myth is generally known as the Heroic Age, and it appears that Heracles (Latin Hercules) himself, whose own name means "the glory of Hera," was the source of the word "hero." Greek writers told innumerable tales of Heracles and of his contemporaries; of Theseus of Athens who slew the bull-headed Minotaur in the labyrinth at Knossos; of Minos, the fabulously wealthy and powerful king of Crete, who controlled the sea lanes of the Aegean; of Jason of Iolcus, who led his Argonauts to the mysterious land of Colchis, where he captured the wonderful Golden Fleece; of the champions who fought and died at Thebes, and, last but not least, of the warriors who besieged the city of Troy to avenge the abduction of Helen, wife of Menelaus of Sparta. The war with Troy, like the other events of the

---

1 Pindar, *Olympian Odes*, x, 43 ff; Hyginus, *Fabula*, 273

Heroic Age, is now believed to have occurred in the second millennium BC, yet around it too there are clues pointing to a time much more recent. Traditions surrounding the Olympic Games clearly show the festival in existence well before the Trojan Campaign. Thus Homer, who cannot have lived more than a couple of centuries after the first Olympiad, describes how both Nestor and his father Neleus won prizes at the festival.[1] Nestor of course was one of the Achaean princes present at Troy. Another tradition held that it was Pelops, the grandfather of Agamemnon, who founded the Games.[2]

Traditions about the alphabet tell a similar tale. Cadmus, who brought the Phoenician script to Greece, was said to have lived about six generations before the Trojan Campaign.[3] Yet the earliest example of alphabetic writing to emerge from Greece dates from around 750 BC and no one would date its introduction to the country much before 800 BC.[4] Palamedes, who fought at Troy, was credited with adding the letters *x*, *ph*, and *ch* to the Cadmean alphabet,[5] whilst Herodotus saw, and read, three inscribed tripods at Thebes, two of which were dedicated by well-known contemporaries of Pelops, namely Amphitryon and Laodamas.[6] The writing on the tripods, Herodotus said, was executed in an archaic form of the Cadmean script, but he was well able to read it.

How could Amphitryon, who reigned at Thebes two generations before the Trojan War, have written an inscription in the Phoenician alphabet if that alphabet only arrived in Greece around 800 BC — and the Trojan War occurred around 1200 BC?

Similarly, the earliest portrayals in ancient art of themes from the war at Troy date from around 700 BC.

The evidence of ancient genealogies stands in agreement. Numerous genealogies of noble Greek families, such as the one linking Pythagoras to Hippasos of Samos, separate the time of the Trojan War from the Persian War by only eight or nine generations — around 200 years, allowing 25 years to a generation.[7] By this reckoning, the war would have taken place sometime between 750 and 700 BC.

---

1 *Iliad*, xi, 671 and 761
2 Pausanias, v, 8, 1 and vi, 20, 8.
3 Herodotus, iv, 47.
4 "The earliest Greek inscription known as yet lie, on the archaeological evidence ... around 750 BC." L. H. Jeffery, "Greek alphabetic writing," in *CAH* Vol. 3 part 1 (3rd ed.) p. 823
5 Hyginus, *Fabula* 277.
6 Herodotus, v, 59 –61.
7 Pausanias, ii, 13, 1.

Then there is the evidence from the east, both from Asia Minor and Phoenicia, linking characters and kingdoms to the Trojan Campaign who did not exist before the eighth or ninth century. Thus the Phoenicians, a race of sailors and traders, were listed among the allies of Troy. Yet the latter people only became a great seafaring nation around 900 BC. Thus too Greek tradition held that Midas, an eighth-century king of Phrygia, was a contemporary of Agamemnon. It was Midas' father, Gordius, a contemporary of Pelops, who founded the Phrygian kingdom, whilst one ancient source tells us that Midas married a daughter of Agamemnon, an Ionian king based at Cyme.[1] It is normally believed that this Agamemnon was different from the High King who led the Achaeans at Ilion, yet it seems that Midas regarded this alliance with the Greeks as so important that he sent a decorated throne to Delphi to commemorate it. Why go to such lengths if the alliance was with an obscure Ionian princeling?

Finally, tradition links refugees from Troy with the founding of Rome, an event placed by the Romans themselves in the middle of the eighth century BC. In his *Aenead*, Virgil makes the hero Aeneas visit queen Dido at Carthage on the North African coast. Yet neither tradition nor archaeology knows of any city of Carthage predating the eighth century. Similarly, investigation of the Aeneas legend in central Italy has shown that it originated with the Etruscan immigrants to the region, whose language was apparently closely related to the Tyrrhenian (or Pelasgian) dialect of the northern Aegean. But archaeology has shown that the Etruscan settlement of northern and central Italy commenced near the end of the eighth century BC.[2]

This then is a tiny sample of the truly enormous body of evidence pointing to a date in the later eighth century as the proper location of the Achaean campaign against Ilion, as well as an eighth or perhaps ninth century location for the characters and events said to have preceded the Trojan War. But if this is the case, how did the Heroic (or Mycenaean) Age ever come to be located in the position it now occupies, namely the fifteenth to the twelfth centuries BC?

THE REDISCOVERY OF HOMERIC GREECE

The land of Greece has played a decisive role in the development of Western civilization. Throughout the centuries, generations of schoolboys in Europe have thrilled to read of the heroes of Troy; of the deeds of the Argonauts and of the exploits of Hercules. Who, even now, upon reading Homer's *Iliad*,

---

1 Julius Pollux, ix, 83, quoting the *Constitution of Kyme*, by Herakleides of Pontus.
2 See e.g., R. M. Ogilvie, *Early Rome and the Etruscans* (Fontana, 1976) pp. 30ff.

can fail to be enthralled by the colorful, strange and violent world described therein?

With the dawn of the scientific age, Europeans developed a renewed curiosity about the past. In the Age of Reason however it seemed that Homer's world belonged more to myth and fable than to history. How could it be else, when the poet describes a war fought over a woman; a war in which commoners played no significant part, with whole battles decided by the appearance in the field of a single hero; a war in which the gods personally intervened, on occasion saving their favorites from certain destruction by miraculous means? True, it was conceded, there may originally have been a grain of truth to the story, yet the account preserved by Homer was far removed from anything factual; distorted out of all recognition by folk tradition and more resembling a fairytale than anything else. But some authorities went much further, denying even the existence of such a place and such an event, decreeing the whole story to be pure fiction.

This was the situation when, in the 1870s, German adventurer and entrepreneur Heinrich Schliemann embarked upon his memorable excavations in northwest Turkey. As a boy, Schliemann had, like so many generations of youths before him, been enthralled by the myths and legends of Greece and had made it his lifelong ambition to find the locations and remains of these ancient events. Troy, of course, the mythic goal of the Achaeans under their mightiest king, was right at the top of Schliemann's list. And so, having made himself a rich man with just that purpose in mind, he set out for Anatolia with Homer and the Greek authors as his guide. Having made his headquarters at Hissarlik, a low hill near the Dardanelles, he publicized his intention of locating there the ancient city of Troy. The announcement was met with disbelief and sarcasm, but mostly with indifference; and yet within no more than a few weeks he had uncovered the remains of Homer's city. Beneath the mound were the remains of seven cities, one on top of the other; and in the second city from the bottom Schliemann found a great treasure of gold and silver jewelry which he described as the "Treasure of Priam."

The academic world was astonished. Although later scholars identified King Priam's city as the sixth city from the bottom, and still later researchers pointed to the seventh, the German adventurer's achievement was rightly celebrated.

Crowned with success, Schliemann then turned his attention to mainland Greece, where, in 1876 he began work at Mycenae, intent on discovering the tomb of Agamemnon. As at Troy, he put his faith in tradition, which insisted that Agamemnon had been buried by his wife Clytaemnestra just within the walls of the citadel. Ancient authors had spoken of a circle of standing stones marking the grave pits; and these were soon located by the diggers. Within a short time there came to light rich burials in five shafts hewn in rock, whose occupants were bedecked with gold jewelry, crowns and masks, along with weapons and vessels of the richest ornament. Upon uncovering the most splendid of these he found, under an ornate golden face mask, the undecayed visage of an ancient king. Excited, and apparently over-come with emotion, Schliemann sent a telegraph to the Greek king announc-ing that he had "looked upon the face of Agamemnon."

Many discordant voices were now heard. One scholar announced that the finds dated from the Byzantine Age; yet in time the royal graves were ac-cepted for what they were — relics of an age and a civilization that preceded the historical age of Greece. For a short time, it was admitted even that these were indeed the graves of Agamemnon and his royal entourage. Yet this was only for a moment, for soon it was found that the citadel of Mycenae had en-joyed its greatest epoch at a time contemporary with the Eighteenth Dynasty of Egypt. In the buildings and tombs of Mycenae the diggers uncovered car-touches of Amenhotep II, Amenhotep III and Queen Tiy, wife of Amenhotep III and mother of Akhnaton. Even worse, artifacts within the Shaft Graves showed them to have been dug in an earlier period still, around the start of the Eighteenth Dynasty. Since the Eighteenth Dynasty began in the latter sixteenth century BC — or so it was believed — the Shaft Graves could not possibly belong to Agamemnon and his followers. For, although just a cou-ple of decades earlier scholars had denied the very existence of Agamemnon and his Trojan opponents, now it was insisted that both could be accurately dated to the twelfth century BC.

THE EARLY DEBATE

Schliemann's discoveries caused a sensation. The colorful and barbaric world described by Homer, it seemed after all, was real. Yet the German ad-venturer had done more than rediscover Homer's world: he had apparently uncovered a whole new civilization. Certainly the artwork recovered at My-cenae, and later at Tiryns and Pylos, and later still in Crete by Arthur Evans, seemed totally un-Greek; completely unlike anything seen before. Indeed, the excavations of Arthur Evans at Knossos, where he found a fabulously decorated palace, seemed to indicate a civilization as alien to Greece and the Greek mind as it was possible to be. The Cretan civilization was termed "Minoan" by Evans, after the legendary king of Crete, and it soon became obvious that the "Mycenaean" culture of the Greek mainland was an offshoot of the insular.

One of the first questions to occupy the minds of scholars was that of dates. Now that the world of Troy and Mycenae, the world of the heroes, had been proved real, it had to be supplied with a chronology. To begin with, Schliemann made no specific recommendations. Yet classicists were well aware of the traditions quoted above which linked the Heroic Age and the Trojan War to the eighth century BC. In particular, it was known that king Midas of Phrygia, who, although sharing many typically "Heroic Age" features — such as meetings with gods, his Golden Touch and his Asses' Ears — was very definitely a historical character of the late eighth and early seventh century BC. Herodotus for example mentioned that Midas had committed suicide rather than be captured by the barbarous Cimmerians, who had attacked his capital Gordion in or around the year 687 BC.[1] In the same way, it was known that Midas' father Gordius, founder of Gordion, was a contemporary of King Priam of Troy.

It is worth noting at this point that many historical characters of the eighth, seventh and sixth centuries, and not just Midas, were linked to the Heroic Age and displayed the mythic characteristics of typical Heroic Age personalities. Thus for example Arion of Lesbos, described as a "son of Poseidon and the nymph Oneaea," who was carried over the waves to Corinth on the back of a dolphin, is a historical character of the seventh century BC; as is Periander the tyrant of Corinth, who was his patron.[2] Similar mythical stories surround the life of another tyrant of Corinth, Cypselus (seventh century), as well as the Messenian hero Aristomenes, who fought against the Spartans in the seventh or sixth century BC, and was carried off by the gods on the wings of an eagle. And we remember queen Dido of Carthage, who cannot have lived much before circa 700 BC (Carthage was founded, according to tradition and archaeology in the ninth or eighth century), met the Trojan hero Aeneas on his way to Italy; whilst Cadmus, the hero credited with introducing the Phoenician alphabet to Greece — which cannot have occurred much before 750 BC — was believed to have lived well before the Trojan War.

These and other traditions seemed to be adequately confirmed by the archaeology. Although the culture unearthed by Schliemann at Mycenae and Tiryns looked strange and un-Greek, it nevertheless revealed traits in common with the cultures and civilizations of surrounding peoples which very

1 Herodotus, i, 6, 15.
2 See e.g., Robert Graves, *The Greek Myths*, Vol. 1 pp. 290-1

definitely dated from the eighth and seventh centuries. Thus for example it was noted that many features of Phrygian art were strongly reminiscent of artistic motifs from Mycenae. At the main entrance to the Mycenaean citadel, for example, the famous Lion Gate, with its twin rampant lions facing a central pillar, found its precise counterpart in Phrygian monuments and artifacts. "The resemblance in idea is complete," wrote W. M. Ramsay in 1888. He considered the theme "so peculiarly characteristic of Phrygia, that we can hardly admit it to have been borrowed from any other country."[1] He found himself "driven to the conclusion that the Mycenaean artists either are Phrygians or learned the idea from the Phrygians."[2] It was not permissible, he thought, to separate the Phrygian and Mycenaean monuments by any great stretch of time. "The view to which I find myself forced is as follows," he wrote, "There was in the eighth century lively intercourse between Argos and Asia Minor: in this intercourse the Argives learned ... to fortify their city in the Phrygian style lions over the gate. Historically there is certainly good reason to assign at least part of the fortifications of Mycenae to the time when the Argive kings were the greatest power in Greece."[3] Eastern influences found in the remains of Mycenae are "precisely what we should expect in a kingdom like Argos in the eighth century," when the realm had intercourse with Asia Minor, Phoenicia and Egypt. "I wish however to express no opinion here about the date of the Mycenaean tombs and about Mycenaean pottery, but only to argue that the fortifications of the Lion Gate belong to the period 800–700 BC."[4]

Ramsay felt it necessary to make the disclaimer about the date of the Mycenaean tombs and pottery because already, by this time (1888), a new factor had entered the debate which had apparently pushed the date of the latter back into the fourteenth and fifteenth centuries BC: the chronology of Egypt.

It was Flinders Petrie who first insisted that the "Mycenaean" age of Greece be dated in accordance with the chronology of Egypt. We have seen that, right from the beginning, Egyptian material of Eighteenth Dynasty manufacture was found in some abundance in association with Mycenaean material. For Petrie and other Egyptologists, who were convinced they possessed a precise and accurate chronology, the debate was thus concluded. Irrespective of what Greek tradition said, and irrespective of the apparent

---

1 W. M. Ramsay, "A Study of Phrygian Art," *Journal of Hellenic Studies*, IX (1888) p. 369
2 Ibid., pp. 369-370
3 Ibid., p. 370
4 Ibid., pp. 370-71

parallels between Mycenae and Phrygia, the great epoch of Mycenae's power must have been in the fifteenth and fourteenth centuries BC. Petrie now engaged in a protracted and at times rancorous debate with Ramsay and various other classicists over the very foundations of the Greek past. In answer to Ramsay's plea that the Lion Gate at least be considered apart from the contents of the Shaft Graves and the Mycenaean pottery found at El Amarna in Egypt, Petrie wrote: "[A] matter which demands notice is Professor Ramsay's conclusion that the lion gateway is of as late a date as the eighth century BC. This results from assuming it to be derived from Phrygian lion groups, on the ground of not knowing of any other prototype. As however we now have a wooden lion, in exactly the same attitude, dated to 1450 in Egypt ... it seems that the Phrygian designs are not the only source of this motive for Mykenae."[1]

Of Petrie's above-mentioned Egyptian antecedent for the lions of Mycenae, Immanuel Velikovsky wrote: "In Egypt of the latter part of the Eighteenth Dynasty a single instance of a rampant lion (not two rampant lions facing each other as at Mycenae and in Phrygia) made Petrie claim Egypt as a possible place of origin of this image rather than Phrygia."[2] As Velikovsky remarked, here was a case where evidence from Anatolia pointed to the eighth century, but the chronology of Egypt demanded a back-dating into the fourteenth or fifteenth centuries. The debate between Ramsay and Petrie took place before Evans' archaeological work on Crete, where rampant lions were found engraved on Minoan gems. This conveyed the idea that Mycenae must have borrowed the motif from there, from a period well preceding the Phrygian age. Yet, as Velikovsky stressed, we must not lose sight of the fact that the chronology of Crete, too, is based on that of Egypt. It cannot be produced as independent corroboration of a Mycenaean civilization in the fourteenth and fifteenth centuries.

After Ramsay retired from the debate, the cudgels were taken up by another classicist, Cecil Torr, who very publicly crossed swords first with Petrie and then with John L. Myers on the issue between the years 1892 and 1897. The discussion, carried out largely in the pages of *The Times* and several other newspapers, was on occasion heated and ill-tempered, though always informative, and Torr's arguments were eventually published in pamphlet form by Cambridge University in 1896 as *Memphis and Mycenae. An Examination of Egyptian Chronology and Its Application to the Early History of Greece*. Like Ramsay,

---

1 W. M. Flinders Petrie, "Notes on the Antiquities of Mykenae," *Journal of Hellenic Studies*, XII (1891) pp. 202-3
2 Velikovsky, *The Dark Ages of Greece*, http://velikovsky.collision.org/dag/lionga.htm.

Torr emphasized the Phrygian links with Mycenae and, being something of a polymath, took the first steps towards a thorough critique of Egyptian chronology. In *Memphis and Mycenae* he highlighted the shortcomings of the supposedly astronomically-based "Sothic Calendar," which the Egyptologists regarded as the foundation of their chronology, and brought forward abundant proofs to show that the Eighteenth Dynasty needed to be brought forward in time by several centuries. In fact, he held that the Eighteenth Dynasty ended around 850 BC (as opposed to the prevailing date of circa 1320 BC), and thereby brought the age of the "Mycenaean" material which was associated with this epoch into the ninth century. Thus, he claimed, the six or seven extra centuries which Petrie wished to install into Greek history were unnecessary.

Such was Torr's energy that, had he persisted, he might well have caused an academic rethink. Unfortunately however his interest in the subject waned, and he retired from the debate early in 1900s without bringing things to a logical conclusion.

In the end, Petrie's arguments were heeded. The early opposition of the classicists was silenced and a totally new view of the Hellenic past emerged.

A "Dark Age" Intrudes

Placing the high point of Mycenaean civilization in the fourteenth and fifteenth centuries BC, which Egyptian chronology seemed to demand, did not bring about the resolution of any puzzles and mysteries. Indeed, it only created new ones.

To begin with, it was regarded as strange that the Heroic Age should be placed so far in the past. Numerous Greek families and cities preserved genealogies and king-lists which linked the Heroic Age to the Classical. None of these contained enough names to cover the nine hundred years which it now appeared had separated the great epoch of Mycenae from the Battle of Marathon. On the contrary, the king-lists and genealogies could only reach back to the eighth or ninth centuries at the earliest.[1] What happened then between the decline of the Mycenaean world in, say, the thirteenth century BC at the very latest, and the rise of historical Greece in the seventh? For the first time, scholars began to speak of a "Dark Age."

Having brought the term into use, the progress of archaeology began to reveal how thoroughly appropriate it was. As archaeologists excavated site after site throughout Greece they became aware of the paucity of remains which could be assigned to the years designated as the Dark Age. Thus

---

1 Several well-known Greek genealogies are examined in Chapter 7 of the present volume.

between the thirteenth (or twelfth) centuries and the eighth, there was, it seems, a general depopulation of Greece: a catastrophic decline in numbers that left whole districts and even kingdoms abandoned. Search as they might, from a period of five centuries, they found almost nothing. Cities, villages, even hamlets, seem to have been deserted — only to be reoccupied, in strikingly similar fashion, with similar material cultures, technologies and economies, five centuries later.[1] In his book *Discontinuity in Greek Civilization*, historian Rhys Carpenter reviews the evidence from the mainland and the islands garnered over the previous three-quarters of the a century of excavation and comes to the conclusion: "Despite the fact that there is no indication that the late Mycenaeans were driven out by any human intervention, they abandoned the south Aegean islands even as they deserted the central Peloponnese. For some reason and for some cause over which they had no control they found life in Greece and on the southern Aegean so unendurable that they could not remain."[2] And he asks: "What caused them to evacuate whole towns and villages?" He notes that G. Welter refers to the complete abandonment of the island of Aegina, whilst V. R. d'A. Desborough holds that the island of Melos had been totally depopulated. Discussing the island of Kos, Desborough "was puzzled at finding 'no clue as to the cause of its final desertion' in Late Mycenaean times." There must, thought Desborough, have been some serious disaster, and yet, "It can hardly be supposed that there was a complete depopulation," though there "is no clear evidence of continuity into the Protogeometric period."[3]

Yet not even a catastrophe of cosmic dimensions would leave a land completely depopulated for four or five centuries and then find the same country repopulated after that time by a people bearing almost the same material culture.

The Dark Age had strange consequences in many areas. From very early it was known that the inhabitants of the Aegean during the Mycenaean Age had been literate. Examples of a syllabic script, later named Linear B, had been found first at Pylos and then at Knossos and various other places. Yet with the destruction of the Mycenaean palaces and citadels, the art of writing had been lost and had not reappeared until the introduction of the Phoenician alphabet in the eighth century. Here was something unprecedented: a

---

1 "[A] fair number of technical processes and decorative motives of Mycenaean art reappear in Greece in the eighth and seventh centuries BC. These include the carving of ivory, the goldsmith's processes of filigree and granulation, the nature deity with animals, sphinxes and griffins." Reynold Higgins, *Minoan and Mycenaean Art* (3rd ed., London, 1997) p. 190.

2 R. Carpenter, *Discontinuity in Greek Civilization* (Cambridge University Press, 1966) p. 58

3 V. R. D'A. Desborough, *The Last Mycenaeans and their Successors* (Oxford, 1964) pp. 157-8

literate people had somehow lost the art of writing. In his book *Homer and his Forerunners*, Maurice Bowra described this as an "astounding state of affairs" and expresses the problem thus:

> There is no evidence whatsoever that the Mycenaean script continued any-where in Greece after c. 1200. There is no trace of writing of any kind in the sub-Mycenaean and Protogeometric periods, or indeed before the middle of the eighth century, when the new and totally different Greek alphabet makes its first appearance. Now, this is surely not an accident. A single scratched letter from this period would be enough to show that writing survived; but not one has been found. This is undeniably a most remarkable phenomenon, for which it is hard to find either a parallel or an explanation. A society seems suddenly to have become illiterate, and to have remained so for centuries. How and why this happened we do not know...[1]

In the years which followed the synchronization of Egypt with Mycenae, desperate attempts were made, in more ways than one, to close the Dark Age gap. Since archaeology had signally failed to do the job, it was thought at least that the four or five empty centuries might be provided with a writ-ten history. Aware that Greek genealogies could not reach back to the four-teenth or fifteenth centuries, scholars sought to stretch them back at least as far as was feasible. This was accomplished by accepting at face value certain inappropriately-used and grossly-inflated classical estimates for the date of the Trojan War. Thus for example it was pointed out that Herodotus, utiliz-ing the king-lists of Sparta, had provided the date for the Trojan War almost eight centuries before his time (i.e., around 1200 BC), and the mathematician Eratosthenes, employing the same lists, had come up with a date correspond-ing to 1184 for the fall of the city. In order to achieve these figures, Herodotus and Eratosthenes had treated the king-lists as reliable (which they almost certainly weren't: they begin with a deity, Heracles); as a list of generations (which they weren't: they were a list of all the kings who reigned at Sparta, some of whom were brothers); and as a list of generations each of which was accorded forty years (but twenty to twenty-five years is more accurate for a real generation).

Although the dates provided by Herodotus and Eratosthenes are still widely quoted — almost as if they were fact — in textbooks, it is nevertheless conceded that they are complete fiction. Thus for example classicist Paul A. Cartledge noted that, "It goes without saying that the absolute dates arrived at by these erudite men [Eratosthenes, Herodotus and others] have no truly scientific foundation, and that differences between their dating and ours are to be expected."[2] In particular, Cartledge noted that there was no justifica-

---

1 Sir Maurice Bowra, *Homer and his Forerunners* (Edinburgh, 1955) pp. 1-2
2 Paul A. Cartledge, *Sparta and Lakonia: A Regional History, 1320–362 BC.* (Routledge, London, 1979) p. 297

tion for assuming that the fifteen kings on Herodotus' list represented fifteen generations, and that quite likely many of the kings named were brothers who inherited the throne after the death of the elder sibling. Cartledge noted that in historical times this was often the case, that succession was "consobrinal — brother succeeding brother," and that "even if Herodotus' lists are adaptations of king-lists drawn up in the joint reign of Kleomenes and Damaratos, we should make allowances for an unknowable number of collateral successions."[1] And even if the king-lists were to be accepted as representing generations, he noted that "it is impossible to accept a generation average as high as forty years over a period of fifteen generations."[2]

So, although the Spartan King-List is not a list of generations and is in any case of dubious historical value, it was somehow latched onto. Accepting the date of the twelfth century for the fall of Troy which these estimates seemed to provide,[3] it could at least be said that the Dark Age had been partially closed.

Yet any honest appraisal of the situation will admit that when historians have been compelled to resort to such desperate measures, there is something truly and terribly wrong.

In fact, as we shall see in the chapter to follow, even the context within which the Mycenaean remains of Greece were discovered should have left not a shred of doubt as to their true age. For not only were they discovered immediately beneath Archaic pottery and artifacts that could be dated to the sixth century BC, they were actually, on occasion, even found along with Archaic material, in the same level. Furthermore, in virtually every site, the Mycenaean Age material was found mixed with an early type of pottery named "Geometric" which was securely dated to the seventh, eighth and ninth centuries, and on occasion it was even found *above and therefore after* this Geometric ware.

The Dark Age in Asia Minor

The progress of excavation during the first half of the twentieth century brought no resolution to the Dark Age question. On the contrary, the mystery only deepened: for it was found, much to the astonishment of the scholarly community, that this epoch of decline had affected not only Greece but Asia Minor and indeed almost the whole of Anatolia. As was the case with

---

1 Ibid.
2 Ibid.
3 Even if the Spartan King-Lists are treated as genealogies (which of course they are not), they would still give a date for the Trojan War no earlier than about 850 BC at the earliest.

Greece, this "darkness" did not represent a period of impoverishment or even barbarism, but one of complete and total depopulation: a span of over four centuries when it seemed no human beings at all had existed in the region we now call Turkey.

This strange anomaly was first noted at Troy, a settlement which was found to be "... barren of deposits which might be referred to the period c. 1100–700 BC. Not one shred of proto-geometric pottery is known to have been found at Troy — not by Schliemann, or by Dörpfeld, or by Blegen himself. We are now in effect asking what happened at Troy during the Dark Ages of Greece, from the [beginning of] the 11th to the [end of the] 8th century BC: and this is the answer that we must accept — that there is nothing at Troy to fill the huge lacuna. For 2000 years men had left traces of their living there; some chapters of the story were brief and obscure, but there was never yet a chapter left wholly blank. Now at last there is silence, profound and obscure for 400 years."[1]

This observation of Denys Page, Professor of Greek at the University of Cambridge, is expressive of the writer's amazement. Yet had he looked further afield he would have found much more to disturb him: For as the years went by and scholars turned their attention to sites in the interior of Anatolia, they encountered the same phenomenon. Thus, by 1961, Ekrem Akurgal, Turkey's senior archaeologist, could write that, "Today, despite all industrious archaeological exploration of the last decades, the period from 1200 to 750 for most parts of the Anatolian region lies still in complete darkness. The old nations of Asia Minor, like the Lycians and Carians, the names of which are mentioned in the documents of the second half of the second millennium, are archaeologically, i.e., with their material heritage, first noticeable about 700 or later.... Hence the cultural remains of the time between 1200 and 750 in central Anatolia, especially on the plateau, seem to be quite irretrievably lost for us."[2]

The cause of the interruption in the flow of history about 1200 BC is assumed to lie in some military conquest. But who could have been responsible? Certainly not the Phrygians, for they did not enter the region until circa 750 BC. Even on the Greek mainland, the attempt to explain the Dark Age as a consequence of the invasion of the supposedly barbarian Dorians had to be abandoned.[3] So it was in Anatolia. According to Akurgal, the effort to close

---

1 D. Page, "The Historical Sack of Troy," *Antiquity*, Vol. XXXIII (1959) p. 31

2 E. Akurgal, *Die Kunst Anatoliens von Homer bis Alexander* (Berlin, 1961) pp. 5-7

3 According to Carpenter, "The Dorians had nothing whatever to do with the collapse of Mycenaean civilization, since they did not enter the Peloponnese until long after the collapse had already taken place." *Discontinuity in Greek Civilization*, p. 52

the hiatus by appealing to the relics of Phrygian art "cannot be harmonized with the results of archaeological study. None of the Phrygian finds and none of the oriental ones found with them can be dated earlier than the eighth century." And, "Such results compel us to exclude from the study of Asia Minor between 1200 and 750 any Phrygian presence and heritage."

If the Phrygians left no trace during this period, what then of other peoples? "It is startling," writes Akurgal, "that until now in Central Anatolia not only no Phrygian, but altogether no cultural remains of any people, came to light that could be dated in time between 1200 and 750." Nothing, it seems, was left by any occupants, not even primitive huts or hovels. Nor did regions on the borders of Anatolia provide anything to fill the gap. Here too the darkness is complete: "In the south of the peninsula, in Mersin, Tarsus and Karatepe, in recent years important archaeological work was done ... here, too, the early Iron Age, i.e., the period between 1200 and 750 is enwrapped in darkness."[1]

We should remind ourselves that this supposed depopulation of a large section of the earth's surface for a period of almost five centuries is not confirmed by any excavated evidence of catastrophic destruction, such as by fire, earthquake, or flood. On the contrary, there is evidence of cultural continuity between the abandoned settlements of 1200 BC and the reoccupied ones of 750 BC. The "depopulation" theory would never have arisen, never even have been thought of, had the chronology of Egypt not been applied to these lands. When however the occurrence of scarabs and other artifacts of the Eighteenth Dynasty were found in association with remains which had otherwise been placed in the eighth century BC, it was necessary to relocate these into the fourteenth or thirteenth centuries and thus create a chasm which separated them from their true location: a chasm which had no archaeology or remains of any kind to bridge it.

1 Akurgal, op. cit. p. 7

Chapter 2. Archaeology and Art

Artistic Anomalies

One of the most serious consequences of applying Egyptian chronology to Greece arose in the interpretation of a variety of pottery which came to be known as "Geometric." The earliest examples of this ware were found to consist of simple incised pots, which later began to be decorated with geometric designs, eventually developing into richly ornate ware which, from the beginning of the seventh century BC, incorporated elements of design from oriental art. By the sixth century Geometric pottery had fully evolved into Archaic, and this was the direct predecessor of the art of the Classic Age, which appeared in the fifth century.

There was thus recognized, from the very beginning, a clear line of descent from Geometric art to that of the Greeks of the historical age; and there was no question whatsoever in the minds of scholars that the Geometric ware was the first historical expression of the Hellenic aesthetic.[1]

But there was a problem. Excavators from Schliemann onwards found, in almost every site, that Geometric ware occurred in the same levels as Mycenaean. Often the two varieties of pottery were thoroughly mixed together. Excavations throughout the nineteenth and twentieth century encountered the same phenomenon. Thus in 1966 Carl Blegen could write in his report of the excavations at Pylos: "In some places ... in the upper black layer ... were

---

1 In the words of Bernhard Schweitzer, Geometric art "was the earliest great and purely artistic achievement of the Greeks." *Geometric Greek Art* (English trans. Phaidon Press, London, 1971) p. 15

found, along with the usual Mycneaean pottery, a few glazed sherds of Late Geometric style, as in so many other parts of the site, where similar deposits were encountered."[1] Such was the case also, three quarters of a century earlier, at Tiryns, which Schliemann, with the help of Wilhelm Dörpfeld, excavated in 1884–85. The two men quickly uncovered, on the acropolis, the foundations of a palace; and it was immediately evident that this Mycenaean structure had been a sacred site into the sixth and even fifth century: Everywhere were little flasks in which libations had been brought.[2] Ancient writers had spoken of a temple to Hera at Tiryns which was deserted when the Argives vanquished the city in 460 BC. Schliemann came to the conclusion that the Mycenaean palace shrine was also a temple to Hera and that it had been used continuously until the seventh century and only replaced by an Archaic temple at the beginning of the sixth century. When excavations at Tiryns were resumed in 1905 by a team headed by A. Frickenhaus, special attention was paid to the time in which the Mycenaean palace was destroyed. It was found that on the site of the palace and, in part, on its original foundations, a smaller edifice was built, identified as the Archaic Age (sixth century) temple of Hera. The excavators felt that many facts pointed to the conclusion that the latter temple was built over the Mycenaean palace very shortly after the palace was burned down.[3] The altar of the temple was an adaptation of the Mycenaean palace altar and the plan of the Mycenaean palace had evidently been familiar to the builders of the temple. The floor of the palace served as the floor of the temple.[4]

After deliberating on the evidence, the excavators refused to accept the end of the Mycenaean Age in the second millennium as the time of the destruction of the palace, and decided that the palace had survived until the seventh century. A continuity of culture from Mycenaean to Greek times was claimed. Even the worship of Hera, they felt, must have been inherited.[5]

The idea that a Mycenaean palace shrine could have been in regular use until the seventh century seemed to fly in the face of everything that was known about the archaeology of the region. Desperate attempts were made to explain the anomaly. Thus Blegen, surveying the evidence, decided that "the later building within the megaron at Tiryns is not a Greek temple" but "a reconstruction carried out towards the end of the Mycenaean Period after

---

1 C. W. Blegen and M. Rawson, *The Palace of Nestor at Pylos in Western Messenia*, Vol. 1 part. 1 (Princeton, 1966) p. 300

2 H. Schliemann, *Tiryns* (London, 1886)

3 A. Frickenhaus, "Die Hera von Tiryns," in *Tiryns*, Vol. 1 (Athens, 1912) p. 34

4 Ibid.

5 Ibid., p. 31

the destruction of the palace by fire."[1] But this explanation still left a gap of several centuries between the "late Mycenaean" building and its undoubted use as a sacred site in the sixth and fifth centuries, which the terracottas and votive flasks showed only too well. Furthermore, in order to maintain the "late Mycenaean" origin of the building, Blegen had to ignore the significance the capital of a Doric column found during the excavations.

Blegen's attempts to explain the anomaly thus failed to convince. The Greek temple which replaced the Mycenaean shrine clearly belonged to the seventh or even sixth century, and everything about the Mycenaean shrine showed that it had been in regular use until immediately before the building of the temple. This came to be accepted by the majority of historians, though they could not explain the fact that a Mycenaean sanctuary would have survived in regular use and completely unaltered for such a long time; even through the supposed five centuries of barbarism that characterized the Dark Age.

Identical problems were encountered in almost every location. The Dictaean Cave on Crete for example was a votive shrine in the Late Minoan (contemporary with Late Mycenaean) Age and it supplied the Cretan Collection in Oxford's Ashmolean Museum with many objects. In 1961 J. Boardman published a study of the Cretan Collection in which he attempted, with reference to the work of previous scholars, to classify the finds by their style of affiliation. Of bronze figurines of men from the votive cave he wrote: "These Cretan figures have been dated, apparently by style, to Late Minoan III. They must be related in some way to the well-known Geometric type of mainland Greece which exhibits the same characteristics."[2] Bronze figures of women from the same cave present a similar problem: "Although no such figures of women have been recovered from the Late Minoan III deposits, it is likely that the cruder specimens from the cave are of this date, although Pendlebury thought some might be Geometric."[3] Animal figures raised question of the same kind: "[T]here is as yet no reason to believe that bronze animal votives were being made uninterruptedly from Minoan to Geometric times. It should then be possible to distinguish the early from the late, but it is not easy."[4]

---

1 C. W. Blegen, *Korakou, a Prehistoric Settlement near Corinth* (Boston, 1921) p. 130
2 J. Boardman, *The Cretan Collection in Oxford* (Oxford University Press, 1961) p. 7
3 Ibid., p. 8
4 Ibid., p. 9

Next came knives with human heads at the end of the handles. "The style of the head is exceptionally fine.... Its superficial resemblance to a group of Cretan Geometric bronzes is noteworthy, and although the shape of the blade and solid handle point to the latest Bronze Age, there is much in the style to be explained." The strata in which it was found "suggest a Middle Minoan III–Late Minoan I context" and this "considerably complicates the problem."[1] Again, a "cut-out plaque from the cave ... is of a woman with a full skirt. The dress and pose, with elbows high, seem Minoan, but the decoration of the small bosses is more Geometric in spirit."[2]

In the words of Velikovsky: "Thus bronze figurines, rings and plaques perplex the art expert when he tries to determine the period from which they date, and the difference frequently amounts to more than half a millennium. Will not then the pottery — vases and dishes, the hallmark of their age — throw some light on the problem?"[3] He answers his own question: "for the storage jars with reliefs (*pithoi*) from the Dictaean Cave, two authorities 'imply a Geometric date,' but two other authorities 'have them Minoan.'" Pendlebury himself viewed it as "tempting to see in these pieces the immediate predecessors of the finely molded and impressed *pithoi* of seventh-century Crete, but for these the independent inspiration of mainland Greece or the islands can be adduced, and the cave fragments are best regarded as purely Minoan in date."[4]

And so the problem could have no resolution. The very same features tended to confuse the experts. Some Cretan vases have a very characteristic decoration on them and it could be expected that this would help solve the question of the age. But it does not. "There are several Cretan examples of heads or masks being used to decorate the necks of vases.... The example from Knossos was published by Evans as Minoan, and the signs on the cheeks thought to be signs in a linear script. The technique and the decoration tell against this. The patterns are purely Geometric ... The outline of the features is common in Cretan Geometric."[5] In other cases the confusion is still greater when a decision has to be made between the Minoan/Mycenaean of the second millennium, the Geometric of the eighth century and the Archaic of the late seventh and sixth centuries. Yet, as we shall see towards the end of the present chapter, evidence both on Crete itself and on Sicily to

---

1 Ibid., p. 20
2 Ibid., p. 43
3 Velikovsky, "A Cretan Votive Cave," *The Dark Age of Greece*. www.varchive.org/
4 Boardman, loc. cit., p. 57
5 Ibid., p. 103

the west finally, by the 1960s, compelled art critics to admit that, in these regions at least, the Mycenaean/Minoan style survived as a living tradition into the sixth century BC.

A BITTER CONTROVERSY

If Geometric ware, clearly of the ninth, eighth and seventh centuries, was regularly located at the same levels — or even underneath — Mycenaean ware, why, it might be asked, was the Mycenaean culture not dated accordingly and placed in the eighth and seventh centuries? Such, after all, appears to be the only rational approach. But this was not done, for it would have meant overturning the entire edifice of Egyptian chronology, which, by the later years of the nineteenth century, was regarded as unassailable. Instead, it was assumed that wherever Geometric and Mycenaean artwork had been found in the same levels and (more especially) when Geometric work had been found underneath Mycenaean, that the ground must have been "disturbed" in antiquity; and that ancient builders had, in leveling the sites and preparing them for new structures, blotted out the original stratigraphic sequence. It thus became part of received wisdom that the epoch of Mycenaean ware came to an end around the twelfth century BC, and that the Dorian Invasion, which apparently occurred two generations after the fall of Troy, introduced the "primitive" art form which subsequently came to be known as Geometric. This scheme, first mooted in the latter years of the nineteenth century, is the credo still tacitly accepted in the textbooks — though it creates insurmountable problems.

But one authority at least would not accept the new consensus. Wilhelm Dörpfeld, who had spent many years excavating in Greece, first with Schliemann in the 1880s, refused to date the Geometric culture after the Mycenaean. How could he — after finding it in the same level as Mycenaean, and even lower and earlier than Mycenaean in so many sites? According to Dörpfeld, two or three cultures met in Greece during the Mycenaean Age.[1] Observing that the Mycenaean Age is contemporaneous with the time of the Eighteenth Dynasty, and that the Geometric period is contemporaneous with the Mycenaean, he placed the Geometric Age also in the second millennium. "The geometrical style," he said, "is very old; it existed before and next to the Mycenaean art, nor was it replaced by it."[2]

---

1 W. Dörpfeld, *Homers Odyssee, die Wiederherstellung des ursprünglichen Epos* Vol. 1 (Munich, 1925), pp. 304ff.
2 W. Dörpfeld, *Alt-Olympia* Vol. 1 (Berlin, 1935) p. 12

Dörpfeld argued his case with particular reference to the sites he had himself played a role in excavating. These included Olympia, Tiryns, Troy and Athens. In all of these he had found Mycenaean and Geometric material at the same levels. In Olympia there was very little Mycenaean ware, but what there was placed it slightly later than the Geometric. Dörpfeld had excavated Olympia along with Adolf Furtwängler, a meticulous researcher who was perhaps the first archaeologist to see the importance of pottery as a chronological guide. Furtwängler spent over a quarter of a century classifying small finds, ceramics, bronzes, and other artifacts. He disagreed with Dörpfeld on all points. In the early days Curtius, one of the excavators of Olympia, was impressed by proofs of the great antiquity of the bronzes and pottery discovered under the Heraion (temple of Hera) at Olympia. He was inclined to date the temple to the twelfth and thirteenth century and the bronzes and pottery found beneath it to a still earlier period, and this view is reflected in the huge published volumes containing the report of the excavation.[1] In order to confirm that the Heraion did date to the second millennium, Dörpfeld undertook fresh excavations at the site. What he found confirmed his belief that the Geometric Age was contemporary with the Mycenaean. Furtwängler however interpreted the new finds as further confirming that the Geometric period belonged in the eighth and seventh centuries and therefore must have come long after the Mycenaean period.

An academic battle as bitter as anything ever waged commenced. Who but an ignoramus, asked Furtwängler, would place in the second millennium the geometric vases found in the necropolis near the Dipylon Gate in Athens, when a whole variety of evidence, including alphabetic inscriptions, showed the cemetery to belong to the eighth, seventh and sixth centuries BC. And how could Dörpfeld dare to place the Heraion at Olympia as far back as the twelfth century BC, when iron tools were found beneath it?

Both disputants linked the question of the Geometric epoch to the date of the Homeric epics. Most scholars claimed of course that the poems originated in the eighth or seventh century, but the dissident Dörpfeld held that they originated five or six centuries earlier, in the Mycenaean Age, which was also the Geometric Age.

The battle between the two continued for decades without any resolution, and a quarter of a century after one of the disputants, Furtwängler, was resting in his grave, Dörpfeld, then an octogenarian, filled two volumes with arguments. Furtwängler had vilified his opponent on his deathbed, and Dör-

---

1 E. Curtius and F. Alder, (eds.) *Olympia, Die Ergebnisse der von dem deustchen Reich veranstalteten Ausgrabungen*, 10 vols. (Berlin, 1890-7)

pfeld did the same; and the pupils of both men participated in the quarrel. In the end however the followers of the dissident scholar, Dörpfeld, deserted him and went over to the camp of his detractors. By that time he had already been discredited, and his obstinacy made him a target for further attacks by the younger generation of scholars "properly" trained in the archaeology of the Aegean, who were able at a glance to tell that sherds of the Mycenaean Age had to be dated before 1100 BC and that those of the Geometric Age had to be dated in the ninth, eighth and seventh centuries BC.

Modern estimations of Dörpfeld and his career tend to be colored by the debate with Furtwängler and its outcome. Yet he is still "considered the pioneer of stratigraphic excavation and precise graphical documentation of archaeological projects."[1] The debate with Furtwängler was all about the Geometric Age and how to date it. Dörpfeld insisted it was contemporary with the Mycenaean and, trusting Egyptian dating, placed it in the sixteenth to twelfth centuries BC. Furtwängler, with equal certainty, placed it in the ninth to seventh centuries BC. It never occurred to either that they could both be right: that the Geometric Age was contemporary with the Mycenaean, and that it belonged in the ninth to seventh centuries. To come to that realization however they would have needed to throw out Egyptian dates, and that was something neither dared to do.

THE EMERGENCE OF GREEK CULTURE

The resolution of the debate between Dörpfeld and Furtwängler in favor of the latter did not resolve the problem of the Geometric Age. On the contrary, it only exacerbated it.

As we have seen, archaeologists of the nineteenth and early twentieth centuries were in no doubt that Geometric art, with its disciplined lines and abstract forms, was the earliest authentic expression of the Greek spirit. The art and culture of Minoan Crete, along with its related "Mycenaean" mainland branch, was viewed as utterly alien to all things Hellenic. Trying to determine what kind of relationship — if any — there was between the two proved to be extremely problematic. Initially, it was argued that the "northern" Geometric art must have been introduced after the Trojan War by the Dorians, with the Mycenaean culture being the product of a supposedly earlier Greek-speaking aristocracy ruling over a largely non-Greek "Minoan" population.[2] But the progress of archaeology soon proved this hypothesis

---

1 "Wilhelm Dörpfeld," at http://en.wikipedia.org/wiki/Wilhelm_D%C3%B6rpfeld

2 See e.g., R. M. Cook, *Greek Painted Pottery* (1997) p. 6. "Ancient Greek tradition makes much of the Dorian invasion of southern Greece, which is dated about the same time that archaeologists now date the end of the Mycenaean period. The proposition that the Dorians brought

false: for the major and most important centers of Geometric culture, such as Attica, were found to be in regions never settled by the Dorians at all.[1]

The discovery of this fact implied that Geometric culture was not introduced by invaders, either Dorian or of any other variety, but that it represented an autochthonous Greek style. This presented a problem which left only two possible solutions: either Geometric art was the work of an indigenous Greek-speaking population which had existed contemporaneously with (or even before) the arrival of the foreigners — Cretans and Cycladic islanders — who had produced the Mycenaean artwork, or Geometric art had somehow evolved out of the earlier Mycenaean. The former option was rejected, notwithstanding the protests of Dörpfeld, because Geometric art and culture so obviously belonged to the Iron Age of the ninth, eighth and seventh centuries BC: it displayed striking parallels with the Celtic Hallstatt culture of central Europe (seventh to fifth centuries), and Archaic art of the sixth century was very obviously in direct line of descent from the Late Geometric art of the seventh. To accept Geometric culture as contemporary with Mycenaean meant bringing the Mycenaean Age also down into the eighth century or even later. But Mycenaean culture was provably contemporary with that of the Egyptian Eighteenth Dynasty, which was dated to the fifteenth and fourteenth centuries BC.

So, the idea that Geometric Greek and Mycenaean cultures were contemporary — which the evidence in the ground seemed to insist upon — was discounted even before it was properly considered.

Scholars were then forced to contemplate something that seemed incredible, even absurd: that Geometric culture had somehow "evolved" out of Mycenaean. A search was made for anything that could in any way be regarded as "transitional" between the two. Sure enough, a species of rough pottery labeled "sub-Mycenaean" was decreed to mark the decline and transformation of the formerly splendid culture. On the other hand another variety of inexpensive pottery, often characterized by concentric circle designs produced by the compass (as opposed to the hand-done spirals of Mycenaean/Minoan work), was designated as "proto-Geometric." In order to account for the many centuries which elapsed between the supposed high point of Mycenaean culture (late 16th to 14th centuries BC) and the irrefutable flowering of Greek Geometric (9th to 7th centuries BC), the periods covered by

---

the Geometric or the Protogeometric style with them from Macedonia or the Danube has therefore been attractive."

1 "[T]he Dorians, have as yet no distinguishing feature in terms of archaeological remains." N. G. L. Hammond, "The Literary Tradition for the Migrations" in *CAH*, Vol. 2 part 2 (3rd ed) p. 706

"sub-Mycenaean" and "Protogeometric" were made to stretch out over five centuries — a span far greater than any archaeological remains could justify. This period of abandonment and decline marks of course the so-called Dark Age.

It will be apparent then that the whole concept of an evolution from Mycenaean to Geometric, as well as the existence of so-called transitional forms, is something which has been forced upon historians by Egyptian chronology, and by it alone. If the latter chronology had not existed, a very different picture of archaic Greece would have emerged.

THE EARLIEST GREEK CULTURE

We have noted that in some cases Geometric pottery seemed to occur below and therefore earlier than Mycenaean. This in fact was the case in many of the excavated sites.[1] Of course, as we have seen, to admit that Geometric Age ware came earlier than the Mycenaean Age would have meant a radical realignment of Greek history, with the Mycenaean Age thus down-dated to the eighth or even seventh century BC. In order to avoid this, it was decreed that the Geometric material found underneath Mycenaean strata had got there owing to the ground being "disturbed," either in modern times or antiquity. Nevertheless, archaeologists do admit that the Mycenaean Age was preceded by a culture which produced pottery and other artifacts decorated with various "geometric" patterns. This is the so-called "Middle Helladic," a culture characterized by "Matt-painted" and "Minyan" types of ceramics, the latter variety deriving its name from the large quantities of its kind discovered by Schliemann in the ancient Minyan city of Orchomenos.

As we have said, Middle Helladic pottery, like Geometric, was decorated with abstract geometric patterns. Thus "Minyan" ware was characterized by "incised parallel semicircles ('festoons') and stamped concentric circles"[2] (both in fact typical of Protogeometric), whilst the "Matt-painted" Middle Helladic ware was characterized by its "rectilinear [i.e. geometric] patterns.[3] We are told that "Geometric Matt painting lasted until the sixteenth century," and that "This geometric [Middle Helladic] phase of Aegean art in the

---

1 As well as the material discovered by Dörpfeld, we should call attention also to the discoveries of C. C. Edgar at Phylakopi on the Aegean island of Melos, where he uncovered Geometric pottery under Mycenaean, as well as mixed with Mycenaean right until the end of the Mycenaean deposit. C. C. Edgar, "The Pottery" in *Excavations at Phylakopi in Melos* [supplementary paper no. 4] of *Journal of Hellenic Studies* (London, 1904) pp. 85-107 and 159-163.

2 Quoted from the internet site of Dartmouth College. "Middle Helladic Greece." See http://www.devlab.dartmouth.edu/history/bronze_age/lessons/9.html.

3 Ibid.

second millennium BC" was found "all over Greece and Anatolia."[1] But the parallels between this pre-Mycenaean Geometric art and the supposedly post-Mycenaean Geometric art of the ninth, eighth and seventh centuries, went beyond similarities of pottery decoration: Just as Protogeometric and Early Geometric burials were in cist-tombs, so were those of the Middle Helladic Age. Thus, "all of the Protogeometric burials [at Athens] are inside cist-tombs of the type used in the pre-Mycenaean or Middle Helladic times. These tombs are not derived from Mycenaean tombs, but, where dated to Middle Helladic times, are considered antecedent to them."[2] So apparently Greek was Middle Helladic culture that historians, revising the earlier consensus about the Geometric culture of the ninth and eighth centuries, now see the Middle Helladic folk as the first true Hellenes. Thus in the *Cambridge Ancient History* John L. Caskey notes how, "Persuasive arguments have been advanced that they [the Middle Helladic people] were the first who can properly be called Greeks, and this conclusion must almost certainly be accepted."[3]

Needless to say, an earlier generation of scholars was much more explicit in its recognition of the parallels between Middle Helladic and Early Geometric. In the words of classicist Eddie Schorr; "Numerous scholars have long noted resemblances between the earliest 'Iron Age' [Geometric] pottery ... to the Middle Helladic ware at the time of, and immediately preceding the Shaft Grave period [of Mycenae], with the earliest writers, like Conze, Gardner, and Schliemann himself, making them contemporaneous."[4] Later scholars of course rejected the idea that the two could be contemporary, because of the problems it raised for (Egyptian-based) Mycenaean chronology. Nevertheless, the striking parallels between the two art forms and cultures continued to impress archaeologists, and Schorr notes that at Asine, just to the south of Mycenae, Swedish excavators in the 1920s described the resemblances between Middle Helladic and Early Geometric pottery as "astounding."[5] And though modern scholars are taught to overlook the parallels, they have not ceased to impress. In Schorr's words, historians "still note closer similarities [of Geometric ware] to MH [Middle Helladic] ware 500 years earlier than

1 Bernhard Schweitzer, *Greek Geometric Art* (Phaidon Press, London, 1971) p. 14

2 Jan Sammer, "New Light on the Dark Age of Greece: The Dark Age Spanned," Appendix to Velikovsky, *The Dark Age of Greece*, at http://www.varchive.org/

3 John L. Caskey "Greece and the Aegean Islands in the Middle Bronze Age" in *CAH* Vol. 2 part 1 (3rd ed) p. 137

4 Eddie Schorr (aka 'Israel Isaacson'). Appendix to Velikovsky's *The Dark Age of Greece*. "Shaft Grave Art: Modern Problems." See http://www.varchive.org/

5 O. Froedin and A. W. Perssons, *Asine: Results of the Swedish Excavations 1922-1930* (Stockholm, 1938) p. 279

the intervening LH [Late Helladic — 'Mycenaean'] pottery, a matter which 'raises a host of problems.'"[1] Even the 'cist tomb' burials of the Middle Helladic period display striking parallels with those of the Early Geometric — but do not resemble those of the supposedly intervening 'Mycenaean' age.[2]

Middle Helladic then is a parallel culture to Geometric Greek. It is not however identical to Early Geometric or Protogeometric: there are important differences. Middle Helladic ware, both "matt-painted" and "Grey Minyan," are unique art forms. Nevertheless, they share features in common with Protogeometric — a culture and epoch normally dated to the ninth or tenth century. We can say then that in all probability these two are contemporary cultures produced by two different, though perhaps closely related, ethnic groups.[3] But if Middle Helladic is contemporary with Protogeometric, it means the abandonment of the entire structure of Mycenaean chronology. Middle Helladic is admitted by all to be older than Mycenaean (or Late Helladic),[4] which means, in essence, that the Mycenaean or Late Helladic period must have commenced in the eighth or even seventh centuries, and that it developed, as early commentators guessed, through the importation into southern Greece, especially the Peloponnese, of craftsmen and artists from Crete and the Cyclades. These craftsmen must have been brought over to Greece by the increasingly powerful and wealthy Achaean war-lords of southern Greece and the Peloponnese during the latter years of the eighth and through the seventh centuries BC to decorate their palaces and shrines.

Before moving on, it should be noted that in many areas the pottery typical of Middle Helladic, "matt-painted" and "Grey Minyan," survived, as did Geometric, into the seventh century BC. This was the case for example in Troy, where Grey Minyan ware first appeared at the beginning of Troy VI (contemporary with the earliest Shaft Graves at Mycenae). The same type of pottery, virtually unchanged, was found in great quantities in Troy VII, which is generally believed to have been the city sacked by the Greeks. And yet Troy VIII, the first settlement displaying an Archaic Greek culture (i.e. in the seventh century), *still* produced Grey Minyan ware. "In the seventh century BC the Trojan citadel, which had been virtually deserted for some four centuries, suddenly blossomed into life once more with occupants who

---

1 Schorr, op. cit.

2 Schorr, op. cit.

3 An attempt is made, in Chapter 6, to identify the ethnic group responsible for "Middle Helladic" ware.

4 Though, incredibly enough, it survived in Troy and other parts of Asia Minor into the seventh century BC.

were still able to make Gray Minyan pottery."[1] And Grey Minyan ware, we are told, made up "the great bulk of pottery at Troy VIII."[2]

The above facts, in themselves, are enough to prove conclusively that the Middle Helladic Age was contemporary with the Geometric.

CONTEMPORARY CULTURES

If what we have asserted thus far is correct, it means that the culture we call "Mycenaean" is little more than a mainland expression of Cretan or Minoan and that this culture was introduced into the Peloponnese and southern Greece during the eighth century BC, when the powerful Achaean chiefs of the time began to import artists and artisans from Crete and the Cyclades to decorate their palaces and shrines. These immigrants from Crete would then have come into contact with an already-existing Greek Geometric culture and the two, for some time, would have coexisted and interacted.

We should find therefore that in many of the details of material culture the Mycenaean and Geometric civilizations resembled each other. Indeed, the resemblances should be striking and detailed. We should find too that with the passing of time the Minoan/Mycenaean style began to influence the Geometric artists and that from, say, the Middle Geometric period (i.e., roughly 800 to 700 BC) there would have been a gradual adoption of "Mycenaean" (Cretan) themes and motifs by the Geometric potters and artisans. And we must expect that, as the expression of a still-thriving culture, "Mycenaean" art would have continued to influence the Greek craftsmen in the period from 700 to 600 BC, and that the work we call "Archaic Greek" should display very pronounced "Mycenaean" influence.

We shall find that all of the above propositions are correct.

In scores of details, the Mycenaean and Geometric cultures display striking parallels. These involve almost every area of life, and many of them are so specific and detailed that they can only be explained as evidence of them being contemporaneous.

- Styles of burial, in cist-graves, were identical in the Geometric Age and in the Middle Helladic through to the Mycenaean Age.
- The megaron, a great communal hall, a classic feature of life in the warrior-societies of northern and central Europe, was a feature of both Mycenaean and Geometric cultures.

---

1 C. W. Blegen, *Troy and the Trojans* (New York, 1963) p. 172
2 C. W. Blegen, J. S. Caskey, and M. Rawson, *Troy* Vol. IV part 1 (Princeton, 1958) p. 251.

• Types of tools and weapons employed during the Mycenaean and Geometric periods are precisely alike, as were many of the types of domestic utensils, such as pottery. Indeed, many pottery forms, such as the krater, were equally typical of the Mycenaean and Geometric Ages. Yet it is above all in the field of weaponry and military usage that the parallels impress. Throughout history, as we know, few other areas of life have evolved as quickly as that of military technology; and for obvious reasons: Any power or society wishing to survive had to be as quick as possible in the adoption of advantageous changes. Bearing this in mind, the parallels between military usage during the Mycenaean and Geometric epochs can only make us wonder.

When Geometric artists, from about 750 BC onwards, began to portray the human figure, many of the themes they chose to illustrate were from warfare. Here we find, for the first time, depictions of Greek warriors in action. They carry, very often, enormous "man-covering" shields. These are the earliest representations of the famous *dipylon*, ("Double-Gated") shield; and they are strikingly similar to the enormous "Figure-of-Eight" shields portrayed so often in early Mycenaean and Minoan art.[1] By late Mycenaean times the large "man-covering" shield had gone out of fashion, to be replayed by a much smaller circular targe. If the Geometric Age followed the Mycenaean, we must wonder why the warriors of that time would return to a form of weaponry that had become obsolete in the early Mycenaean Age.

• The Geometric Age warrior was often armed with two throwing spears, as was the Mycenaean warrior.

• The Geometric warrior wore a plumed helmet: The Mycenaean warrior sported a similar headdress.

• The Geometric warrior carried a slashing-sword with a peculiar T-shaped pommel. The Mycenaean warrior carried a similar weapon.

• The Geometric warrior rode a light, wicker-work chariot with four-spoke wheels: The Mycenaean warrior rode in a chariot of precisely the same design.

Even tiny details of military usage match. Consider for example the horses which pull the chariot of the Geometric warrior: Very often these animals have their manes tied into a series of small "pony-tails" which stretch from the ears down to the end of the mane. Yet Mycenaean Age horses were

---

1 The large Geometric Age shield is admitted to be identical to the Mycenaean figure-of-eight. A late 8th century amphora from Athens, for example, portrays marching warriors of whom only the helmeted heads and legs are visible: "everything else is covered by a large shield, which has the Mycenaean figure-of-eight shape, stylized in the Geometric manner." Ronald Hampe and Erika Simon, *The Birth of Greek Art* (Thames and Hudson, 1981) p. 157

done up in precisely the same way. So compelling are these parallels and so obvious is the relationship between the two cultures, that it is now widely admitted that Mycenaean culture had an extremely important impact upon historical Greece; and yet, in the words of one authority, "it seems to me that the degree of continuity between Mycenaean and Classical Greece, and the importance of the Bronze Age heritage, have even now never been stated with sufficient force."[1] The same writer asked, with evident perplexity: "Has the vase-painting of sixth- and fifth-century Athens nothing to do with the fresco paintings at Thebes, Tiryns and Pylos? It is more individual ... and it is therefore less purely decorative. Yet those rather remote, pensive-looking ladies with their slightly hung heads that appear in the frescoes, their hair and dress carefully exploited for decorative effect, surely find significant echoes in Classical painting."[2]

Being in many ways a more advanced and sophisticated culture, it is to be expected that the Minoan/Mycenaean style would have begun to influence that of the Geometric artisans almost as soon as they were exposed to it. Thus we might expect to find, for example, that by the Early Geometric Age (circa 800 to 750 BC), potters and other craftsmen had begun to import Minoan/Mycenaean decorative motifs. Further, as contact between the two cultures increased and the Geometric artisans became more familiar with the work of the Cretans, the influence of the latter would grow exponentially.

In fact, this is precisely what we do find. Perhaps the most detailed examination of Geometric Art and its development was undertaken by Bernhard Schweitzer in the 1960s. His *Greek Geometric Art*, published first in German and, in 1971 in English, presented to the reader the result of many years of meticulous research. Schweitzer noted that by the eighth century, in the Early to Middle Geometric epoch, "Attic potters and painters came into contact for the first time with places with stronger Mycenaean traditions than Athens," as a result of which, "A few motifs which were not part of the basic Attic [Geometric] ornamentation found their way into the indigenous vase painting."[3] Schweitzer identified the source of this "Mycenaean" influence as the Cycladic Islands, though that was evidently not the only one, since we know that "Crete has a pottery record all her own. Minoan and sub-Minoan survived [into the Geometric period]."[4]

1 Jacquetta Hawkes, *Dawn of the Gods* (London, 1968) p. 249
2 Ibid., p. 274
3 B. Schweitzer, *Greek Geometric Art* (London, 1971) p. 33
4 John Boardman, *Early Greek Vase Painting* (Thames and Hudson, 1998) p. 52

The first Minoan or Mycenaean motif incorporated was the false spiral, described as "a frieze pattern of circles connected in a continuous chain by tangents." This, according to Schweitzer, can be "taken as a Geometric version of the Mycenaean running spiral." Its origin, he notes, "can be traced back to the Cyclades in the Early Bronze Age, where spiral chains and spiral nets, incised on stone and clay ware, formed the basic decoration."[1] In addition, from "the same source," we are told, "comes the leaf pattern, the only plant motif which occurs in Attic Geometric art .... The leaf rosette is clearly derived from Mycenaean gold discs while its combination with false spirals indicates that it probably came via the Cyclades." This indicated that "Alien ornamental motifs now begin to merge into the world of the Attic painter."[2] Another decorative feature mentioned by Schweitzer, the metope-and-triglyph frieze, "grew out of the Mycenaean octopus motif."

By the year 700 BC, as Geometric artists introduced more and more figurative work, the borrowings from Minoan/Mycenaean art became a virtual flood. Schweitzer admits to these, and mentions several examples, such as portrayals of recumbent ibexes with their heads turned, which "betray Mycenaean origins." "It is instructive," he writes, "to compare the fragments of the older fresco cycle in the *megaron* of Mycenae with the [Late Geometric] cup from Kerameikos and the [Late Geometric] skyphos from Eleusis." Although, in conformity with the prevalent system of dating, it is "futile to look for the connecting link between the composition of Mycenaean frescoes and the oldest Geometric figured vases," nevertheless, we can "hardly doubt that such a link must have existed."[3]

Now the seventh century is normally known as the "Orientalizing" period and, as the name would imply, it is seen as an era during which powerful influences arrived from the east, mainly from Syria/Phoenicia and from Anatolia. And there is no question that some influences did indeed reach Greece from these areas. Yet, we shall see, the term Orientalizing is a deceptive misnomer; for it is designed to explain-away those evident echoes of the Mycenaean Age which would otherwise have to be admitted. By claiming that the decorative and figurative motifs which crowd Greek art by the seventh century came from the East, it is possible, in part at least, to ignore the obvious Mycenaean influences. The view is expressed thus fairly typically by R. Higgins: "[A] fair number of technical processes and decorative motives of Mycenaean art reappear in Greece in the eighth and seventh centuries BC.

---

1 Schweitzer, loc. cit.
2 Ibid., p. 34
3 Ibid., p. 36

These include the carving of ivory, the goldsmith's processes of filigree and granulation, the nature deity with animals, sphinxes and griffins. But these and other processes and motives are best explained as reintroductions from the East, where they had been adopted in the days of the Mycenaean empire and kept alive through the Dark Age."[1] In this way then the Mycenaean influence can be swept under the carpet. Yet an honest examination of Archaic art brings one to a very different conclusion: Namely that the predominant influence upon Greek craftsmen of the time was not from the East, but from the south; and that the "Mycenaean" stylistic influences had no need to be "reintroduced from the East," for they had never passed out of use in Greece herself. We shall find in fact that the culture we call Archaic was basically the result of Greek artisans having adopted the forms and motifs of the Minoans/Mycenaeans wholesale.

During the later Mycenaean period, normally described as Late Helladic III, the predominant mode of decorating pottery is the so-called "Close Style," a term which art historians use to describe compact designs arranged in friezes of water fowl, rosettes, triangles, loops, semi-circles and other motifs, which fill all the exposed surface area of the pots. Lacey found it "interesting to notice that the same phenomenon occurred again four hundred years later in the profusion of ornaments" that covered the so-called Dipylon pottery of the eighth century.[2] In the words of Eddie Schorr, "It is even more interesting that the individual motifs on the [Mycenaean] Close Style vases, as in the case of the Warrior Vase, find their most striking parallels in the designs on the seventh-century 'Orientalizing' pottery of Greece, Crete, Rhodes, Cyprus, Sicily, Italy and the Eastern Aegean. That interest heightens when we recall that at a number of excavations throughout the same area (including Wace's trench by the Lion Gate) eighth-seventh century pottery immediately overlay, was mixed with, or even lay *beneath* L.H. III B-C [Late Mycenaean] ware"[3]

By around the year 600 BC Greek artists were regularly depicting the human form, in scenes from Heroic Age myth and legend. Male figures are typically "long-haired" and bearded Achaeans; yet it is the portrayal of the face, both male and female, that strikes us most. If we compare the face of the goddess from a Knossos fresco, supposedly executed around 1400 BC, (fig. 11) with the faces of the maenads from an Archaic amphora of c. 540 BC

---

1 Reynold Higgins, *Minoan and Mycenaean Art* (3rd ed., London, 1997) p. 190.

2 A. D. Lacy, *Greek Painted Pottery in the Bronze Age* (London, 1967) p. 223

3 Edwin Schorr, "Applying the Revised Chronology: Other LH III Figural Pottery," in *Velikovsky's Dark Age of Greece*, http://www.varchive.org/

(fig. 12) we can only be impressed by the similarities. The way that the eyes, nose, mouth, and ears are shown are so similar in both works that we could almost imagine them having been executed by the same artist. Yet, according to conventional ideas, these two examples of Aegean art are separated from each other by almost a thousand years — during which time the skill of figurative portrayal was completely lost for about four centuries.

Compare also the so-called "Warrior Vase" from Mycenae (fig. 5), supposedly dating from circa 1150 BC and the Archaic Crater of Aristonothos (fig. 6), dating from about 650 BC. The parallels are obvious enough, even at a glance, and in fact have been the subject of much scholarly conjecture over the years. Actually, for some time after its discovery, historians dated the Warrior Vase to the seventh century. They considered the registers of spearmen as a development of the eighth century (Geometric Age) processional friezes on funerary jars found near the Dipylon Gate at the Kerameikos cemetery of Athens. They thus unhesitatingly attributed the soldiers on the bowl to the Protoattic Period (early 7th century) and of course compared them to the warriors painted on the Archaic Krater, signed by Aristonothos. Some even ascribed both bowls to the same man.[1]

As well as the processions of warriors, scholars were struck by a feature of the Mycenaean Warrior Vase not normally shown in textbook illustrations: the so-called "bull's head handles." (see fig. 7) These were found to have precise parallels in Geometric and Archaic vessels of the seventh and sixth centuries – as for example in the seventh-century Cypriot vase pictured in figure 8. Not only do both vessels display this feature, the details of the two are strikingly similar. Note in particular the crane-like birds placed underneath the bull's head handles on both pieces.

Now scholars had always considered bull's head handles to be a later development from Protogeometric and Early Geometric double-loop handles, now artistically rendered as horns surmounting a bovine face. But the discovery of bull's head handles on work (the Warrior Vase) supposedly preceding the Geometric Age by several centuries now forced a rethink. The bull's head handles could not, after all, be a development of the double-loop, rather the double-loop must be a degeneration of the earlier Mycenaean bull's head.[2] Yet the proponents of this view never explained how it was that the Archaic

---

1 See e.g., E. Pottier, "Observations sur la ceramique mycenienne," *Revue Archéologique*, 28 (1896) pp. 19-23.
2 N. R. Oakeshott, "Horned-head Vase Handles," *Journal of Hellenic Studies*, 86 (1966) pp. 114-5, 121.

artists of the seventh century should return to the bull's head form — in precisely the same design — five centuries after it was abandoned.

There is thus little doubt, even from an examination of the figurative and decorative art on Greek ceramics, that Archaic period artisans, in the sixth century, continued to borrow "Mycenaean"-style motifs and ideas from a still-living "Mycenaean" culture. This is indicated by the evidence and fully admitted by scholarship. In fact, it is now freely conceded — though never discussed a great deal in the popular and popularizing literature — that until the sixth, fifth and even fourth centuries BC, the people of eastern Crete maintained their ancient "Minoan" culture, including its language and its art. It is admitted that Cyprus too, even in the fifth and fourth centuries, retained many Minoan/Mycenaean features, including the use of its ancient syllabic script and the retention of ancient art forms. And, as we shall see, the Thracians and the Scythians, to the north of Greece, continued to display, as late as the fifth, fourth and third centuries BC, artistic and cultural traits that can only be described as Mycenaean. The same holds good too for the regions of the west. In Etruria, to the north of Rome, and in southern Italy and Sicily, Mycenaean-style art and architecture was still being produced in the sixth and fifth centuries. Thus, looking at the evidence from Sicily and southern Italy, where Mycenaean-looking material is regularly found in seventh and sixth-century contexts, Ernst Langlotz noted, "even if surviving finds [of Mycenaean-type pottery in Italy] do not go back to the second millennium BC, they may well be genuine Cretan products of the seventh or sixth century BC, made by Cretans in their characteristic latest Minoan style. This seems to be confirmed at least for the city of Gela (founded c. 690 BC by Cretans and Rhodians) by the finds made there. Even in a city as remote as Cerveteri, very late Mycenaean vases have been found in graves of the sixth century BC."[1]

---

1 Ernst Langlotz, *The Art of Magna Graecia* (Eng. Trans, Thames and Hudson, 1965) p. 15

Above: Fig. 1. The Lion Gate at Mycenae, dated to the thirteenth century BC.

Below: Fig. 2. Phrygian rock-cut tomb at Arslantas, dated to c. 670 BC.

Fig. 3. Cycladic amphora, c. 660 BC, showing rampant felines - an extremely popular motif in Late
Geometric and Archaic art.

Fig. 4. The so-called Treasury of Atreus at Mycenae, as it would have originally appeared. Note the geometric patterns and palmetto-designs, all typical of Late Geometric/Archaic art of the seventh century BC.

Above: Fig. 5. The Warrior Vase, from Mycenae, dated to the thirteenth century BC.
Below: Fig. 6. The Aristonothos crater, dated to c. 650 BC.

Above: Fig. 7. Bull-head handle from the Warrior Vase.

Below: Fig. 8. Bull-head handle of seventh-century vase from Cyprus. Note also the bird, as on the Warrior Vase.

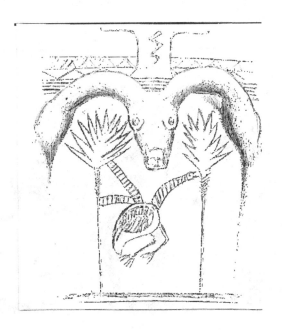

Above: Fig. 9. Silver cup from Mycenae, showing long-haired and bearded Achaeans. Dated to the thirteenth century BC.

Below: Fig. 10. Long-haired and bearded titans, from the Athenian Acropolis. Circa 550-540 BC.

Fig. 11. Female figure from Mycenaean fresco, Tiryns, fourteenth century BC.

12. *Detail from amphora, c. 540 BC, showing maenads. Note the striking similarities with the female figure on the Tirnys fresco, particularly with regard to the eyes, nose, mouth, and ears. It is evident that the sixth-century artist was heavily influenced by Mycenaean/Cretan representations of the human face.*

Fig. 13. Mycenaean sword with
T-shaped pommel.

Fig. 14. Detail from Archaic amphora showing Heracles using a sword with T-shaped pommel. Sixth century BC.

CHAPTER 3. THE QUESTION OF LITERACY

EPIC POETRY

The two epic poems ascribed to Homer, the *Iliad* and the *Odyssey*, occupy a central place in western culture. For the pre-Christian Greeks they were revered almost religiously. The Romans too, even before they had incorporated Greece into the Empire, became enthralled by the tales of heroism and savagery with which the verses are filled. The Romans claimed descent off the Trojans, so these events had for them a particular resonance. From the Romans, Homer's epics entered the culture of all of Europe.

By the beginning of the scientific age, especially after the Enlightenment, Europeans began to cast an increasingly skeptical light on these stories. Although in many respects the *Iliad* appeared to describe incidents in a real war, the *Odyssey* was agreed by all to be little more than a fantasy adventure. But there were major problems even with the *Iliad*, the greatest of which, perhaps, was the routine encounters with gods and the involvement of these beings in the action. This especially was regarded as damning evidence, and by the second half of the nineteenth century, it was generally agreed that Homer's works had no basis in fact: they were imaginative creations of the poet. True, Homer may have had the fabulous stories of earlier poets to work on, but the story of Troy, with its ten-year siege, was without historical foundation. It was believed that the world described by Homer was that of his own time, the eighth or perhaps seventh century BC.

Then along came Schliemann: Trusting the word of the poets and ancient authors, the self-taught German uncovered first the remains of Troy
and then, on the other side of the Aegean, the vastly wealthy burials in Mycenae, fully confirming thereby Homer's epithet for the city, *polykhrusos* —
"rich in gold." The interments at Mycenae were located by the same method
used in Troy — trusting tradition. Very soon, both at Mycenae and other
sites throughout Greece, Schliemann was uncovering the remains of a whole
new and hitherto unsuspected civilization. The artwork found at these sites,
termed "Mycenaean," bore little or no resemblance to the art of the ancient
Greeks as traditionally understood by Europeans. There was, for one thing,
a freedom about it unknown to the disciplined Greeks; and there was a con-
cern for nature and natural things unknown to the Hellenes. Animals, plants
and landscapes were portrayed with a richness and freedom of expression
that excited the archaeologists.

Subsequent excavations, especially those of Sir Arthur Evans at Knossos
in Crete, were to show that this "Mycenaean" culture was in fact (in its origins at least) a Cretan, or at least insular phenomenon. It appeared that Cretan craftsmen and artists had migrated to the mainland of Greece (especially
the Peloponnese) at some time, and there settled in fairly large numbers. But
what astonished scholars most was not the brilliance of this culture or the
mystery of its origin, but the way in which it reflected, in incredible detail,
the world described by Homer. Thus for example the poet had described
several of his heroes as defended by a helmet of wild boars' tusks. Since no
such equipment was ever seen in Greek art of the historical age, classicists
had no idea of what he meant: not at least until they found numerous examples of just such helmets in Mycenaean settlements, and portrayed on Mycenaean artifacts. According to one writer, "It is difficult to imagine Homer
transmitting a description of an object which we could not visualize.... For
four centuries at least no one could possibly have seen a boar's tusk helmet."
Again, when Homer described the "man-covering" shield of Ajax, it was not
known what he meant, until numerous portrayals of such targes were found
in Mycenaean artifacts. The technique of metal inlay of the shield of Achilles
was found to be practiced in the Mycenaean period, though it "disappeared
before its close, and apparently never returned there." Even tiny details, it
emerged, of Mycenaean culture and technological usage, were known to
Homer. Thus Nestor's cup with the doves on its handles had an exact counterpart in one excavated on the Peloponnese, whilst the swords with "silver-
studded" handles described by Homer were actually uncovered.

None of these things, it was (and is) believed, could possibly have been seen by Homer, who was apparently separated from them by a barbarous dark age of five centuries' duration, in which time even the art of writing was lost. How, it has been asked again and again, could Homer have known about these things? Whence came his detailed knowledge of Mycenaean life and customs? As a solution, some have suggested that the poems were not written by Homer at all, but were relics of the Mycenaean Age which were handed down by wandering bards by word of mouth for five centuries before finally being committed to writing in the eighth or seventh century. In defense of this position, poets and bards of various regions (but especially Albania) are cited, who are able to recite very long epics which they have learned by heart from their predecessors. It is suggested then that by these means Homer derived his uncanny knowledge of Bronze Age civilization. Yet even should we admit the existence of a bardic college in Dark Age Greece, the problem remains unresolved: For Homer's poems reflect not only Mycenaean Greece but also Greece of the seventh century. Objects are described "which cannot have found a place there before the 7th century." One such artifact is the clasp which fastens the cloak of Odysseus when on his way to Troy. "It points to the second decade of the 7th century as the time of the composition of the *Odyssey* (unless it is an interpolation, the dates of which could not be much earlier or later than the first half of the 7th century)."

If then Homer merely wrote down or repeated epics he learned by word of mouth from his predecessors, why did he corrupt them with material from his own time? In the words of Velikovsky: "The blending of elements testifying to the Mycenaean Age together with elements the age of which could not precede the seventh and certainly not the eighth century is a characteristic feature of the *Iliad*. Some scholars have expended enormous efforts in trying to separate passages of the epics and ascribe their authorship to different generations of poets, from contemporaries of the events to the final editor of the poems in the seventh century. But all these efforts were spent unprofitably, and their authors at the end of their labors usually declared their perplexity." Classicist M. P. Nilsson expresses it thus: "To sum up. There is considerable evidence in Homer which without doubt refers to the Mycenaean Age .... The Homeric poems contain elements from widely differing ages. The most bewildering fact is, however, that the Mycenaean elements are not distributed according to the age of the strata in the poems." Nilsson continued: "The Mycenaean and the orientalizing elements differ in age by more than half a millennium. They are inextricably blended. How is it credible that the former elements were preserved through the centuries and incorporated in poems whose composition may be about half a millennium later?"[1]

The answer to the puzzle has already been given: the two cultures and artistic styles of the *Iliad* and the *Odyssey* do not reflect two different ages, but two different peoples; the Cretans and islanders who worked for the Achaean chieftains in the coastal regions of the Peloponnese (and Crete) and the native Greeks, who occupied the central Peloponnese and all of the rest of Greece north of the Isthmus of Corinth. Yet even taking such a radical solution into account, the precise date of the composition of the poems remains a problem, and it is a question we shall return to in due course.

THE LOSS OF LITERACY

Although it was suggested that Homer's detailed knowledge of Mycenaean life had been transmitted to his time through an oral tradition of bardic poetry, this did not solve the problem of how an entire society had managed to lose the art of writing for a period of almost five centuries. We know that Mycenaean society was fully literate, as the discovery of the Linear B tablets made very clear; and we know that writing played an important part in the culture of the time: It is even mentioned by Homer, who tells how Bellerephon was given a letter of introduction for King Iobates of Lycia, written by Proteus of Tiryns, urging him to slay the bearer of the note, for the crime of attempting to violate his wife.[2] Ignoring the fact that Homer thus displays his own familiarity with writing, the very preservation of so many other details of Mycenaean life through epic poetry speaks of a culture which valued, even revered, the relics of the Mycenaean Age. And in fact the cults of the Heroic Age characters were still very much alive in Archaic and Classical times. If the heroes who fought at Troy and their predecessors were so highly regarded, how is it that one of their most important skills, that of writing, was utterly lost?

In his *Homer and His Forerunners*, M. Bowra puts the problem thus: "There is no evidence whatsoever that the Mycenaean script continued anywhere in Greece after c. 1200. There is no trace of writing of any kind in the sub-Mycenaean and Protogeometric periods, or indeed before the middle of the eighth century, when the new and totally different Greek alphabet makes its first appearance. Now, this is surely not an accident. A single scratched letter from this period would be enough to show that writing survived; but not one has been found. This is undeniably a most remarkable phenomenon,

1 M. P. Nilsson, *Homer and Mycenae* (1933) pp. 158-9
2 *Iliad*, vi, 160.

for which it is hard to find a parallel or an explanation. A society seems suddenly to have become illiterate, and to have remained so for centuries. How and why this happened we do not know."[1]

Bowra expresses his wonder that "this astounding state of affairs," which "undermines any hope that the transmission of heroic poetry was maintained by a succession of written texts from the time of the Trojan War."

Returning to the well-known problem of Homer's sources, Bowra emphasized that "the Homeric poems contain material which is older than 1200," though we can be "reasonably confident that Homer worked in the latter part of the eighth century, since this suits both the latest datable elements in his details and his general outlook." This required the existence of a tradition of purely oral poetry, transmitted for centuries by word of mouth without the assistance of writing. This, in fact, is the solution now generally accepted; though it is one that scholars baulk at. How could poems of the size and detail of Homer's works have survived so long without the assistance of any writing? It was an idea that Alan J. B. Wace could not countenance. In his preface to Ventris' and Chadwick's *Documents in Mycenaean Greek* (1956), he wrote that future discoveries and study would "undoubtedly make clear" whether the Dark Age was really dark: "the orthodox view of classical archaeologists is that there was a 'Dark Age' when all culture in Greece declined to barbarism, at the close of the Bronze Age and in the early period of the ensuing Iron Age. Even now, when it is admitted that the Greeks of the Late Bronze Age could read and write the Linear B Script, it is still believed by some that in the transition time, the Age of Bronze to that of Iron, the Greeks forgot how to read and write until about the eighth century when they adapted the Phoenician alphabet. It is incredible that a people as intelligent as the Greeks should have forgotten how to read and write once they had learned to do so."[2]

Where then are the documents? The answer apparently is that, "Letters or literary texts may well have been on wooden tablets or some form of parchment or even papyrus; some fortunate discovery will possibly one day reveal them to us." A half century since this was written nothing has been found that would substantiate this hope. Wace's words "it is still believed by some that ... the Greeks forgot how to read and write" refers in fact to the opinion of virtually every classicist and specialist on Greek history, not, as Wace obviously wanted to believe, to just one hypothesis among many.

---

1 Sir Maurice Bowra, *Homer and His Forerunners* (Edinburgh, 1955) pp. 1-2

2 P. xxviii; cf. J. Chadwick, "The Linear Scripts and the Tablets as Historical Documents" in *The Cambridge Ancient History* Vol. 2 part 1, (3rd ed., 1971) pp. 609-617.

The contention that during the Dark Age the Greeks wrote only on perish-able material does not carry weight, and has been decisively refuted by L. H. Jeffrey in his work, The Local Scripts of Archaic Greece.[1] In Mycenaean times, and again from the eighth century on, the Greeks left many examples of writing on imperishable materials, such as baked clay or stone, as well as on perishable ones, such as papyrus or wood. In Velikovsky's words, "The view that *all* writing during the Dark Ages was on perishable materials, none of which was found, is rather difficult to uphold."[2]

"There is not a scrap of evidence," writes Denys Page in History and the Ho-meric Iliad, "and no reason whatever to assume that the art of writing was practiced in Greece between the end of the Mycenaean era and the eighth century BC."[3] And yet, according to the same writer, "The *Iliad* preserves facts about the Trojans which could not have been known to anybody after the fall of Troy VIIa [supposedly c. 1200 BC]." How then, asks Page, "did the truth survive through the Dark Ages into the *Iliad*?"[4]

THE LINEAR B TABLETS

At a very early stage archaeologists discovered strange inscriptions on clay tablets among the ruins of Greece and Crete. The tablets had not been baked deliberately, but accidentally, by the fires which had destroyed the palaces and fortresses in which they were found. It was thus to an accident that we owe their preservation.

It was soon recognized that in Crete at least two separate writing-sys-tems were represented. The earliest of these, termed Linear A, apparently served as a model for the later, Linear B, which was found both on Crete and the Greek mainland. To begin with, only a few of these were uncovered at Pylos and other places, but others appeared in due course, and to date more than 4360 Linear B tablets have been found at Knossos, 1087 at Pylos, 337 at Thebes, 73 at Mycenae, 27 Tiryns, 4 at Chania, as well as 170 inscriptions on pottery vessels and an enigmatic inscription on a pebble from Kafkania, which was found in 1994. The latter may well be oldest of all, preceding the others by a considerable period of time.[5]

Deciphering the Linear inscriptions proved problematic. Since they were all held to date from the twelfth century BC at the latest, no one imagined

1 L. H. Jeffrey, *The Local Scripts of Archaic Greece* (Oxford, 1961) p. 17

2 Velikovsky, "Why no Literary Relics from Five Centuries?" *The Dark Age of Greece*, http://www.varchive.org/

3 Denys L. Page, *History and the Homeric Iliad* (Berkeley, Ca, 1959) p. 122

4 Ibid., p. 120

5 See e.g., "Linear B" http://en.wikipedia.org/wiki/Linear_B.

that the language would be Greek. Such was the consensus even into the 1950s. Thus for example in 1950 classicist Helen L. Lorimer stated that in the case of Linear B: "The result is wholly unfavorable to any hope entertained that the language of the inscriptions might be Greek."[1] There was however one notable dissenter. In 1945 Immanuel Velikovsky wrote the following: "I expect new evidence from the Minoan Scripts and the so-called Hittite pictographs. Texts in the Minoan (Linear B) script were found years ago on Crete and in Mycenae and in several other places on the Greek mainland. I believe that when the Minoan writings unearthed in Mycenae are deciphered they will be found to be Greek. I also claim that these texts are of a later date than generally believed. No 'Dark Age' of six centuries' duration intervened in Greece between the Mycenaean Age and the Ionian Age of the seventh century."[2]

The above passage, written originally in 1945, was quoted again by Velikovsky in an address to the Forum of the Graduate College of Princeton on October 4, 1953. As he read it, he was unaware of the researches of a young architect on the other side of the Atlantic that were about to cast a dramatic new light on the subject. Finally, in April 1954, the story broke in a front page article in the *New York Times*. The reader heard how Michael Ventris, an "amateur" and "leisure-time scholar of pre-classic scripts," who had served as a cryptographer during World War 2, had found that the language of the Linear B tablets was Greek.

As a boy, it seems, Ventris had attended a lecture by Sir Arthur Evans on the Minoan tablets and, like the young Schliemann, was captivated by the mystery of the Hellenic past. But he was not immediately on the right path. In his *The Languages of the Minoan and Mycenaean Civilizations* (known as the 'Mid-Century Report,' privately distributed in 1950), Ventris revealed that all the leading authorities of his time, whom he had questioned in 1949, were convinced that the language of Linear B could not be Greek. In 1962 Leonard R. Palmer testified as to the opinion of Ventris and the classicists before the breakthrough. In his book *Mycenaeans and Minoans*, Palmer wrote: "Evans ventured no guess at the possible affinities of the Minoan language. That it was Greek never entered his head." Also Blegen, who was the first to find the tablets on Greek soil, "was 'almost certain' that the language of his tablets was 'Minoan'.... Nor did the possibility that the Linear B tablets concealed the Greek language occur to Michael Ventris." He "guessed that the

---

1 Helen L. Lorimer, *Homer and the Monuments* (1950): cited from Velikovsky's *Dark Age of Greece*.
2 Velikovsky, "Theses for the Reconstruction of Ancient History," first published as a monograph in *Scripta Academia* (Jerusalem, 1945)

language was related to Etruscan .... This wrong diagnosis was maintained by Ventris right up to the final stages of his decipherment." "It figures in the so-called 'Mid-Century Report,' which records what could be deduced by the most eminent living authorities from the archaeological and other evidence available at the time preceding the decipherment of the script. The remarkable fact stands out that not one of the scholars concerned suggested that the language could be Greek."

In fact, the tablets, which some had hoped would provide information on political events of the Mycenaean Age, proved to be nothing more, in general, than inventories and accounts kept for taxation and other purposes. Nevertheless, they were very definitely written in Greek, and that fact alone was to provide scholars with an astonishing array of important, even sensational, information. But their being Greek raised first of all the question, mentioned above: How could a literate people in the thirteenth and twelfth centuries become illiterate for five centuries, before regaining literacy in the eighth century?

The documents raised other problems and some were urgent. It was found, for example, that many, very many, of the place- and personal names found in Homer also recurred in the tablets. The list included those of gods. Thus it was discovered that Hera, Artemis and Hermes were worshipped at Pylos, whilst Zeus and Poseidon were worshipped in Pylos and Knossos. Athena was honored at Knossos, and Dionysus' name was found on a Pylos document.[1]

The occurrence of these called for a re-examination of Mycenaean art, and it was recognized that a figure on one vase might be Apollo singing among the Muses, whilst Poseidon appeared to be portrayed driving a chariot over the sea and Zeus with Europa in the depiction of a bull carrying a woman. The Minotaur and centaurs were likewise recognized as probable Mycenaean images.[2]

The names of Achaean heroes familiar from the Homeric epics occurred with great frequency, as did a "wealth of Trojan names."[3] Ajax, called by his patronymic "Telamonian," along with his brother Telamonian Teucer, occurred in the tablets, "and between them they killed two Trojans with tablet names Pyrasos and Ophelestas, and a third Simoeisios, whose father's name, Anthemos, occurs at Knossos." Hector's name and Priam's, and that of Tros,

---

1 M. Ventris and J. Chadwick, *Documents in Mycenaean Greek* (London, 1956) Xa 06 and Xa 1419.
2 See T. B. L. Webster, *From Mycenae to Homer* (London, 1958)
3 Ibid.

are found at Pylos. Achilles' name is found both at Knossos and at Pylos, and Castor's at Knossos.[1] In the *Iliad* Laodokos' father is Antenor and on a Pylos tablet one Laodokos holds land in a village where Antenor is mayor. In Homer Laodokos is from Pylos, where the tablet with his name was found.

Characters from other legendary cycles, mentioned by Homer, also occur in the tablets. Amongst these are some from the Theban Cycle. "Mycenaean names in the story are Amphiaros (Knossos), Adrastos, Eteocles, Polyphontes (Pylos)."[2] One of the sons of Eteocles in Pylos was called Alektryon, a name known from the *Iliad* (xvii, 602). A man names Theseus lived at Pylos and men at Knossos bore the names Selenos and Iakchos, known from the *Odyssey*. The name Aeneas was read on a tablet from Mycenae. Phegeus' name, found in the *Iliad*, occurs also on a tablet from Mycenae. The Trojan Pedasos had a namesake at Knossos.

Incredibly, attributes and epithets accompanying names in Homer are also found on the tablets. "The evidence of the tablets" is "that such formulae as Telamonian Ajax were Mycenaean titles."[3] Nestor of Homer "has Mycenaean titles."[4] Agamemnon's title *wanax* is "certainly Mycenaean,"[5] whilst "king of men" was a title most probably "remembered from Mycenaean poetry" half a millennium before Homer.[6] "The epithet *hippiocharmes* (chariot-fighter), which is applied to Troilos in the *Iliad* and to Amythaon (a name found on the Pylos tablets) in the *Odyssey*, has been recognized as derived from the Mycenaean word for chariot."[7]

If Homer thus displayed an astonishing knowledge of Mycenaean names, titles and cults long vanished, his knowledge of Heroic Age geography was no less impressive. In his famous Catalogue of Cities and Ships, where the poet describes the cities and princes contributing men and equipment to Agamemnon's expedition, Homer provides a treasure-trove of information about the land and people of Bronze Age Greece. Towns, localities and even villages, many of which were uninhabited and even forgotten during the classical period, are described in detail. It was long believed that this information described the Hellas of the poet's own time, namely the eighth or seventh century BC. But the decipherment of the Linear B tablets changed

---

1 Ibid.
2 Ibid.
3 Ibid., p. 286
4 Ibid., p. 218
5 Ibid., p. 121
6 Ibid., p. 107
7 Ibid., p. 103

all that, for there scholars found, to their astonishment, many of these long-abandoned settlements. In the words of Denys Page, "There is no escape from this conclusion: the names in the Catalogue afford proof positive and unrefuted that the Catalogue offers a truthful, though selective, description of Mycenaean Greece."[1] Nevertheless, "there is no scrap of evidence, and no reason whatsoever to assume, that the art of writing was practiced in Greece between the end of the Mycenaean era and the eighth century BC."[2] Yet "it is inconceivable that such a list should have been first compiled during or after the Dark Ages."[3]

With growing wonderment, Page continues: "Descriptive epithets are attached to some fifty of the place names.... Many of the epithets are distinctive, not generally applicable. One place is a meadowland, another is rocky; one place is rich in vineyards, another is famous for its sheep; one place is rugged, another had many flowers; one place is on a riverbank, another on the seashore." "Let us ask," Page continues, "how could an Ionian poet living in the 10th or 9th or 8th century BC know how to describe so many places — some of them very obscure places — all over Greece? How could he know that there were many doves at Messe (if anyone could still find the place); and vineyards at Hine (if it had not yet been swallowed up by the lake); that Aegylips was rugged, Olosson white, Enispe windy, Ptellos a meadowland, Helos on the coast."[4]

How indeed! In the words of Velikovsky: "The problem of the Mycenaean heritage in the Homeric poetry is staggering and remains unresolved through hundreds of volumes dealing with it; it is the despair of anyone endeavoring to solve it within the framework of the accepted chronological timetable."

Yet the Linear B tablets revealed a final and utterly incomprehensible mystery.

THE LANGUAGE OF LINEAR B

When the Linear B tablets were finally read, and found to be Greek, it was naturally assumed that they would represent an extremely archaic form of the language; and it was accordingly proposed to name it "Old Achaean." These were, after all, documents supposedly five or six centuries older than Homer. By the standards of Classical Greek, Homer's language itself is markedly archaic — and the poet's compositions were placed only a couple of cen-

---

1 D. Page, *History and the Homeric Iliad* (1959).
2 Ibid.
3 Ibid., p. 123
4 Ibid., p. 123

turies before the time of Herodotus. The Mycenaean tablets, it was assumed, would display an extremely ancient form of the language.

Astonishingly, this was far from being the case. In the words of A. Tovar: "But contrary to what we expect from Greek documents of the fourteenth and thirteenth centuries BC, the Mycenaean dialect is not seen to be closer to proto-Greek than are Homer or Thucydides. If sometimes Mycenaean shows primitive features, it also sometimes appears more advanced that the dialects of the first millennium."[1] John Chadwick, who co-operated with Ventris in the decipherment of Linear B, wrote: "Since 1952 important new work has modified the general view and this has entailed a shift of emphasis, and the abandonment of the name proposed for the dialect, 'Old Achaean.'"[2]

In terms of its actual affinities, the Linear B language was most closely related to the Greek still spoken in Classical times in Arcadia (central Peloponnese) and Cyprus — the so-called Arcado-Cyprian dialect. Mycenaean was in fact very closely related to Arcado-Cyprian; but it was not the ancestor of other Greek dialects, such as the Ionian. In Tovar's words, "Mycenaean presents many dialectical phenomena of quite recent aspect and is in some traits as far from 'common [early] Greek' as the dialects known a millennium later."[3] There had indeed been one or two authorities who, because of the chronological imperative, persisted in trying to see Mycenaean as an ancestral form of the Greek spoken by the Ionians and others in the fifth century BC. One of these was E. Risch. Against him, Tovar writes: "The weak point in Risch's argument is that it ignores the fact that against the innovations which appear in Mycenaean (and Arcado-Cyprian), Ionic shows many old forms." In other words, in many respects the Ionian dialect of the historical age, of the sixth and fifth centuries, looks *older* than the Mycenaean! Risch was also criticized by E. Benveniste: "It must be admitted," he said, "that according to the hypothesis maintained by Risch during this period [the four or five hundred years between the last Mycenaean texts and the first literary testimony in eighth-century Greek] a remarkable conservation of Mycenaean was upheld in its Arcado-Cypriote dialect and a profound evolution of Mycenaean in its Ionian dialect took place. Is it not more plausible to assume that in the epoch of our tablets the Ionian (not represented in the tablets) already substantially differed."[4]

1 A. Tovar, "On the Position of the Linear B Dialect," *Mycenaean Studies*, ed. E. L. Bennet, Jr. (University of Wisconsin Press, 1964).
2 J. Chadwick, *The Decipherment of Linear B* (1958) p. 78
3 Tovar, op. cit., p. 146
4 E. Benveniste, in *Études myceniennes* (Paris, 1956) p. 263

The language of the tablets suggests that they were written, not in the thirteenth or twelfth centuries BC, but near the middle of the or even later seventh.

At this point we must pause. The Linear B tablets were recovered from the remains of Mycenaean palaces supposedly burned in the twelfth century BC. They were found however to be written in the Arcado-Cypriote dialect of Greek, and to be no more archaic in form than other Greek dialects of the seventh and perhaps even the sixth century BC.[1] Information contained in the tablets proves that they were written very close to the time of Homer and the composition of the Iliad and Odyssey. This brings to our attention once again the question of Homer's date.

Even in antiquity there was disagreement about Homer and his lifetime. Some were inclined to believe he lived shortly after the Trojan War, though others placed him several generations later. Depending on where one placed the Trojan War, this could make Homer live anywhere between the eleventh and eighth centuries. In more modern times, beginning with the Enlightenment, scholars began to question not only these early dates, but even the existence of such a person. Thus in 1715 the French scholar Abbé d'Aubignac Hédelin came to the conclusion that "Homer as a person never existed and that the epics as we have them are a sixth century compilation of poems not previously connected."[2] The next important salvo was fired by Robert Wood, whose book *Essay on the Original Genius of Homer* had immense repercussions for classical scholarship. Wood argued that, since prose writing was unknown before the sixth century, and since the Iliad and Odyssey could not have been preserved without the aid of writing, the two poems must date to that time.[3]

Wood's reasoning was admirable, and the tendency, until the discovery of Mycenaean civilization by Schliemann and the translation of the Linear B texts, had been to accept this late date, with many historians assuming that they had been compiled in the sixth century by either Solon or Peisistratos, or perhaps by the latter's son Hipparchus.[4] With the archaeological discoveries of the nineteenth and twentieth centuries however there were renewed attempts to place the epics further back in time, as near as possible to the

---

1 The earliest Greek inscriptions, in any dialect, are from the seventh and sixth centuries BC.
2 H. L. Lorimer, "Homer and the Art of Writing: A Sketch of Opinion between 1713 and 1939," *American Journal of Archaeology* 52 (1948) p. 12
3 Ibid., p. 15
4 See e.g., the arguments presented Karl J. Beloch, *Griechische Geschichte*, Vol. 1 (Strassburg, 1913)

end of the Mycenaean period. Thus we hear once again of a Homer in the eighth or even ninth century.

Yet the progress of textual criticism and exegesis has continued to add new proofs for a later date. Thus it is admitted, even by the advocates of an early Homer, that a number of verses can only be dated to the sixth or even fifth centuries. These however, as for example the "Athenian" verses of *Iliad* ii, 557 and 558, are explained as "interpolations" of the sixth century.[1] This explanation however has been vigorously countered by Erich Bethe, who argued that the unified style of the texts do not permit us to delete lines we do not like. He accordingly dated the entire *Iliad* and *Odyssey* to the sixth century.[2] In the words of Benny Peiser:

> A 6th century edition of the so-called Athenian verses in the second book of the Iliad is accepted today — but with one proviso — that the Athenian editors did not, in any case, compile the Iliad and Odyssey for the first time, but instead wanted to prevent much older versions from being distorted. The question thus remains how the controversial Athenian verses — in all versions of Homer — were able to be perpetuated without competition. "Out of all the wonders related to the 'Homeric Question,' this is without doubt the most noteworthy" [E. Heitsch, *Epische Kunstsprache und Homerische Chronologie* (Heidelberg, 1968), p. 659].

> If one accepts the existence of a pre-6th century Homeric text, then it is surprising that the supposed Athenian interpolation could be found in all Greek Homer editions — even in the competing non-Athenian ones. It is clear, however, that the Greeks never knew any other version of the Homeric Epics.

Peiser concludes that "there never was a written version of the Iliad before the [sixth century] Athenian edition."[3]

The present writer agrees. As we shall see, the Linear B tablets, whose language is in some ways less archaic than Homer, were composed shortly before the destruction of the palaces in which they were found. But this occurred in the late seventh and sixth centuries; not in the twelfth.

The sixth century was the great age of epic writing. Solon himself was a notable poet, and Plato informs us that he had intended to compose a poem on the destruction of Atlantis using notes he had taken whilst in Egypt. Whether a man named Homer existed or not is beside the point. The works attributed to him were compiled and almost certainly composed in the sixth century, probably the late sixth century. This does not mean that his subject, the war against Troy, must be brought down to that date. As we have seen, themes from the Trojan War occur in pottery and other art from at least the

---

1 See e.g., Alfred Heubeck, *Die homerische Frage* (Darmstadt, 1988) p. 235

2 E. Bethe, "Troja, Mykene, Agamemnon und sein Grosskönigtum," *Rheinisches Museum* 80 (1931) p. 219

3 Benny Peiser, "Re-Creating the Dark Ages of Greece: Fatal Flaws in the New Chronology,"

beginning of the seventh century. Yet the war was not many centuries in the past when the epics were composed. Popular songs and poems dealing with the conflict were probably by then an integral part of Greek culture. The poet of the *Iliad* and *Odyssey* would have used these lays for his own purposes, and preserved also their slightly archaic language. And his intimate knowledge of "Mycenaean" or more accurately Cretan culture is to be explained by the simple fact that Minoan civilization, with all its unique characteristics, survived on Crete and the islands even into the fifth century.

CADMUS AND THE PHOENICIAN ALPHABET

The legend of Cadmus (Kadmos) raises profound difficulties for textbook chronology. Here we meet the whole Dark Age problem head on: For Cadmus, who, according to Herodotus, lived eight generations before the Dorian Invasion and therefore six before the Trojan War, was responsible for introducing the Phoenician alphabet into Greece.[1] If the Trojan War is placed in the twelfth century BC, this means that Cadmus and his Phoenicians must have arrived in the Aegean region in the thirteenth or even fourteenth century BC. Yet no authority would place the existence of a Phoenician alphabet, in the form we now understand it, much before the ninth century; whilst the earliest alphabetic inscription to be recovered from Greece dates from the eighth century: Even worse, Herodotus records seeing, and reading, three Cadmean or early alphabetic inscriptions at Thebes. The problem is that all of these are attributed to known characters of the Heroic Age. One inscription, on a tripod, stated how Amphitryon, reputedly the father of Heracles, dedicated the vessel in thanksgiving for his victory over the Teleboans.[2] Herodotus explains that the style of writing was archaic, but was nevertheless "Cadmean," whose "characters look for the most part like Ionian letters."[3] Amphitryon is supposed to have lived three generations before the Trojan War, therefore sometime in the thirteenth century BC, according to accepted timescales. This has led scholars to reject the authenticity of the inscriptions, or alternatively to suggest that they were written in the syllabic Linear B. The writing, it is suggested, was simply translated for Herodotus by the temple priests.

The same expedient has been called upon to explain the entire Cadmus myth. Thus, it is suggested that the script introduced to Greece by the Phoenician adventurer was the syllabic Linear A or perhaps the slightly later Lin-

1 Herodotus, v, 57
2 Ibid. v, 59
3 Ibid.

ear B. This was a solution accepted, for example, by Robert Graves.[1] Yet it is an explanation that has little to recommend it. The Linear scripts, both A and B, had no Phoenician or Semitic antecedents, and seem to owe far more to the primitive syllabary of the Old European Script, which existed from Neolithic times onwards throughout much of the Balkans. On the other hand, the Greek alphabet really did come from Phoenicia. This alone would suggest that the Cadmus story cannot, irrespective of what textbook chronology says, be separated from the introduction of the Semitic alphabet. Yet once this is admitted, it means that the whole of the Mycenaean/Heroic Age be brought down into the ninth, eighth and seventh centuries: for the Cadmus story was placed by the Greeks *very early* in the Heroic Age.

The problem does not end in Greece, but extends even to the Latin alphabet. Scholars recognize the latter as an adaptation from one of the Greek systems, introduced to the Italian peninsula during the eighth or perhaps seventh century. And sure enough, legend tells how the alphabet was brought to Italy from Arcadia in Greece. The problem is that Evander, the hero-figure who taught it to the Latins, was a contemporary of Heracles and placed very clearly in the Heroic Age.[2]

Linguistic and mythological evidence suggests that there was a culturally significant Semitic or Phoenician impact on Greece in early times. This is demonstrated not least by the number of characters of Greek myth who have Phoenician/Hebrew names and also occur in Palestinian and Syrian legend: Below are just a few of these; and the list is confined only to some of those with identical names. If we were to include those with similar or identical characters, though with different names, the list would be extended almost indefinitely:

TABLE 1. CHARACTERS OF GREEK MYTH WHO ALSO OCCUR IN HEBREW/PHOENICIAN LEGEND

GREEK	HEBREW/PHOENICIAN
Adonis	Adonai (title of Tammuz)
Anax (giant)	Anakim (giants of Joshua, xiv, 13)
Asterion (fem. Asterië)	Astarte, Ashtaroth
Belus	Bel, Baal
Danaus	Dan (son of Jacob)

---

1 R. Graves, *The Greek Myths*, Vol. 1 (Penguin, 1955) p. 183. According to Graves, "The Greek alphabet was a simplification of the Cretan hieroglyphs [i.e., Linear A]," a manifest absurdity.
2 Plutarch, *Symposiacs*, ix, 3; and Scholiast on Homer's *Iliad*, xix, 593.

Iapetus	Japheth (father of Greeks and Europeans)
Leto, Leda, Latona	Lot, Lotan, Leviathan
Melicertes	Melkarth
Nephele (wife of Athamas)	Nefilim
Ogyges	Agog (Amalekite king)
Phineus	Phinehas (grandson of Aaron)
Salmoneus (king of Elis)	Shalman (god of wisdom)
Tyro (daughter of Salmoneus)	Tyre

To the above could be added others who, although having a Greek etymology, such as Niobe, sound suspiciously — in terms of both name and characteristics — to personalities from Hebrew/Phoenician story (in this case Naomi).

The Cadmus legend itself is connected to several of the above characters, and it is evident that his story recalls a Phoenician settlement — not necessarily a numerically large one — in Greece during the Mycenaean or perhaps immediate pre-Mycenaean Age. We are told that Cadmus was the son of Agenor, who, along with the Danaids left the land of Egypt and settled in Canaan. It was there that Cadmus, along with his brothers Phoenix, Cilix, Thasus and Phineus, as well as his sister Europa (Heb. "west"), was born. After Europa's abduction by Zeus, the brothers were ordered by Agenor to set out in search of her.

Elsewhere I have argued in detail that the legend of Agenor contains a garbled account of the Israelite Exodus from Egypt.[1] This is made apparent by the fact of Agenor quitting Egypt, apparently in extreme conditions, and settling in Canaan: Also by the involvement of Phineus and the Danaids. The occurrence of the name Phineus in particular provides perhaps the most unmistakable link with the Exodus. There seems little doubt that this character is identical to the Hebrew Phinehas or Pinehas, grandson of Moses' brother Aaron, who slew the Israelite Zimri along with his Midianite bride in their tent.[2] In the corresponding Greek legend Phineus (or Phineas) attacked Perseus along with his bride Andromeda, daughter of the king of Joppa (Jaffa), at their wedding-feast, but was slain by the Gorgon's head, which Perseus exposed.[3] Again, in another tradition the Greeks told how Phineus, who had been plagued by harpies, was rescued by two of the Argonauts, Calais and

---

1 In my *Pyramid Age* (1999)

2 Numbers, 25: 6-15

3 Ovid, *Metamorphoses*, v, 1-230

Zetes, who pursued the harpies through the air.[1] This accords with a Jewish tradition about Phinehas which has the flying swordsman Zaliah pursue Balaam through the air, on the orders of Phinehas.[2]

It seems clear that the story of the Danaids, as well as that of Agenor and Phineus, must have arrived in Greece through the same channels as the Phoenician alphabet. After their entry into Canaan the Twelve Tribes were allocated separate territories. The tribe of Dan, the Danites, settled in the very north of the country, regions now part of eastern Lebanon (Judges, 18: 7-28). It is known that they became closely associated with the Phoenician kingdoms of the region. Some of the Phoenician traders and settlers who brought the alphabet to Greece might have come from this tribe.

I would suggest therefore that the Cadmus *mythus* relates to a Phoenician settlement in Greece in one of the great population movements which followed the Israelite Exodus. Although Cadmus himself (Heb. *Kedem*, "the east"), cannot be regarded as a historical person, his story records a real event. That there was a Phoenician penetration of Greece at this time is borne out also by the fact that various cities throughout southern Greece, and not just Thebes, had legends of rulers with Semitic names. Thus we note that the Danaids, grandchildren of Belus (Phoenician 'Baal') gave their name to the Argives, who by Homer's time were known as Danaioi ('Danaans'), and the grandson of Danaus, first king of Argos, was known as Abas (Heb. *Aba*, "father"). We note also a king Salmoneus (Heb. *Shalman*, "Wisdom") of Elis, whilst in Corinth one of the ruling king's titles was Melikertes (Heb. *Melkarth*, "Guardian of the city"). Indeed, Phoenician influence in the Corinthian area was substantial, and Robert Graves notes how one legend from Megara, where a king sacrificed his son to Melikertes (biblical Moloch), has a precise parallel in Joshua 6:26, where a king of Moab does the same. Moreover, as Graves notes, the Greek hero, "like Samson and David ... had killed a lion in ritual combat." All of which demonstrates how "Corinthian mythology has many close affinities with Palestinian." [3]

It is worth pointing out, at this stage, that the connection between Cadmus and the Israelite Exodus cannot be used to support a fifteenth or fourteenth century date for the former and for the Greek Heroic Age in general. If Egyptian history was responsible for distorting Greek history, it was the Bible that threw Egypt herself into confusion. As I have demonstrated in

---

1 *Argonautica*, ii, 178ff.

2 L. Ginzberg, *Legends of the Jews* Vol. 1 (1961 ed.) p. 508

3 R. Graves, *The Greek Myths*, Vol. 2 p. 43. We should note too how Scylla, daughter of (supposedly Egyptian) king Nisus of Megara, cut off her father's hair and thereby brought his downfall, just as Delilah did to Samson.

great detail in my *Genesis of Israel and Egypt* and *The Pyramid Age*, it was application of the chronology provided in the Old Testament which originally caused the distortion of Egyptian chronology. This was because, from a very early stage, scholars had sought to "tie-in" the history of Egypt to that of the Bible, with a view to vindicating the latter. Thus as early as the fourth century AD the Christian writer Eusebius had made the second Ramses pharaoh live at the time of the Exodus: this because the Book of Exodus mentioned a city "Ramses" constructed by the Israelite slaves. Following the chronology of the Old Testament, which no one, it seems, bothered to question, Ramses II was then placed in the fifteenth/fourteenth century BC. And this chronology, established by the early Christian chronographers, is still the one found in the textbooks. True, Ramses II has now been reduced in date by a century or two; but then, so has the Exodus.

All the evidence, which is voluminous, demonstrates that the chronology of the Old Testament in so more reliable than that of pre-Classical Greece or pharaonic Egypt, and that virtually all of the events and characters placed by the Old Testament in the second millennium BC need to be brought forward into the first millennium. Thus, for example, it can be demonstrated in great detail that the Exodus should rightfully be placed in the ninth century, and that the period of the Judges, contemporary with and culturally parallel to the Heroic Age of Greece, belongs in the eighth century BC. The Cadmus legend, therefore, along with the introduction to Greece of the Phoenician alphabet, provides a very specific chronological gauge for the Heroic Age, a gauge which places it firmly in the ninth and eighth centuries BC.

Chapter 4. Evidence from Abroad

Thrace and Scythia

It is a common and false assumption that the art and culture associated nowadays with the "Mycenaean" civilization came to an end at some remote time in the past. We have already seen, for example, that Mycenaean, or more accurately Late Minoan art-styles survived on Crete until the sixth and even fifth centuries BC. The same apparently holds good for Cyprus, where not only Mycenaean-style artwork, but even a version of the Linear B script survived until the fourth century BC. And so it is too with regions further to the north and to the west.

One area in particular which displays an altogether mysterious connection with Greece of the Mycenaean period is Thrace. Here, in a region anciently inhabited by a people of apparently Scythian or Sarmatian linguistic affiliations, there appeared in later Classical times, i.e. in the fourth and third centuries BC, a wealthy civilization whose royal and aristocratic burials have caused something of a sensation over the past half century.

In 1931 the peasants of the village of Mezek in southern Bulgaria stumbled upon the entrance to a tomb located in the Mal Tepe Mound. The archaeologist who later explored the tomb, Bogdan Filov, "was amazed by its resemblance to the ancient Mycenaean *tholoi*, or 'beehive' tombs."[1] It was found that "The tomb's central chamber, with its round floor-plan and cor-

---

[1] Ivan Venedikov, "Thracian Royal Tombs," in Ivan Marazov (ed.) *Ancient Gold: The Wealth of the Thracians* (Harry N. Abrams, Inc., 1997) p. 77

belled vault, was shaped like those of the Mycenaean tombs, and like them, its entrance was through a corbelled arch. Similarly, the approach to the tomb was through a twenty-seven-meter-long *dromos*, a straight passageway cut through the mound."[1] Yet this tomb was not to be placed in the Mycenaean Age, for the items found in the interior included "gold earrings and a *tetradrachm* (a silver four-drachma coin) bearing the name of Alexander the Great," as well as "a set of bronze ornament for the yoke of a chariot of a type known from several Celtic burials in Western Europe."[2] It is known that Celtic tribes settled in Thrace in 279 BC.

Filov, the excavator of the tomb, initially postulated that *tholos* tombs must have existed both in Mycenae and Thrace during the Mycenaean Age, and that, while the *tholos* form disappeared from Greece after the twelfth century BC, it continued in use in Thrace for more than a thousand years afterwards.[3] Yet the progress of archaeological investigation soon revealed a very different picture. Of the fifteen or so Thracian *tholos* tombs now known, "Most ... can be dated to the fourth or third century BC. A few appear to be from the fifth century BC, and none can be dated earlier."[4] The "surprising difference" in the ages of the Mycenaean and Thracian *tholos* tombs prompted a search for anything that might bridge the gap. As a solution, archaeologist Vassil Mikov suggested a species of mound-tombs from the Bronze Age, the so-called dolmens, as an intermediate form. Yet these dolmens "were made of five roughly hewn stone monoliths (four walls and a roof), which together form a chamber with an entrance."[5] Hardly a good model for the advanced *tholos* tomb. And it appears that the dolmens too went out of fashion long before the fifth century; so that still left an enormous gap to account for.

Another variety of tomb, chambers hewn from rock, have also been advanced as an intermediate form. Like the dolmens, these have certain features in common with the *tholos* tomb — yet here again chronology stands in the way: For these tombs too came to an end in the twelfth century.[6] Furthermore, "neither corbelled vaults nor corbelled domes were used in dolmens or rock tombs, and the Thracian builders were not familiar with these structures before the fifth century BC.... One must therefore ask what role Greece might have played in introducing corbelled construction to Thrace."[7]

---

1 Ibid.
2 Ibid.
3 Ibid., p. 73
4 Ibid., p. 74
5 Ibid.
6 Ibid.
7 Ibid., p. 75

Greece then was the source: but how could the Thracians have copied an architectural technique that went out of fashion in Greece in the twelfth century? As a partial answer, the writer quoted above cited evidence for the continued existence of corbelling in the Greek world as far as the Hellenistic period. Historian Angelos Orlandos, for example, refers to ten examples of corbelled vaulting used in the construction of fountains and wells during Hellenistic times.[1]

Yet this too fails to solve the problem: for just as in Thrace, we have in Greece no examples of corbelled tombs or the use of corbelling at all between the end of the Mycenaean Age and the Classical.

However, the problem is solved instantly by an adjustment of chronology. The *tholos* tombs of Mycenae, as we shall see, do not date from the second millennium BC, but from the seventh and sixth centuries; and they are thus only a century removed from the earliest Thracian *tholos* structures.[2]

Since the above-writer penned his comments, new discoveries in Thrace have revealed fabulously rich royal burials, several of them completely undisturbed, in Bulgaria's so-called "Valley of the Kings," a region in the centre of the country which is dotted with dozens of burial mounds or tumuli. The excavations, conducted throughout 2004 by Professor Georgy Kitov of the University of Sophia were to reveal some very disturbing things. Several of the royal dead were surrounded, as in Mycenae, with a rich variety of ornaments and weapons. One of these had the head covered by a golden face mask strikingly similar to those found by Schliemann in the Shaft Graves at Mycenae. This mask, "unprecedented" in Thracian archaeology, is now in the Bulgarian Academy of Science in Sophia. The mask almost certainly belongs to Seuthes III (circa 330–300 BC), though it displays an "astonishing" similarity with the face masks from Mycenae, particularly with the so-called Mask of Agamemnon, with which it is routinely compared.[3] Yet the Mask of Agamemnon is conventionally dated to around 1600 or 1590 BC, about 1,300 years earlier than the mask of Seuthes III; and from this long stretch of time, not a single example of another such face mask has been found.

. Are we really to believe that 1,300 years separate these two examples of Balkan art?

---

1 Ibid.
2 Tholos-type tombs are however reported from Thessaly during the Archaic Age (sixth-fifth century), which neatly provides the link to Thrace — but not to Mycenae of the fourteenth to twelfth centuries.
3 See www.theage.com/articles/2004/09/24/1095961855479.html

To the north and east of Thrace stretched the lands of the Scythians, ancient nomad warriors who were apparently related, in terms of language, to
the Thracians themselves. They were also, it seems, like their Balkan cousins, enthusiastic students of Greek culture — Mycenaean Greek culture. Yet,
"According to the account which the Scythians themselves give," wrote Herodotus, "they are the youngest of nations."[1] It was only in the eighth and seventh centuries BC that these nomadic tribesmen migrated from the depths
of Asia to the doorstep of the civilized nations. Formerly they had dwelt east
of the Araxus (either the Oxus or the Volga), and their earliest settlements
in southern Russia date to the end of the eighth century. According to Herodotus, they pursued their arch-foes the Cimmerians south of the Caucasus
around the start of the seventh century BC, and, crossing Anatolia, entered
Mesopotamia, where they participated in the battle for Assyria then rag-
ing. Later the powerful Persian Empire succeeded in confining them to the
steppes north of the Caucasus.

The appearance of the Scythians on the political scene in the ancient
East coincides, in the chronology proposed here, with the very peak of Mycenaean civilization: They must have entered Anatolia within a decade or
two of the end of the Trojan War. In the conventional scheme however they
would have arrived fully four centuries after the last of the Mycenaean citadels had been abandoned. And yet, the tombs of the Scythian kings of the
Crimea, which are dated to around 700 BC, are "surprisingly reminiscent
of Mycenaean constructions."[2] The burial chamber consisted of "enormous
blocks of dressed stone set to overlap each other so as to meet at the centre
in an impressive vault."[3] In the words of Velikovsky, "To explain the use by
the Scythians of the corbelled vault of the type common in the Mycenaean
period, it was suggested that there must have been a continuing tradition
going back to Mycenaean times, despite the lack of even a single exemplar
between the twelfth and seventh centuries."[4] Russian historian Rostovzeff
expressed his confidence that "although we possess no example ... the corbelled vault was continuously employed in Thrace, and in Greece and in Asia
Minor as well, from the Mycenaean period onwards."[5] Velikovsky however
remarked that we "must begin to have doubts about a scheme which needs
to postulate a five hundred year tradition of work in stone for which not a

1 Herodotus, v, 5.
2 E. H. Minns, *Scythians and Greeks* (Cambridge, 1913) p. 194
3 T. T. Rice, *The Scythians* (1957) p. 96
4 Velikovsky, "Mycenae and Scythia" *The Dark Ages of Greece*, http://www.varchive.org/
5 M. Rostovzeff, *Iranians and Greeks in South Russia* (Oxford, 1922) p. 78

thread of evidence exists. Stone constructions of the type, had they existed, would have survived."[1]

The Scythians copied not only the funerary architecture, but also the fine art of the Mycenaeans. Gregory Borovka, in his book Scythian Art, writes of "the striking circumstances that the Scytho-Siberians animal may exhibit an inexplicable but far-reaching affinity with the Minoan-Mycenaean. Nearly all its motifs recur in Minoan-Mycenaean Art."[2] At an even earlier stage Solomon Reinach called attention to these affinities. For instance, the design of animal bodies portrayed in a "'flying gallop' in which the animal is represented as stretched out with its forelegs extended in a line with the body and its hind legs thrown back accordingly, is at once characteristic of Minoan-Mycenaean art and foreign to that of all other ancient and modern peoples; it recurs only in Scythia, Siberia and the Far East."[3]

Strange echoes of Mycenaean art were noticed too in Scythian portrayals of fighting animals. Borovka supplies his description with illustrations. "How often are the animals depicted with the body so twisted that the forequarters are turned downwards, while the hind quarters are turned upwards? Can the agonized writhings of a wounded beast or fury of his assailant be more simply rendered?"[4] Also, "Other motives if the [Scythian] animal style, too, reappear in Minoan and Mycenaean art. We may cite the animals with hanging legs and those which are curled into a circle. Conversely, the standard motif of the Minoan-Mycenaean lion, often represented in the Aegean with reverted head, reappears in Scythian and Siberian art."

These idiosyncrasies in the portrayal of animals are unusual. But what appeared most surprising to the art historians was the fact that two such similar styles should be separated not only by a vast geographical distance, but also by an enormous gulf in time. "How are we to explain this far-reaching kinship in aim between the two artistic schools? It remains, on the face of it, a riddle. Immediate relations between Minoan-Mycenaean and Scytho-Siberian civilizations are unthinkable; the two are too widely separated in space and time. An interval of some 500 years separates them .... Still, the kinship between the two provinces of art remains striking and typical of both of them."

---

1 Velikovsky, op. cit.

2 G. Borovka, *Scythian Art* (London, 1928) p. 53

3 S. Reinach, "La représentation du galop dans l'art ancient et moderne," in *Revue archéologique*, 3e série, tome XXXVIII (1901) fig. 144 p. 38

4 Borovka, loc. cit. pp. 53-4

Magna Graecia

Sicily and southern Italy were heavily colonized by Greek settlers during the eighth and seventh centuries BC. The various Greek cities of the region all had strong traditions regarding their origins and founding. None of them dated that earlier than the eighth century. Nevertheless, many of them, perhaps even the great majority, were said to have been founded by Achaean princes in the wake of the Trojan Campaign. Strabo the Roman geographer puts it thus:

> For it came about that, on account of the length of the campaign, the Greeks for a time, and the barbarians as well, lost both what they had at home and what they had acquired by the campaign; and so, after the destruction of Troy, not only did the victors turn to piracy because of their poverty, but still more the vanquished who survived the war. And indeed, it is said that a great many cities were founded by them along the whole seacoast outside of Greece, and in some parts of the interior also.[1]

The cities founded by the "barbarians" (the Trojans) who survived the war were mainly those of Etruria; of which more will be said shortly. Those founded by the Greeks were in Sicily and southern Italy. The most important settlement in the latter region was Brundisium, reputedly established by Diomedes. The Greek warrior's golden armor was said to have been preserved by the priests of Athena at Apulian Luceria, and he was worshipped as a god in Venetia and throughout southern Italy.[2]

Idomeneus, king of Crete, was banished upon his return from Troy and settled in the Sallentine region of Calabria, where he lived until his death.[3] Again, the hero Philoctetes was expelled by rebels from his city of Meliboea in Thessaly, and fled to southern Italy, where he founded Petelia, and Cremissa near Croton, and sent some of his followers to help the hero Aegestes fortify Sicilian Aegesta.[4]

The problem for conventional scholarship is that none of these settlements claimed to be older than the latter eighth century, and none of them can produce archaeology older than circa 700 BC.

The earliest of the Greek settlements on Sicily was at Syracuse, a city dating, according to the general consensus, from 735 BC. Gela on the southern coast, founded by migrants from Crete and Rhodes, was said by Thucydides to have been "built in the forty-fifth year after Syracuse," thus in 689 or 690

---

1 Strabo, i, 3.
2 Pausanias, i, 11; Servius on Virgil's *Aenead*, viii, 9 and xi, 246; Strabo, vi, 3, 8-9.
3 Virgil, *Aenead*, 121ff. and 400ff.
4 Tzetzes, *On Lycophron*, 911, quoting Apollodorus' *Epitome*; Homer, *Iliad*, ii, 717ff; Strabo, vi, 1, 3.

BC.[1] And yet tradition also stated that Gela's founder was Antiphemos, one of the Greek warriors who fought at Troy. A fragment of a lost work, *On the Cities of Asia*, by Philostephanos, apparently stated that Gela had been founded by a brother of Lacius, the founder of Phaselis, and that both brothers had been in the company of Mopsus, one of Agamemnon's allies, as he made his way to Cilicia in the aftermath of the Trojan War.[2] We shall have more to say on this Mopsus in due course. Thus, according to Jan Sammer, "In the chronology of Philostephanos ... Gela was founded in the same generation that saw the fall of Troy, by one of the warriors who took part in that war; since ... the historical date of Gela's establishment is acknowledged by the best authorities to be ca. 690 BC, Priam's city could not have fallen more than two or three decades earlier."[3] Virgil has Aeneas, the Trojan hero, sail along the southern coast of the island and admire flourishing Gela and two other Greek settlements.[4] None of these could have existed before the early seventh century, though Aeneas' voyage is held to have occurred almost five hundred years earlier.

A little to the north of Agrigento, a little to the west of Gela on Sicily's southern coast, are found *tholos* tombs of Mycenaean type.[5] Inside one of the tombs were discovered gold bowls and seal rings manufactured in a style that derives from Mycenaean gold work.[6] Astonishingly, however, neither the tombs nor the objects found inside could be dated before the end of the eighth century. Archaeologists regard it as a puzzle how "splendid gold rings" with incised animal figures, so reminiscent of Mycenaean objects presumably five centuries older, could have been manufactured by Greek colonists in the seventh century if "a real Dark Age" of five hundred years' duration did in fact separate them from the latest phase of Mycenaean civilization.[7] In Sicily the time between the end of the Mycenaean Age and the beginning of Greek colonization is an absolute void, with a total lack of archaeological remains. Even the "Protogeometric" pottery which elsewhere is claimed to span the Dark Age is absent.[8]

---

1 Thucydides, vi, 4.

2 Athenaeus, *Deipnosophistae*, vii, 298.

3 Jan Sammer, "New Light on the Dark Age of Greece: The Western Colonies." Appendix to Velikovsky's *The Dark Ages of Greece*. http://varchive.org/

4 *Aeneid*, iii, 671-73

5 P. Griffo and L. von Matt, *Gela: The Ancient Greeks in Sicily* (Greenwich, Connecticut, 1968) p. 47

6 L. B. Brea, *Sicily Before the Greeks* (New York, 1966) p. 175

7 Ibid., p. 130

8 T. J. Dunbabin, "Minos and Daidalos in Sicily," *Papers of the British School in Rome*, Vol. XVI. New Series, Vol. III (1948) p. 9. The absence of "Protogeometric" in Sicily is of course answered by the fact that Protogeometric, or Early Geometric, is in fact, as we saw in Chapter 2, a

As is the case elsewhere, the decorative motifs used by these Greek colonists of the seventh century display strong Mycenaean influence: A detailed comparison of the motifs in use in the seventh century with those on Mycenaean ware caused amazement among art historians, though they refrained from even attempting an explanation as to how these motifs could have been transmitted through the Dark Ages.[1]

ETRURIA

The Etruscans, according to ancient tradition, arrived in northern Italy from Asia Minor in the wake of a devastating famine in their homeland. The historical land of Etruria bordered on that of the Latins, and the Tiber itself formed the southern boundary of Etruscan territory during a long period of history. Sometime in the sixth century, Rome itself became virtually part of Etruria and an Etruscan dynasty ruled at the city for many years. The Etruscans, as well as the Romans, regarded Aeneas, one of the greatest heroes of Troy, as their ancestor, and we are told that "Numerous depictions of Aeneas, or Aeneas with Anchises, have been found in Etruria dating from the sixth and fifth centuries BC," whilst it is certain that Aeneas was viewed as "a founder-hero in S. Etruria towards the end of the sixth century, especially at Veii and Vulci."[2]

There is no question that the Etruscans regarded themselves as having a Trojan or at very least Asian origin. This was an opinion shared by Herodotus, who described them as descendants of Tyrsenos, son of the Anatolian god Atys and brother of Lydos, eponymous ancestor of the Lydians.[3] Herodotus' claim had always, until the advent of modern archaeology, been viewed with skepticism; not least since it was contradicted by the Lydian historian Xanthus. Yet it has now received the support of archaeologists. In the words of A. R. Burn,

> Numerous resemblances have been traced between Asian art [of Asia Minor] and the earliest Etruscan, even in such important matters as dress, weapons and armor. A type of heavy-armed pikeman, with horse-hair-crested helmet and round shield, who could pass either as an Etruscan warrior or an early Greek hoplite, makes his first appearance in Hittite sculptures of the Dark Ages, from North Syria. The Etruscan tracing of descent through the mother, one may here note, is most easily paralleled from Lydia, and their method of taking omens from the entrails of sacrificed beasts was learnt from Babylonia by the Hittites.

---

variety of Middle Helladic — i.e., pre-Mycenaean. It therefore dates from well before the beginnings of Greek settlement in Magna Graecia.

1 G. Karl Galinsky, *Aeneas, Sicily and Rome* (Princeton, 1969) p. 83
2 R. M. Ogilvie, *Early Rome and the Etruscans* (Fontana Books, 1976) p. 34
3 Herodotus, i, 94.

Even the Etruscan physical type and many of their names are redolent of Asia Minor.

The presence of Etruscans on Lemnos at some very early period is now attested by archaeological evidence that is practically conclusive; not only by the sculptured tombstone, long well-known, the epitaph on which is a language "at least closely akin" to Etruscan, but also by the weapons and pottery from an extensive cemetery excavated by Della Seta on the island, and datable, by the character of the jewellery found, to the Geometric period.[1]

Thus the Etruscans, who regarded Aeneas as a founder-hero, apparently really did come from the region of Troy. The island of Lemnos, where the Etruscan-type inscription was found, is within sight of the famed city. The problem for historians of course is that archaeology is quite unequivocal in placing the arrival of the Etruscans in Italy the seventh century or late eighth century at the earliest. In the words of R. M. Ogilvie, the region of Etruria was settled "around 700 BC by a new wave of immigrants, probably displaced from Asia Minor by the troubled conditions of the Cimmerian invasions. The new arrivals brought with them many fertile ideas, including a taste for Greek and Phoenician artistic styles, new techniques for working metals ... and, it seems, a sophisticated non-Indo-European language ... which we call Etruscan."[2]

So we are presented with the following enigma: Aeneas, whom tradition in Italy regarded as one of the founders of Rome, a man who was said to have called into Carthage on his journey west — a city which did not exist (according to the archaeologists) till sometime near 800 BC — also helped found the Etruscan states adjacent to Rome, states which did not exist until circa 700 BC!

Here again we find two diametrically opposed views of the past, two views separated by a chasm of five centuries.

Many Etruscan tombs have been found. They are richly-decorated and often extremely well-preserved. In the region to the north of Rome as far as the river Arno, there exist many vaulted structures erected by the Etruscans. They date from the seventh and sixth centuries BC, yet they are strikingly reminiscent of Mycenaean funerary architecture. According to O. W. von Vacano, "The Mycenaean corridor design and *tholos* structures are related

---

1 A. R. Burn, *Minoans, Philistines and Greeks* (1930) p. 61. One of the well-known Asiatic names also occurring among the Etruscans is that of the god Tarkhun or Tarhun, names which "reappear in that of the Etruscan culture-hero Tarehon, that of the town Tarquinii, and that of the famous Etruscan dynasty of early Rome." Burn, loc. cit., p. 241

2 Ogilvie, loc. cit. p. 13

to the vaulted buildings which make their appearance in the orientalizing period [sixth century] in Etruria — and here it is even more difficult to solve, even though the connection itself is undisputed."[1] Yet it is not only tombs which display this Mycenaean echo: "The remains of the city walls of Populonia, Vetulonia and Rusellae, consisting of huge stone blocks which have a 'Mycenaean' look, do not date further back than the end of the sixth century BC: their gateway may well have had arches rounded like the entrance doors to the *Grotto Campana*, on the outskirts of Veii, which dates from the second half of the seventh century BC, and is one of the earliest painted chamber-tombs of Etruria."[2] So, like the Mycenaeans, the Etruscans employed megalithic masonry very similar to, indeed almost identical to, the megalithic work found at Mycenae and Tiryns: enormous blocks of stone either cut square (*ashlar*), or polygonal.

Associated with these megaliths, small artifacts such as pottery and jewelry have been found in abundance. All of this material is typically Archaic-Greek-looking, and without question dates from the seventh and sixth centuries BC. Yet these remains too often bear striking comparison with the pottery and jewelry of Mycenae. This was illustrated most strikingly in the case, already mentioned in Chapter 2, of a vase fashioned by a Greek master who signed it with his own name, Aristonothos. It is known that between 675 and 650 BC this man studied in Athens and then migrated to Syracuse (Sicily) and later to Etruria. The vase was found at Cerveteri, in southern Etruria. In the words of one historian, "There is an obvious link between the design of the Aristonothos crater and another earthenware vessel, scarcely less often discussed and more than five hundred years older, the vase known from the principal figure decorating it as 'the Warrior Vase of Mycenae.'"[3]

The work of this adopted Etruscan, Aristonothos, would cause further problems for historians, this time in far-off Cyprus.

CYPRUS AND THE EAST

When we look to Cyprus, the problems for conventional chronology are perhaps at their most acute. Here we find a society where apparent echoes of the Mycenaean Age existed well into the fourth century BC. It is not denied, for example, that the linear script employed in Cyprus into the fourth century BC was in direct line of descent from the Linear A and B syllabaries

---

1 O. W. von Vacano, *The Etruscans in the Ancient World* (trans. S. Ogilvie, Bloomington, 1965) p. 81
2 Ibid., p. 82
3 Ibid., p. 81

of Crete and mainland Greece during the Minoan/Mycenaean epoch.[1] But real problems arise when we come to material remains which are, through association with Egyptian New Kingdom artifacts, very definitely dated to the Mycenaean Age. Yet, as with everywhere else, these pieces of pottery, jewelry and weaponry, prove themselves, in a thousand ways, to be stylistically identical to artifacts of the seventh, sixth and fifth centuries BC.

As was the case in various other regions of Hellenic archaeology, this evidence led to a prolonged and bitter academic dispute, with one authority claiming the Mycenaean material could not be dated earlier than the eighth or seventh centuries, and another demanding that Egyptian chronology be respected and the Mycenaean material be dated in the second millennium BC. The most important dispute centered round Enkomi, the location of an ancient Cypriot metropolis. In 1896 the British Museum began excavations at the site, under the direction of A. S. Murray. Within a short time a Mycenaean Age necropolis, with numerous sepulchral chambers, was uncovered. The entire necropolis was in use for as little as one century, according to Murray, and there was "no question that [it] ... belonged to what is called the Mycenaean Age." The pottery, gems, glass, ivory, bronze and gold found in the tombs all displayed the characteristic marks of the Mycenaean epoch and they were accompanied, in case there should be the slightest doubt, by artifacts of the Eighteenth Dynasty. These included a scarab of Queen Tiy, wife of Amenhotep III, a ring with cartouches of Akhnaton, and a gold collar or pectoral inlaid with glass of a design very peculiar to the time of Akhnaton.[2]

Murray was convinced, notwithstanding the Egyptian material in the tombs, that they could not be dated much before the seventh or eighth centuries BC. In the published report on the excavations, he examined many different artifacts in detail, demonstrating their close affinity with Greek material of the eighth, seventh, and, on occasion, of the sixth centuries. He looked at a vase, typical of those found at Enkomi, decorated with figures drawn in dark outlines and accompanied by white dotted lines, making the contours of men and animals appear to be perforated. But, "The same peculiarity of white dotted lines is found also on a vase from Caere [in Etruria],

---

1 See e.g., The Cypriot Syllabary was a "... script used in Iron Age Cyprus, from ca. the 11th up to the 4th century BC, when it was replaced by the Greek alphabet. A pioneer in that change was king Evagoras of Salamis. It is descended from the Cypro-Minoan syllabary, in turn a variant or derivation of Linear A." "Cypriot Syllabary" http://en.wikipedia.org/wiki/Cypriot_syllabary

2 A. S. Murray, "Excavations at Enkomi," in A. S. Murray, A. H. Smith, H. B. Walters, *Excavations in Cyprus* (London, 1900)

signed by the potter Aristonothos which, it is argued, cannot be older than the seventh century BC." We have already encountered this master crafts-man before, whose Caerean vase was the cause of much wonder due to its close similarity to the Mycenaean Warrior Vase, supposedly of the twelfth century BC. Murray continues: "The same method of dotted lines is to be seen again on a pinax [plate] from Cameiros [in Rhodes] in the [British] Museum, representing the combat of Menelaos and Hector over the body of Euphorbos, with their names inscribed. That vase also is assigned to the seventh century BC. Is it possible that the Mycenae and Enkomi vases are seven or eight centuries older?"

Analyzing the workmanship and design of sphinxes and griffins with human forelegs on the vase, the archaeologist stressed "its relationship, on the one hand, to the fragmentary vase of Tell el-Amarna (see Petrie, *Tell el-Amarna*, Plate 27) and a fragment of fresco from Tiryns ... and on the other hand to the pattern which occurs on a terracotta sarcophagus from Clazom-enae, [in Ionia] now in Berlin, a work of the early sixth century BC." The con-nection between the Mycenaean and Aristonothos vases caused "a remark-able divergence of opinion, even among those who defend systematically the high antiquity of Mycenaean art."

A great many golden objects were found in the tombs, and these too caused immense problems. There were a number of gold pins, and, "One of them, ornamented with six discs, is identical in shape with the pin which fas-tens the chiton on the shoulders of the Fates on the Francois vase in Florence (sixth century BC)." A pendant "covered with diagonal patterns consisting of minute globules of gold soldered down in the surface of the pendant" was made by "precisely the same process of soldering down minute globules of gold and arranging them in the same patterns" that "abounds in a series of gold ornaments in the British Museum which were found at Cameiros in Rhodes" and which were dated to the seventh or eighth century.

Porcelain objects were found. These "may be fairly ranked" with the se-ries of Phoenician silver and bronze bowls from Nimrud (Assyria) of about the eighth century. A porcelain head of a woman from Enkomi "seems to be Greek, not only in her features, but also in the way in which her hair is gath-ered up at the back in a net, just as on the sixth century vases of this shape." Greek vases of this shape "differ, of course, in being of a more advanced ar-tistic style, and in having a handle. But it may be fairly questioned whether these differences can represent any very long period of time."

It was the same story with glass: "In several tombs, but particularly in one, we found vases of variegated glass, differing but slightly in shape and fabric from the fine series of glass vases obtained from the tombs of Cameiros, and dating from the seventh and sixth centuries, or even later in some cases. It happens, however, that these slight differences of shape and fabric bring our Enkomi glass vases into direct comparison with certain specimens found by Professor Flinders Petrie at Gurob in Egypt, and now in the British Museum. If Professor Petrie is right in assigning his vases to about 1400 BC, our Enkomi specimens must follow suit. It appears that he had found certain fragmentary specimens of this particular glass ware beside a porcelain necklace, to which belonged an amulet stamped with the name of Tutankhamen, that is to say, about 1400 BC." Surveying the evidence which apparently pointed in two diametrically opposed directions, Murray came to the conclusion that the "Phoenicians manufactured the glass ware of Gurob and Enkomi at one and the same time." Consequently, "the question is, at what time? For the present we must either accept Professor Petrie's date (about 1400 BC) based on scanty observations collected from the poor remains of a foreign settlement in Egypt, or fall back on the ordinary method of comparing the glass vessels of Gurob with those from Greek tombs of the seventh century BC or later, and then allowing a reasonable interval of time for the slight changes of shapes or fabric which may have intervened. In matters of chronology it is no new thing for the Egyptians to instruct the Greeks, as we know from the pages of Herodotus."

Of this last remark of Murray, Velikovsky noted that "the excavator of Enkomi came close to the real problem, but he shrank from it. He did not dare to revise Egyptian chronology; all he asked was that the age of the Mycenaean period be reduced. How to do this he did not know. He quoted an author (Helbig) who thought that all Mycenaean culture was really Phoenician culture, the development of which remained as a standstill for seven centuries."[1] Yet, as Velikovsky remarked, Murray's proposals were flatly rejected. Arthur Evans, at that time having just embarked on his famous series of excavations at Knossos on Crete, came out against Murray's work, "so full of suggested chronological deductions and — if its authors [Murray and his collaborators] will pardon the expression — archaeological insinuations, all pointing in the same direction," namely, "a chronology which brings the pure Mycenaean style down to the Age of the Tyrants" of the eighth century, and makes it "the immediate predecessor of the Ionian Greek art of the seventh

---

1 Velikovsky, "The Scandal of Enkomi," *The Dark Age of Greece*, http://www.varchive.org/

century BC."[1] He concluded with regret that "views so subversive" should come from to high an authority in classical studies.

Yet Evans himself had to admit that "nothing is clearer than that Ionian art in many respects represents the continuity of Mycenaean tradition," and that a number of objects from Enkomi, like the porcelain figures, seemed to present the "most remarkable resemblances" to some "Greek painted vases of the sixth century BC." But he could not ignore the manifold connections of Mycenaean art with Egypt of the Eighteenth Dynasty. Are not the flasks of the Enkomi tombs, he asked, almost as numerous in Egyptian tombs of the Eighteenth Dynasty? A fine gold collar or pectoral inlaid with glass paste, found at Enkomi, has gold pendants in nine different patterns, eight of which are well-known designs of the time of Akhnaton, "but are not found a century later." The metal ring of Enkomi, with cartouches of the heretic Akhnaton, is especially important because "he was not a pharaoh whose cartouches were imitated at later periods," and so on.

This dispute, which echoed that between Petrie and classicists such as Ramsay and Torr a generation earlier and mirrored the contemporaneous debate between Dörpfeld and Furtwängler, was, like the others, settled in favor of the Egyptologists. Murray was accused of failing to distinguish between Mycenaean Age material of Eighteenth Dynasty date and later Iron Age material "of the Dipylon period."[2] A generation later other excavators opened more graves at Enkomi and passed the following judgment: "The burials in the graves belong to the second or Bronze Age, its Late or third period, the second part (out of three) of this third period, more precisely to the subdivisions A (9 graves), B (10 graves) and C (8 graves) also a few belong to Late Bronze IA and IB. Thus the graves on the acropolis are 'all intermingled with each other in a seemingly arbitrary way.'"[3] "What does this mean?" asked Velikovsky, "It means that simple and great questions are eclipsed by nomenclatures."[4]

And yet, in the end, not all of the jargon or redefining could conceal the simple fact that as late as the fourth century BC Cypriot society held onto its Mycenaean and Minoan heritage, and not just its Linear script. Thus in the words of A. R. Burn, "Cypriote society and government ... like Cypri-

1 A. Evans, "Mycenaean Cyprus as Illustrated in the British Museum Excavations," *Journal of the Royal Anthropological Institute*, XXX (1900) pp. 199ff.

2 H. R. Hall, *Aegean Archaeology* (London, 1915) pp. 23-4

3 Velikovsky, *The Dark Age of Greece*, in the Velikovsky Internet Archive, quoting E. Gjerstad and others, *The Swedish Cyprus Expedition, 1927-1931* (Stockholm, 1934), I. 575

4 Velikovsky, loc. cit.

ote art, were recognizably 'Minoan' even in Hellenic times ... the houses in which these [Cypriot] princes dwelt we have learnt something of late from the excavations of the Swedish expedition under Dr. Gjerstad. At Vouni, the ancient Sŏloi where the friend of Solon, king Philokypros, reigned, a sixth-century Cypriote prince's palace was laid bare. It was a well-built masonry building of imposing size — over 100 meters square; and many of its details — its light-wells, staircases, magnificent rooms, above all its capacious magazines — are all thoroughly Minoan in style as if it had been built six centuries earlier."[1]

---

1 A. R. Burn, *Minoans, Philistines and Greeks* p. 239

GREECE AND THE EAST

Archaeology proves that during the Mycenaean epoch Greece was in close contact with the nations of the Near East. Mycenaean pottery and artifacts have been found in great quantities in Egypt, Cyprus, the Phoenician coast and the shores of Asia Minor. As noted earlier, scholars found that links between early Greece and Egypt were strongest during the Eighteenth Dynasty. Throughout that period large amounts of Mycenaean pottery were imported into Egypt, as were Mycenaean-looking weapons and other artifacts. In addition, Mycenaean or Minoan-type characters are portrayed in Eighteenth Dynasty art, the most famous example of which are the "Keftiu" shown in the tomb of Rekhmire, an official of Thutmose III. Conversely, Egyptian artifacts of Eighteenth Dynasty date were discovered with great frequency in a Mycenaean context in Greece, whilst Eighteenth Dynasty-style weaponry was also found in Mycenaean Greece.

It goes without saying then that any attempt to date the Mycenaean Age in Greece must pay close attention to the date assigned to the rise of the Eighteenth Dynasty; and, as we shall see, the two lands and two epochs are connected in an even more intimate way: For there is good evidence to show that elements from Greece played a crucial role in the actual establishment of the Eighteenth Dynasty.

The Eighteenth Dynasty rose to power after a desperate struggle against the Hyksos, a dynasty of foreigners, apparently Asiatics, which had ruled the land of the Nile for several generations.

The rise of the Eighteenth Dynasty in Egypt was contemporary with the appearance in northern Mesopotamia of a new superpower: the Mita, or Mitanni. This folk, whose rulers bore Indo-Iranian names and who assumed the title "Great King," were famous for having conquered the "Old Assyrian" kingdom whose most famous rulers were named Sargon and Naram-Sin. It seems that, just at the moment the Theban princes of the Egypt ousted the Hyksos, the Mitanni were simultaneously overwhelming the Old Assyrians a thousand miles to the north. The apparent synchronicity of the two events, combined with the fact that the Mitannians and Eighteenth Dynasty Egyptians were — at a later stage at least — close allies, makes us wonder: Could the Egyptians and Mitannians have had a common enemy?

They could, and they did.

Elsewhere I have presented a great quantity of evidence showing that the Hyksos foes of the Egyptians and the Old Assyrian foes of the Mitannians were one and the same people. It would be impossible to go into a detailed examination of this material here, though a couple of salient points should be mentioned. To begin with, in the so-called "Memphite Genealogy" of Priests, the name of the first Hyksos pharaoh is given as Sharek, identical almost to Sharru-kin (Sargon), the name of the first Old Assyrian ruler. Secondly, a large number of technical innovations, particularly associated with the art of war, were introduced into Egypt by the Hyksos. Three of these were: (a), the two-wheeled chariot; (b), the bronze scimitar; and (c), the composite bow. These three innovations revolutionized warfare, and gave the Hyksos a decisive advantage when they attacked the Nile Kingdom. Yet all three were also associated with Mesopotamia, particularly with a line of kings whose two most famous representatives were named Sargon and Naram-Sin — identical in name to the "Old Assyrians".[1]

So, in the opinion of the present writer, the Eighteenth Dynasty Egyptians and the Mitanni fought a common Assyrian enemy. Now, the Greek historians of the Classical end Hellenistic Age knew of only one Assyrian Empire — that of the Imperial Assyrians, conquered by the Medes, sometimes known as the "Mighty Medes," during the seventh century BC. As early as 1987, Professor Gunnar Heinsohn suggested that these Old Assyrians

---

1 As I have shown in my *Pyramid Age*, these innovations are normally accredited to the Akkadian kings Sargon I and Naram-Sin. Yet these are alter-egos of the Old Assyrian kings of the same names.

(and the Hyksos) were in fact identical to the Imperial Assyrians, and the Mitanni king who first challenged the Old Assyrians — Parattarna — was none other than the Mede king who first waged war against the Assyrians — Phraortes. Following on from this, Heinsohn identified the Mitannian ruler who sometime later sacked Nineveh — Shaushtatar, or Shaushatra — with Cyaxares (Khwashatra), the Great King of the Medes who sacked Nineveh in the seventh century.

For reasons I have given elsewhere, I date Shaushtatar, a contemporary of Thutmose III, to circa 680 BC, and I place the overthrow of the Old Assyrians in Egypt (the Hyksos) several decades earlier; around 720 BC. But if all this is correct, if the Mitanni are the same people as the Medes and the conquest of the Old Assyrian Empire occurred between 720 and 680 BC, this has profound consequences for the whole of ancient history. For one thing it means that the fall of Assyria was almost contemporary with the date we have already identified as marking the Fall of Troy — around 720 BC. And it is surely significant that it is right at the start of the Eighteenth Dynasty, right at the time of Troy's downfall, that large-scale Mycenaean penetration of Egypt begins.

This is a topic of immense importance to which we shall return presently.

Contemporary with the fall of the Hyksos/Old Assyrians there arose throughout the Near East a number of regional powers — apparently on the ruins of the fallen empire. One of these was that of the Hittites, a mysterious people of central Anatolia who are mentioned in the pages of the Old Testament and occur in the records of the other peoples of the region variously as Kheta, Khatti, or Hatti. It appears that they also warranted a brief mention by Homer, who speaks of the Ketioi as Trojan allies. After the discovery of the Hittite capital at Boghaz-koi, on the Halys River, there came to light an immense archive of cuneiform documents which proved to be the royal archives of the Hittite Kings. These documents, composed in several languages, proved that the Hittites were heavily influenced by the peoples of Mesopotamia; many of the tablets were written in Akkadian. Yet the language of the Hittites themselves, known as Nesha, or Neshili, proved to be an early dialect of Indo-European: And with the discovery of this fact the "Hittite" language was declared the oldest example of Indo-European in existence.

The translation of the Boghaz-koi archive was an immense task that took many years. What it revealed was a mighty and previously unsuspected empire in the middle of Anatolia, which was a major player in the political arena in the time of the Eighteenth and Nineteenth Dynasties. Indeed, Hittite kings came into conflict with Egypt and fought a protracted war against the Egyptians in the earlier years of the Nineteenth Dynasty. They also made war against the peoples of Mesopotamia, and Suppululiumas I, one of the greatest of all Hittite monarchs, gained a decisive victory over the Mitannian king Tushratta, whose empire he reduced to a state of dependency.

The language of the Hittites, Neshili, proved to display striking similarities with Lydian, and many cultural features of the Hittites seemed to point to an age much more recent than that assigned to them — the fifteenth to thirteenth centuries. This chronology, of course, was built upon the synchronization of Hittite and Egyptian history.

The progress of translation of the Boghaz-koi texts threw up a number of surprises, the most sensational of which was the names of cities and towns, as well as individuals, known from Greek tradition. Thus in the west of Asia Minor Hittite documents spoke of regions like Lukka (Lycia), Assuwa (Asia), Masa (Mysia), Karkisa or Karkiya (Caria?) and Pitassa (Pisidia?) as well as cities such as Apasa (Ephesus) and Millawanda (Miletus). The last in particular was not expected, since Greek tradition had insisted that Miletus was established by Greek colonists sometime in the ninth or tenth century. Even more exciting however was the appearance of names of individuals that seemed to be Greek. Thus on a document from the time of Mursilis II, son of the great Suppiluliumas I (a contemporary of Akhnaton) there occurred a Tawalagawas, described as "the Ayawalawas," recognized by some scholars as "Eteokles the Aeolian,"[1] whilst another document of the same king makes reference to a certain Antarawas, king of Ahhiyawa; seen by some as Andreus, king of Achaea (Homeric Greek *Akhaiwoi*). And place-names such as Wilusa and Taruisa, agreed to be located in north-west Asia Minor, brought to mind both Troy and Ilion (archaic Greek *Ilios*). The latter city was, early in the reign of Mursilis II's successor Muwatallis, ruled by a prince Alaksandus, calling to mind one of the names of Paris — Alexandros.[2] The identification of the latter with the prince who eloped with Helen and fought against the Achaeans is highly improbable, but there were other characters mentioned in the archives whose connection with the events related in the *Iliad* could scarcely be denied. Amongst, these, as we shall see, was a character named Mopsus; one of the chiefs who accompanied Agamemnon to Troy.

The identification of this man with the Homeric warrior of the same name is without question one of the sensations of modern archaeology; yet

1 Burn, loc. cit. p. 119
2 Ibid., p. 121

it is a discovery that is not widely celebrated, for the chronology of Egypt, as we shall discover presently, has again caused confusion.

ACHAEAN WARRIORS FIGHT THE ASSYRIANS

In his history of Egypt Herodotus informs us that the Egyptians of his time were well acquainted with the story of the Trojan War. They also told of a violent incursion into Egypt by Menelaus, husband of Helen, immediately after the sack of Ilion.[1] Greek tradition too referred to the arrival of Menelaus in Egypt, though it insisted that the Spartan prince's sojourn in the land of the Nile was a peaceful one. Although both traditions, Greek and Egyptian, are now generally dismissed as fable, they apparently find some kind of echo in the very real contacts between Mycenaean Greece and Egypt discovered by archaeology.

It appears that regular Mycenaean contacts with Egypt were established just before the beginning of the Eighteenth Dynasty. Some Minoan or Cretan artifacts have been located from earlier epochs, but the earliest finds that unquestionably speak of contact with mainland Greece appear to come at the start of the Eighteenth Dynasty. Indeed, the Mycenaeans seem to have been particularly linked to the rise of the Eighteenth Dynasty. Inlaid daggers, for example, found in the coffin of Ahhotep, mother of Ahmose (founder of the Eighteenth Dynasty), were almost identical in design to the daggers taken from the Shaft Graves at Mycenae. Ah-hotep herself is of the greatest interest. On a number of inscriptions she is identified as a princess of the Haunebu (or Haunebt), the "Lords of the North."[2] Now, on the Canopus Decree, the Rosetta Stone, and other documents of the Ptolemaic epoch, the name Hellenes is translated as Haunebu[3] and is apparently a direct translation of the Greek term "Hellenic coast." Indeed the word now transcribed as "Haunebu" was originally given as "Helou-nebut." However, with the discovery of the term in documents of the early Eighteenth Dynasty, supposedly in the middle of the second millennium BC, the phrase Helou-nebut was quietly dropped and replaced with Haunebut. Nevertheless, the use of the term to denote the lands of the Greeks in the Ptolemaic documents is unequivocal, and scholars are thus compelled, notwithstanding the name change, to link the earlier, Eighteenth Dynasty occurrence of the name, to the Mycenaean

---

1 Herodotus, ii,119
2 Frank H. Stubbings, "The Rise of Mycenaean Civilisation," in *CAH* Vol.2 part 1 (3rd ed.) p.634
3 Cecil Torr *Memphis and Mycenae* (Isis, 1988) p.50

Greeks.[1] Such a conclusion has been underlined by the Mycenaean-style weapons associated with Ah-hotep. Could it be then that Ahhotep, a founding member of the Eighteenth Dynasty, was a Greek princess?

On the Karnak stela of Ahmose, her son, Ah-hotep is described as "one who cares for Egypt. She has looked after her soldiers; she has guarded her; she has brought back her fugitives, and collected together her deserters; she has pacified Upper Egypt, and expelled her rebels."[2] According to T G H James: "These words suggest that Ahhotpe had at some critical moment seized the initiative in restoring order in Egypt when control had been lost, possibly on the death of Seqenenre or of Kamose. The terms of her praise are unusually precise and they may well signify that her behavior had been crucial to the establishment of the unified kingdom at the time of the expulsion of the Hyksos."[3] The evidence then, in the words of Frank Stubbings, seems to suggest that "forces from Greece may have served in Egypt, against the Hyksos, as mercenaries."[4]

But to state that the Eighteenth Dynasty rose to power with Greek help raises enormous problems for orthodox chronology. Greek intervention in Egypt at the beginning of the conventionally dated Eighteenth Dynasty (16th century BC) seems historically impossible, though if the Eighteenth Dynasty rose to power near the end of the eighth century, as we argue, all is explained. These events, then, must be dated to the last quarter of the 8th century BC, probably around 720 BC, very close to the period of the Trojan campaign. As such, it seems virtually certain that Ahhotep's Greek warriors probably arrived in Egypt fresh from the sack of Ilion, and she may well have formed part of Menelaus' entourage. Since these Greeks were of such crucial importance in the war to liberate Egypt from the Hyksos/Assyrians, it is little wonder that the Egyptians were familiar both with the story of the Trojan War and the wanderings of Menelaus.[5]

---

1 Stubbings, loc. cit.

2 T. G. H. James, "Egypt: From the Expulsion of the Hyksos to Amenophis I," in *CAH* Vol.2 part 2 (3rd ed.) p.306

3 Ibid., pp.306-7

4 Stubbings, loc. cit.

5 Herodotus records a tradition that Greek warriors helped a king named Psammetichus expel the Assyrians. Although no king named Psammetichus (Psamtek) lived in the epoch under discussion, it appears that Herodotus' Egyptian sources had tapped into an authentic tradition dating from the late eighth century BC. Why they confused Psamtek, a fifth-century ruler, with the founders of the Eighteenth Dynasty is a question discussed at length in my *Ramessides, Medes and Persians* (New York, 2001)

THE SHAFT GRAVES OF MYCENAE

This fresh perspective has exciting consequences for Greek history. Most importantly, it means that the whole question of the Shaft Graves in Mycenae must be re-examined. Heinrich Schliemann fervently believed these to represent the actual burials of Agamemnon and his attendants who were murdered by Aegisthus and Clytemnestra upon their return from Troy.

In should be remembered that Schliemann was drawn to the Shaft Graves by tradition. According to a legend reported by Pausanias, Agamemnon and his followers had been buried by Clytemnestra inside the citadel walls, just to the right of the Lion Gate. The spot, said Pausanias, was marked by a circle of marker-stones, still visible in his time. And in fact, within days of starting work, Schliemann was able to confirm the existence of the stone circle, for the diggers struck upon several of them almost immediately. Soon a large circular enclosure was revealed and the workmen began removing tons of earth, gravel and rock. They had discovered what is now known as Grave Circle A, a series of royal and aristocratic burials, dating from the very beginning of the Late Helladic epoch. This was quickly synchronized with the beginning of the Egyptian Eighteenth Dynasty, for many of the artifacts unearthed bore striking comparison with Egyptian work of that precise time.

It should be noted that a further Grave Circle, B, was discovered outside the walls of the fortress during the 1950s.[1] This Circle contained burials of an earlier age than A, belonging generally to the latter part of the Middle Helladic Age.

About eight feet down, Schliemann came across the first of thirteen separate cist graves, containing altogether about nine adult males, eight females, and two juveniles. The bodies had been covered in shrouds before being lowered into the graves, and many of them richly attired and equipped with vessels, jewelry, and weapons of the richest design. Some of these were swords and daggers, beautifully fashioned and on occasion inlaid with scenes of hunting and war. The heads of the men were covered in magnificent golden face masks. One of these, aesthetically the best, showed the face of a bearded and mustached warrior, which Schliemann took to be Agamemnon himself. It was after removing this mask — under which, for a brief moment, he could discern the partly undecayed features of the dead man — that Schliemann, apparently overcome with the emotion of the moment, telegrammed the Greek king with the message, "I have looked upon the face of Agamemnon." And to this day, the death-mask is known as the "Mask of Agamemnon."

---

1 Excavated between 1952 and 1954 by Papadimitriou and Myloas.

For all that, Schliemann's claim to have discovered the burial of Agamemnon and his entourage is now dismissed out of hand. Stylistically the material in Grave Circle A has to be placed near the beginning of the Eighteenth Dynasty. Indeed, it appears to date almost exactly to the beginning of that period. Since it is believed that the Eighteenth Dynasty came long before the Trojan War (conventionally dated to 1184 BC), it is assumed that the Shaft Graves could not possibly belong to Agamemnon and his followers. In vain did Schliemann protest that the burials conformed in detail to what tradition had said of Agamemnon's interment, even down to the number of persons, their age and sex. And, after all, was it not tradition that had led to him to the spot in the first place? But all such protests were swept aside.

Thus the Shaft Graves are now said to have been the resting places of unknown kings who lived centuries before the dynasty of Atreus.

Armed with our new knowledge such ideas can at last be "laid to rest." The rise of the Eighteenth Dynasty did not precede the Trojan Campaign, it followed it by about five years or perhaps a decade. The Shaft Graves must date to around 720 or 710 BC and are almost certainly the final resting places of Agamemnon and his unfortunate entourage. Who knows, it may even be that the so-called "Mask of Agamemnon" does indeed portray the legendary lord of Mycenae and that the face behind the mask, which had lain in its airtight tomb all those centuries before being uncovered by an astonished Heinrich Schliemann, really was that of Atreus' famous son.

A more fitting end to the tale of Troy could not have been imagined by Homer himself.

At this point we need to say something about the other burial-places of Mycenae, the great "beehive" tholos tombs, which stand without the citadel and which are now associated with the Dynasty of Atreus, given names such as the Tomb of Clytaemnestra and the Treasury of Atreus.

Not long after the Shaft Grave burials, a Mycenaean ruler disturbed one of the interments in (Middle Helladic) Circle B, enlarging its shaft to form an entrance for a new kind of tomb with a stately chamber and saddle-shaped roof constructed of stone blocks. Pottery from the burial identified the epoch of this structure as Late Helladic II, corresponding with the reign of Thutmose III. The new tomb was foreign to Greece, though a similar one from roughly the same period was found on Crete. The style seems to have originated in Syria, though excavations have uncovered comparable structures of the Iron Age in Cyprus, Asia Minor, Palestine and Carthage. Most of these however belong to the ninth-seventh centuries, and none are earlier than c. 950 BC.[1]

The "built tomb" of Grave Circle B marks the last burial inside the Grave Circles. After this, the rulers of Mycenae turned from simple, stone-lined shafts and began constructing immense tholos tombs with typically "bee-hive" shaped roofs of cut-stone which formed a great corbelled arch. All of these structures are from Late Helladic IIIA and IIIB, contemporary with the second half of the Eighteenth Dynasty and the period of the Nineteenth Dynasty. They are therefore, from our point of view, to be dated from circa 670 to 550 BC. Since we date the Dorian Invasion to c. 680 BC, this means that the tholos tombs have nothing whatsoever to do with what is generally considered "Heroic Age" Mycenae, and must have been constructed by the powerful Dorian kings who ruled at Argos during the seventh and sixth centuries BC. Evidently Mycenae still remained a site of immense prestige after the Dorian Conquest, and the Argive aristocracy would have maintained the citadel as a royal residence.

It should be noted that the artistic motifs and designs engraved on the entrances to the tholos tombs, rosettes and palmettos arranged in strict geometrical patterns and separated from each other in triangular panels and zig-zags, represent an art-style typical of the Late Geometric and Archaic Age of the seventh and sixth centuries.

During the period of Late Helladic IIIB, corresponding to the time of the Nineteenth Dynasty, both Grave Circles, A and B, experienced renewed activity. Circle B, the farthest from the citadel, suffered an ignoble fate when the workmen excavating the last of the great tholos tombs (the so-called Tomb of Clytaemnestra), sliced through the eastern portion of the Grave Circle and heaped the earthen mound to cover over the rest of Circle B.[2]

Disrespect for the graves of the Pelopids is to be expected, if the tholos tombs were constructed by Dorians, as we suggest.

Circle A, on the other hand, enjoyed a completely different fate during the same period. Like Circle B, the beehive tombs, and all the other graves of rich and poor residents of Mycenae, Circle A originally lay west of, and outside, the settlement proper. When the Late Helladic IIIA Mycenaeans decided to enlarge their city by building another longer wall in the area of

---

1 Eddie Schorr, "Applying the Revised Chronology: Later Use of the Shaft Graves," in Velikovsky, *The Dark Age of Greece* http://www.varchive.org/

2 G. Mylonas, *Mycenae and the Mycenaean Age* (Princeton, 1966) p. 98

the prehistoric cemetery to the west, they faced the problem of what to do with Circle A. In the words of Eddie Schorr:

> We already saw some evidence of the disrespect for their dead predecessors which the Mycenaeans displayed at Circle B, when the owner of the built tomb violated the earlier Shaft Grave he expropriated, only to have his own tomb pillaged after his death, and again when the excavators of the beehive tomb destroyed part of Circle B and heaped dirt over the rest of it. In fact, they were notorious for their lack of piety towards the deceased, building structures over earlier tombs, robbing the dead, and casting aside their bones.
>
> Unlike Circle B and so many other graves in the vicinity, the Mycenaeans treated Circle A, which lay directly in the path of their urban expansion, with a reverence singular for that age. They extended their fortification wall farther than mere concern for defense or for urban planning dictated, enclosing Circle A within the city proper. They made sacrifices and dedicated idols inside the circle. Although space inside the citadel was at a premium, and the inhabitants crowded buildings around that area, many of them over older graves, some of which they plundered, they spared Circle A. In fact, they decided to raise its level as a whole, to correspond to the higher grade of the city's interior—a massive engineering feat, requiring the construction of a giant retaining wall to the west over five meters high, adding tons of earth above the graves until they formed a higher, even surface, then raising the old grave stelae to the new level to designate the individual burials below. At the new surface they constructed a new enclosure wall of two concentric rings of stone slabs filled with earth and capped by horizontal stone slabs.
>
> Considering the lack of respect for other, neighboring, tombs, the building all around but not above Circle A, the vast labor that went into deflecting the city fortification around the circle, and into creating the circle as it now appears, as well as the contemporary sacrifices and dedication of idols, some scholars have considered Circle A as a sacred burial precinct, unique for thirteenth century Greece.[1]

In short, the reverence shown to the burials in Circle A is evidence of the emergence of a "Hero Cult," a phenomenon familiar enough in Greece, but not before the seventh century or eighth at the very earliest.

Again, we might wonder: Why would the seventh or sixth century inhabitants of Mycenae have accorded these burials, and these alone, such reverence? Could it be because they contained the remains of the greatest king of the entire Heroic Age?

Pelops and Chariot Warfare

The end of the Hyksos (Old Assyrian) Empire thus seems to have been roughly contemporaneous with the fall of Troy. Yet the establishment of that same Empire was also marked by events which had a direct impact upon Greece and the Aegean world. In order to understand these however we need to say something more about the Hyksos.

---

1 Schorr, op. cit.

We have already identified the Hyksos, who worshipped Semitic deities like Ishtar and Baal and whose first king was named Sharek, with the Old Assyrians, whose chief deities were Ishtar and Baal and whose first king was named Sharru-kin — Sargon. Even conventional scholarship admits that the Old Assyrians and Hyksos were contemporaries, for the rise of the Mitanni, conquerors of the Old Assyrians in the north, was precisely contemporary with the rise of the Eighteenth Dynasty, conquerors of the Hyksos in the south. So, the Hyksos and Old Assyrians were one and the same. Yet they were also identical to the so-called Akkadians, an imperialist nation based in Mesopotamia who rose to prominence under a king named Sargon, and who are described by historians as the first military world power. Why the Akkadians (whose major kings were named Sargon and Naram-Sin) are differentiated from the Old Assyrians (whose major kings are also named Sargon and Naram-Sin) is a question that would require a whole chapter in itself to elucidate. Suffice to say that both the present writer and Professor Heinsohn have elsewhere examined the question in depth, and that evidence from every discipline confirms the identification of the Akkadians with the Old Assyrians.

Now the Akkadians were above all a nation of conquerors. Their subjugation of virtually the entire ancient east was accomplished with the aid of that quintessentially Mesopotamian invention, the chariot. Indeed, it is accepted that it was the utilization of the fast, horse-drawn and two-wheeled chariot by king Sargon that gave him a decisive advantage over his opponents. But the Hyksos too are believed to have gained decisive military superiority over the Egyptians through their use of the chariot, and it is evident that the Hyksos weapon, introduced to Egypt by king Sharek, was one and the same as the Mesopotamian weapon employed elsewhere by king Sharru-kin/Sargon. An Egyptian tradition, recorded by Manetho, relates how the people of the Nile dared not venture to offer the Hyksos invaders battle. One tradition about Sargon, recorded in an epic called *The King of the Battle*, told how he overran much of Anatolia after merchants from the city of Purushkhanda appealed for his assistance against a rival named Nur-daggal. To the astonishment of everyone, Sargon advanced through the mountainous lands of the west and routed Nur-daggal.[1]

---

1 C.J. Gadd, "The Dynasty of Agade and the Gutian Invasion," in *CAH* Vol.1 part 2 (3rd ed.) p.427

That Anatolia, or at least large parts of it, were incorporated into the Ak-kadian Empire is now accepted wisdom, with some historians suggesting Akkadian hegemony stretching as far west as the Aegean coast.[1]

Placing both the Akkadian Empire and the Heroic Age of Greece in the eighth century, we might expect Greek tradition to allude in some way to Sargon and his empire. The arrival of chariot warfare, for example, would scarcely have gone unnoticed among the Greeks — particularly if the Greeks actually learned the use of the chariot from the Akkadians.

Before going a step further, it should be remarked that the chariot used in Greece during the Mycenaean period was virtually identical in almost every detail to that employed by the Hyksos invaders of Egypt; and it is common-ly surmised that the chariot was introduced to Greece during the Hyksos epoch. Indeed, this is more than a surmise, for it is supported by a wealth of archaeological data. Only one question remains unanswered: by which route did the Hyksos chariot reach Hellas? Was it from Egypt, or did it arrive through Anatolia? Both theories have supporters.[2]

It so happens that the Greeks themselves recalled very clearly the arrival of the chariot. It was brought to the land of the Achaeans by a king of Ana-tolia named Pelops. This man, from whom the Peloponnesian Peninsula de-rived its name, established a mighty dynasty centered in the Argive Plain, a dynasty whose most famous scion, the legendary Agamemnon, was to launch the celebrated war against Ilion two generations later.

Pelops, it was said, had been ruler of the fabulously wealthy kingdom of Paphlagonia, and had been driven from his home by "barbarians." These *bar-baroi* (Grk. "foreigners") are not named, but we may hazard a very good guess as to their identity. Pelops and his entourage fled westwards to the Aegean, where they sought refuge with Ilus, the king of Troy. Finding no welcome there, the fugitives crossed the sea to Greece, where Pelops set out to win the hand of Hippodameia, daughter of King Oenomaus of Elis. Before he could wed the girl, however, Pelops had a test to pass. He had to beat Oenomaus in a chariot race — a race across the Peloponnesian Peninsula. Defeat meant death, and many previous suitors had paid for their ardor with their lives. It was said that Oenomaus boasted he would eventually build a temple of

---

1 Ibid. "If the King of the Battle has any historical foundation, Sargon did not stop short at the mountain barrier [of Cappadocia], but extended his sway deep into Asia Minor."

2 See, e.g., Frank Stubbings, op. cit. p. 639. "He [Pelops] does at least represent a dimly remem-bered event or period of events — the conquest of part of the Peloponnes by invaders from Asia Minor, perhaps indeed owing their success to their war-chariots. Such an event we can hardly place very much later than the era of the Mycenaean Shaft Graves."

human skulls.[1] With the help of Oenomaus' treacherous charioteer Myrtilus, Pelops duly defeated his rival and claimed the throne of Elis as his prize.[2]

Myrtilus (whose name is Hittite) had his image set among the stars as the constellation of the Charioteer.[3]

The story of Pelops provides the earliest reference to the chariot in Greek tradition, and the central role of horses and chariots in the narrative has long led scholars to believe that it marks their introduction into the country. However, if we are on the right track, if it was the onward march of Akkadian/Assyrian arms that had forced Pelops westwards, we might expect the Greeks to have recalled it in some way. The presence of such a mighty empire in Anatolia and Asia Minor could scarcely have escaped their attention.

As a matter of fact Greek tradition insisted that during the Trojan campaign (two generations after Pelops) all of Asia Minor was part of the Assyrian Empire. One tradition, recounted by many of the Classical authors, stated that after the death of Hector, the Assyrian king Teutamus sent a powerful force of Ethiopian troops, under the leadership of Memnon, to support the Trojans. Memnon, it was said, marched to Troy at the head of a thousand Ethiopians and a thousand Susians (Mesopotamians), and the people of Phrygia, many centuries afterwards, still showed the rough, straight road by which he travelled.[4]

The assistance was belated and ineffective, and after some initial success, Memnon was slain in single combat by Achilles.[5]

This story of Assyrian and Ethiopian involvement in the Trojan campaign has always seemed puzzling, and has generally been dismissed as little more than a romantic fiction. The very concept of Nubian and Mesopotamian troops coming to the assistance of Troy is regarded as fantastic, whilst no king of Assyria named Teutamus, it is claimed, existed. However, from the perspective of history outlined in the present work, it will be obvious that with Sargon's conquest of Anatolia, Assyrian participation in the Trojan War is a real possibility. Furthermore, having identified the Egyptian Hyksos Dynasty as an alter-ego of the Old Assyrians (or Akkadians), it may be possible to name the king who sent Memnon to the ringing plains of Ilion.

Teutamus, it should be noted, bears a name reminiscent of Teti, first pharaoh of the Sixth Dynasty, and elsewhere I have argued in great detail

---

1 Lucian, *Charidemus* 19
2 Pausanias, viii,14,7
3 Apollodorus, *Epitome* ii,8
4 Diodorus Siculus, ii, 22 and Pausanias, i,42,2
5 Philostratus, *Heroica* iii,4

that the Sixth Dynasty, whose two most important kings were named Pepi I and Pepi II, is an alter ego of the Great Hyksos Fifteenth Dynasty, whose two most important kings were named Apepi I and Apepi II.[1] The Sixth Dynasty's first pharaoh is known as Teti, and it will be obvious that he must be one and the same as Sharek/Sargon, the Hyksos conqueror who apparently occurs in Manetho's account of the invasion under the name of Tutimaeus. Thus Teti or Tutimaeus, the Hyksos/Assyrian master of Egypt, seems to be identical to Teutamus, the Assyrian king who sent aid to the Trojans.

Having said all that, it is unlikely, or should I say impossible, that Teti/ Sargon could have been an ally of Troy against the Achaeans. We have already synchronized the fall of Troy with the end of the Hyksos/Assyrian Empire, sometime between 715 and 720 BC. The first ruler of that empire, Sargon, must have ascended the throne sometime between 780 and 770 BC. If any Assyrian king sent aid to the Trojans, it can only have been one who reigned near the end of the Hyksos/Old Assyrian Age, when the ruling pharaoh was Naram-Sin or perhaps Shal-kali-sharri, either of whom could be Pepi/Apopi II.

It must have been at this time or shortly thereafter that the chariot was introduced to Western Europe, where it became a favored weapon of the Celts. It would no doubt have reached these regions along the same trade routes that conveyed tin bronze, a Western European invention, to the Near East. King Sargon himself records expeditions to the mysterious "tin lands" of the west. Elsewhere I have argued in great detail how the art of tin-bronze manufacture was developed in Britain towards the end of the ninth century BC, and that it was to gain access to this valuable resource that the Phoenicians opened up the western sea routes and established their Mediterranean and Atlantic colonies (e.g. Carthage and Gades) to service the trade. But this only occurred at the start of the eighth century BC, which means, in effect, that the Bronze Age begins then. Attempts to suggest that the ancients knew other sources of tin much closer to the Near East founder on the economics. If such sources existed (and there is in any case no evidence of them), Phoenician traders could scarcely have found it profitable to fund the vastly expensive expeditions to Britain, an island 3,000 miles distant.

The folk of Britain's Wessex culture, who raised Stonehenge III, derived their fabulous wealth from the tin and bronze trade; and their rich tombs on Salisbury Plain still yield artifacts (such as faience beads) of Near East-

---

1 See my *Pyramid Age* (1999)

ern manufacture. But the trade in luxuries was not all one-way. Bronze and gold trinkets manufactured in the British Isles at the time found their way to Greece, Phoenicia, Egypt and Mesopotamia. Thus Flinders Petrie discovered a series of gold earrings, of obviously Irish manufacture, in a Hyksos-period Egyptian tomb.[1]

Truly astonishing is the picture that emerges once the chronology of antiquity is put right; unsuspected and even undreamt of connections become apparent. Homer's Achaeans visited not only Egypt at the height of her Pyramid Age, but pushed their dark ships much farther, into the dangerous and mysterious waters of the west, even into the mighty "Sea of Atlas" that lay beyond the brooding Pillars of Hercules. They knew however what they were looking for; the "tin isles," the mysterious archipelago associated with the mystical Hyperboreans, the folk said to dwell beyond the North Wind. This race of sorcerers and alchemists, dwellers at the edge of the world, alone held the secret of forging bronze; and the national myth of their island home told how their own Hercules, the Bear hero Artos, pulled a bronze sword from a stone whilst still a young man. The wealthy Hyperboreans were known also to be astronomers of the highest order, in virtue of which they had raised, not far from the tin-bearing regions, a great circular temple to the heavenly deities.

AGAMEMON IN THE RECORDS OF THE HITTITES

The Hyksos Empire thus collapsed roughly at the time of the Shaft Grave burials. This is common knowledge and denied by no one. As we have stated, out of the ruins of the Hyksos Imperium there arose, as well as the Mitanni and Egyptian Empires, the Hittite state, whose capital city Hattusas was discovered on the banks of the Halys River just over a century ago. As noted above, the rich cuneiform archive discovered at Hattusas was to provide fascinating insights into Hittite life, enabling scholars to piece together a fairly comprehensive history of this "forgotten empire." Whilst the Hittite kingdom is recognized as rising to the status of world power only in the time of Suppiluliumas I, who was a contemporary of Amenhotep III and Akhnaton, the empire was already an important power a century earlier. Thus Suppiluliumas's great-grandfather, Tudkhalias II, controlled a wide-reaching territory that stretched almost from the Aegean coast to the borders of Assyria. Tudkhalias II was a contemporary of the first pharaohs of the Eighteenth

---

1 F. Petrie, *The Making of Egypt* (1939) p.144. "Trade brought products from Persia and from Ireland in the Hyksos age."

Dynasty, and he seems to have witnessed the titanic struggle that rent the Near East during the time of Parattarna, first of the Mitanni Great Kings, and the Old Assyrian (Hyksos) monarch Naram-Sin. Tudkhalias II, it seems, left a large number of documents at Hattusas and many of these dealt with relations between him and various potentates in western Anatolia and Asia Minor.

Sifting through and translating the vast number of clay texts discovered at Hattusas was a herculean task that even now is not fully completed. At an early date however scholars found reference to events apparently taking place on the shores of the Aegean. Names familiar from Classical tradition were encountered. Thus the city of Apasa was easily identified as Ephesus, whilst Millawanda (or Millawata) was clearly the same as Miletus, an Ionian settlement not far to the north of Ephesus. Some names, though suggestive, were not so certainly identified. Thus Wilusa, which appeared to be located in north-west Asia Minor might have been Ilion, or Ilios (early Greek Wilios), but there was no agreement. One group of scholars however was fairly vociferous in this identification and, with mounting excitement, began to see names even of individuals known from Homeric tradition.

Several of the most exciting discoveries had to wait a number of decades after initial translation to be fully appreciated.

A document named the Madduwattas Text, dealing with events during the reign of a Hittite king named Tudkhalias, perhaps Tudkhalias II, as well as his successor Arnuwandas, caused great excitement from the very beginning because of its mention of characters apparently connected with Heroic Age Greece. Thus, for example, the document complains of the activities of a king of Ahhiya (Achaea?) named Attarsiyas (Atreus?) in the land of Zippasla Khariyata, identified as a mountainous region of western Asia Minor: the word Zippasla apparently being cognate with the classical Sipylos, a peak close to Ephesus. In the document, commonly known as "The Sins of Madduwattas," we hear how the latter prince had been driven from Zippasla by Attarsiyas and how he had been rescued by Tudkhalias.

> Attarissiya, the Man of Ahhiya, chased you, Madduwatta, from your land. [Moreover] he was right behind you, and he kept pursuing you. He kept seeking an [evil] death for you, Madduwatta. He [would have] killed you, but you, Madduwatta, fled to the father [of My Sun], and the father of My Sun saved you from death. He cut off Attarissiya behind you. If (he had) not, Attarsiya would not have let you be, and he would have killed you.
>
> When the father of My Sun cut off [Attarissiya] behind you, the father of My Sun [took] you, Madduwatta [for himself], along with your wives, your children, your troops, and your chariotry. He gave you chariots, [. . .] grain,' and seed' in heaps. He gave you beer and wine, malt, beer-bread, rennet, and [cheese'] in

heaps. The father of My Sun saved you (from) hunger, Madduwatta, along with your wives, your [children] and your troops.

The father of My Sun saved you from the blade of Attaršiya. The father of My Sun saved you, Madduwatta, along with your wives, your [children], your household servants, and along with your troops and chariots. If (he had) not, dogs would have devoured you from hunger. Even if you had escaped from Attaršiya, you would have died from hunger.

Then it came about that the father of My Sun made you, Madduwatta, into his own sworn subject. He made you swear an oath. He put these matters under oath for you; "I, the father of My Sun, have just saved [you], Madduwatta, [from the blade] of Attaršiya. Be (a man) of the father of My Sun and of the land of Ḫatti! I have just given you the land of Mt. Zippašla [in lordship]. You, Madduwatta, remain in the land of Mt. Zippašla along with your [troops], and afterwards keep yourself on patrol within the land of Mt. Zippašla." The father of My Sun repeatedly spoke in this very way to you, Madduwatta, "Come! Settle yourself in the land of Mt. Ḫariyati, and be near to the land of Ḫatti." You, Madduwatta, refused to occupy the land of Mt. Ḫariyati, so then the father of My Sun proceeded to speak in this way to Madduwatta, "I have now given you the land of Mt. Zippašla. Occupy only that place! Again, do not further occupy another vassal state or another land on your own initiative. Stay within the borders of [the land of] Mt. Zippašla. May you be my servant, and may your troops be my troops."[1]

Later, we hear how Madduwattas had, against the oaths he had sworn, tried to bring Arzawa Land (western Asia Minor, roughly the region of Lydia), under his rule, but had been defeated by local prince Kupanta-Inaras. Again, it had been the Hittite king who had saved him; providing in addition aid against renewed attacks by Attarsiyas, who advanced against him, famously, with a hundred chariots.[2] In spite of all this, Madduwattas persisted in his faithlessness and even came to terms with Attarsiyas, with whom he attacked Alashiya (Cyprus).

Could this document refer to events surrounding the Trojan War? It seemed a real possibility. The action took place in the right location. We know, for example, that the Achaeans under Agamemnon really did attack allies of the Trojans far beyond the immediate vicinity of Troy, sending raiding parties both along the coast and inland. In addition, contingents from Agamemnon's forces also attacked Cyprus in the immediate aftermath of Troy's defeat, whilst a mysterious figure named Muksas was linked to Attarsiyas, and this seemed to be a reference to Mopsus, one of Agamemnon's allies, who did in fact lead a great army of Achaeans along western and southern Asia Minor after the collapse of Ilion.

We shall have more to say on Mopsus presently.

1 Albrecht Götze, "The Sins of Madduwata," *Madduwattas* (Wissenschaftliche Buchgesellschaft, Darmstadt, 1968).
2 A. Götze, "The Hittites and Syria (1300-1200 BC)," in CAH Vol. 2 part 2 (3rd ed.) pp. 264-5.

As regards the name Attarsiyas, there was no linguistic objection to it being related to the Greek Atreus, and Götze suggested that it might be a possessive adjective meaning something like "belonging to Atreus." The Greeks themselves spoke in such terms and throughout the Iliad the more usual name for Agamemnon is Atreides, "son of Atreus."

Such an interpretation was perfectly legitimate, but failed to gain widespread support because of the chronology. Scholars accepted unquestioningly the "traditional" date for the fall of Troy (1184 BC), whereas this document was assigned, initially, to the time of Tudkhalias IV, a great-grandson of Suppiluliumas I and a contemporary of Ramses II and Merneptah of the Nineteenth Dynasty. Thus the text was placed in the thirteenth century BC and Attarsiyas of Ahhiya could not possibly be either Atreus or his son Agamemnon. Scholars had in fact associated this and related documents with Tudkhalias IV, near the end of the Hittite Empire, but the trend in recent years, apparently even more damning for any attempt to synchronize with Greek history, has been to "backdate the whole of this group of texts to the 15th century BC," owing to the fact that they "exhibit certain archaic features of language and orthography."[1] The writer of these words suggested dating the Madduwattas Text to the time of Tudkhaliyas II, the great-grandfather of Suppiluliumas I, and thus a contemporary of the early Eighteenth Dynasty kings. As such, the Madduwattas Text would describe events very close to the defeat and expulsion of the Hyksos. Since conventional history regards the Eighteenth Dynasty as having risen in the late sixteenth century and the Trojan War in the twelfth, the postulated Greek links are now regarded as a non-starter.

For us however it is a very different story. Since we have already placed the Trojan campaign very close in time to the rise of the Eighteenth Dynasty, we would have expected Hittite documents of that period to have referred it. And this is precisely what we do find. The Madduwattas Text therefore provides spectacular confirmation for the reconstruction of history presented in these pages; and we can now say, with a reasonable degree of certainty, that a contemporary reference to the Trojan Campaign has been found!

Those scholars who wished to identify Attarsiyas of Ahhiya with Agamemnon were absolutely correct. The term Attarsiyas almost certainly denotes "son of Atreus." Similarly, the King Mita of Pahhuva (or Piggaya), who also occurs in the Madduwattas Text, is of course Agamemnon's famous contemporary, Midas of Phrygia.

---

1 O. R. Gurney, "Anatolia, c.1600-1380 BC," in *CAH* Vol.2 part 1 (3rd ed.) p.678

MOPSUS

Among the enigmatic characters appearing in the Madduwattas Document was a freebooter named Muksus, or Mukshush. This man, it seems, caused immense problems for the Hittite king's vassals in various regions of western and southern Asia Minor. The significance of this character only became apparent with H. T. Bossert's discovery in 1945 of the famous bilingual Karatepe inscription, where the name Muksus is rendered in the Hittite hieroglyphic version as Muksas, but in the alphabetic Phoenician as Mps. The monument on which the inscription was carved dated from the Neo-Assyrian Age and named Muksas/Mps as an ancestral figure. Nevertheless, it implied that Muksus of the Madduwattas Document was the same person as Mps, which also meant that Muksus of the Madduwattas Text was "identical in name with Mopsus, a strange figure of Greek legend."[1]

Greek tradition stated that after the sack of Thebes (traditionally ten years before the start of the Trojan War), Manto, daughter of the seer Tiresias, led a group of refugees to Colophon in western Lydia, just to the north of Ephesus, where she set up a shrine to Apollo.[2] Her son Mopsus, born at Colophon, led "the peoples" across Mt Taurus into Pamphylia, where some settled, while others scattered to Cilicia, Syria and Phoenicia.[3] According to the Cretan *Diktys*, Mopsus' warlike career began as an ally of the Achaeans at Troy, but he parted company with Agamemnon a year before the end of the war, marching southwards with a band of followers. After the fall of Ilion he was joined by various other Achaean chiefs, including Amphilocus, Calchas, and Podaleirius. Arriving in Pamphylia, south-west Asia Minor, Mopsus and his companions founded its most notable cities, Aspendus and Phaselis. It was then, so the legend went, that Calchas died, after being "out-prophesied" by Mopsus.[4] Shortly thereafter, the motley band of freebooters set out for Cilicia, where they established Mallus and Mopsou-hestia (Mopsus' hearth). Another dispute then arose, this time between Mopsus and Amphilocus, over who should rule Mallus. It was said that Amphilocus had temporarily returned to his own city in Greece, leaving Mopsus in charge, but had become dissatisfied with affairs at home and come back after twelve months to Mallus. Arriving once again in Asia, he expected to resume his former powers, but was rebuffed by Mopsus, who told him to be gone. When the embarrassed Mallians suggested that the dispute be decided by single combat, the

1 R. D. Barnett, "The Sea Peoples," in *CAH* Vol.2 part 2 (3rd ed.) p.364
2 Pausanias, viii, 3, 1-2.
3 Herodotus, vii, 91.
4 Strabo, xiv, 642.

rivals fought and killed each other. The funeral pyres were so placed that Mopsus and Amphilocus could not exchange unseemly scowls during their cremation, yet the ghosts somehow became so tenderly linked in friendship that that they set up a common oracle; which in classical times had gained a higher reputation for truth even than Delphic Apollo's.[1]

It should be remarked that the Lydians also remembered Mopsus, where his name was rendered as Moxus (identical to Muksus in the Boghaz-koi texts) and according to their historian Xanthus, he "was a mighty and popular warrior ... who overthrew the hated tyrant Mêles and won great glory by many warlike expeditions. The most famous of these was against the city of Krabos, which he took after a long siege, and — with a piety he had already shown by his offerings to the gods after the fall of Mêles — drowned all the inhabitants 'as atheists' in the neighboring lake."[2] The Lydians held that he ended his days in Ashkelon, where he threw the statue of the goddess Astarte into her own lake.

It seems evident that the communities established in this region by Mopsus and his allies were the ancestors of the *Hypachaioi* ("Lesser Achaeans") from Cilicia who formed a contingent of Xerxes' army and who, according to Herodotus, were descended from Greeks who had come thither in the Heroic Age.[3]

The many warlike exploits attributed to Mopsus in the Lydian tradition recall the complaints about him in the Madduwattas Text, and his importance in the region is further illustrated in the Karatepe monument, where he was honored as the forefather of the kings of Adana. But it is above all the occurrence of his name on the Madduwattas Text that has transformed "for the first time a figure of Greek legend ... into an undeniable historical personality."[4] The writer of these words could not deny that the Muksus of the Madduwattas Document was the same as Mopsus of Greek legend, for the names were clearly interchangeable in the Karatepe Inscription (many languages confuse the "p" and "k" sounds); yet he did not dare to look at the chronological implications of his own words. If the Madduwattas Document really belonged to the time of Tudkhalias II, as the linguistic and stylistic evidence seemed to indicate, then it meant that Mopsus, an undoubted contemporary of the Trojan War, lived (according to conventional timescales)

---

1 Apollodorus, iii, 7, 7 and *Epitome*, vi, 19; Tzetzes, *On Lycophron*, 440-42.
2 Burn, loc. cit. pp. 151-2.
3 Herodotus, vii, 92.
4 R. D. Barnett, loc. cit. p.365

in the late sixteenth or early fifteenth century BC. How this could be justified he did not care to explain. Equally, if Muksus of the Madduwattas Text
is Agamemnon's lieutenant Mopsus, this would also imply that Attarsiyas of
Ahhiya, who occurs in the same document, was Atreides of Achaea — Agamemnon, King of Men.

But these questions were not examined: For to do so would have perchance unhinged the whole of ancient history.

From our point of view, the Madduwattas Text adds yet another welcome detail to the picture built up in the preceding pages. Once more, this is
confirmation for our proposal that the Trojan campaign, ending around 720
BC, directly preceded the collapse of the Hyksos/Assyrian Empire and the
rise of Egypt's Eighteenth Dynasty.

CHAPTER 6. THE COURSE OF HISTORY

MYTH AND HISTORY

Moving the whole of the Minoan/Mycenaean, or more appropriately, Heroic Age, down into the ninth, eighth and seventh centuries, might persuade us that the myths and legends of Greece could contain real history. After all, if Agamemnon and Priam were contemporaries of Midas, who was very definitely a real person, the same may possibly be said of them. And we have indeed shown that Agamemnon's ally Mopsus figures in the records of the Hittites (whom we regard as Lydians), whilst it seems almost certain that the legendary Mycenaean king himself is mentioned in the same records. We noted too that the Shaft Graves at Mycenae probably really did contain the bodies of Agamemnon and his entourage, whilst the traditions surrounding Agamemnon's grandfather Pelops seem to recall the introduction of the chariot and chariot-warfare into Greece. If all this is correct, it means that Greek tradition, at least as far back as the time of Pelops, which we have placed sometime between 780 and 770 BC, contains much that must be regarded as genuine history.

Having said that, the very nature of the Greek myths, especially those dealing with events before the Trojan War, make us skeptical of their value as history, properly speaking. The routine intervention of the gods, for example, warns us to proceed with extreme caution. The names of many characters reveal themselves to be personifications or eponyms, whilst many others, who at first glance might appear quite human, reveal themselves, upon closer inspection, to be deities. This is certainly the case with individuals such as Perseus and Salmoneus, as well as all the earlier heroes like Deucalion and Phoroneus. Even characters such as Cadmus, who can be linked to an undoubted historical event — the introduction to Greece of the Phoenician alphabet — can in no way be regarded as a flesh and blood person. He is, rather, to be seen as a composite figure comprising elements of two or three individuals intermixed with the characteristics of several deities. Even personalities of the later Heroic Age, such as Heracles, cannot be viewed as real people. The latter was — with a couple of minor provisos — virtually one and the same as the god Ares, or Mars.

Having said all that, there is no question that within the body of Greek tradition there exists a logical progression, with characters who lived nearer the end of the Heroic Age becoming progressively more real, more human. Thus by the time of the Trojan War, meetings with deities seem less common than before and the people we encounter definitely more mortal. This development continues afterwards, until we meet, at the time of the Dorian Invasion — two generations after the Trojan War — characters who seem in all essentials to be ordinary human beings.[1]

What then of the myriad other characters who fill the legends of ancient Hellas? Which of them might be regarded as real? And how far back can we go? Is there, after all, any kind of gauge, such as an astronomical event, that might assist us in providing some kind of historical narrative for the eighth or perhaps even the ninth century BC?

In fact, Greek history had a very definite starting point.

A Dramatic Beginning

In Chapter 2 we noted how scholars regard the Middle Helladic Age, with its "geometric" pottery and art-styles, as the first culture that could reasonably be described as Greek. In the same place, we saw that Middle Helladic ware is, to all intents and purposes, indistinguishable from that otherwise known as Protogeometric, a culture securely dated to the early part of the first millennium, commencing perhaps around 1000 or 900 BC.

The Middle Helladic Age began in dramatic circumstances: a terrible catastrophe, apparently a vast fire accompanied by earthquake, destroyed virtually every Early Helladic settlement in Greece. The Early Helladic period was an epoch of high culture, and is described as "a prosperous era, a time

---

1 It has to be admitted however that even after the Dorian Invasion, in the seventh and sixth centuries BC, many individuals who were very definitely historical, still display typically mythic characteristics, such as meetings with deities and divinely-inspired prophecies. This topic is examined more closely in the following chapter.

of enterprising men who sailed the seas." These were "sensitive imaginative people ... who brought home wealth and new ideas from their journeys. Some were rich enough to attain a measure of power in their districts and presumably to rule as princes from their palaces at centers like Tiryns and Lerna, or from forts like the one at Chalandriani in Syros, maintaining contact with their royal cousins in the Hellespont."[1] This was a culture which spread throughout the Aegean, establishing close links to the peoples of Asia Minor. Early Helladic settlement was particularly concentrated in central Greece, in Attica and the Argolid, where was located Lerna, one of the richest centers. Like the others, it succumbed to a fierce conflagration: "An era ended at Lerna with the burning of the [Early Helladic] House of the Tiles; and in the whole surrounding region there are evidences of a similar catastrophe ... it is extremely probable that the great round building at Tiryns, which has a roof of similar tiles, fell at the same time as the palace of Lerna III. There was a disaster also at nearby Asine, where one of the burnt buildings had been roofed likewise with tiles .... A few miles further north, at Zygouries in the valley of Cleonae, houses of the same age were destroyed in a general conflagration."[2]

This disaster was not confined to the Greek mainland: The Early Minoan sites in Crete, as well as those on the Cylcades, were leveled in the same way. And yet further afield, the Early Bronze Age settlements of Asia Minor and Anatolia were annihilated in a similar conflagration. Claude Schaeffer, one of the greatest field archaeologists of the twentieth century, examined scores of sites throughout the Near East and came to the conclusion that all of the Early Bronze settlements of the region were destroyed simultaneously by some form of vast upheaval of nature.[3]

Elsewhere I have examined the evidence Schaeffer presented in some detail, and any further comment here is superfluous.[4] We need only remark that an honest examination of the archaeological evidence, whether it be from the Greek mainland, from Crete, from Thera or from Anatolia, makes it evident, even to a superficial consideration, that in the Bronze Age the earth suffered a period of seismic and volcanic activity much more intense than anything in the experience of modern man.

---

1 John L. Caskey, "Greece, Crete, and the Aegean Islands in the Early Bronze Age," in *CAH* Vol.1 part 2 (3rd ed.) pp. 805-6

2 John L. Caskey, "Greece, Crete, and the Aegean Islands in the Early Bronze Age," in *CAH*, Vol. 1 part 2 (3rd ed.) p. 785

3 Schaeffer presented the evidence in his encyclopaedic *Stratigraphie comparée et chronologie de l'Asie occidentale* (Oxford, 1948).

4 In my *Genesis of Israel and Egypt* (1997, 2008), as well as *The Pyramid Age* (1999 and 2007).

Now the surprising fact is that these events occupy a very prominent position in the Greek myths (though one would never guess it from reading modern "popular retellings" of them): the original myths are replete with references to catastrophic fires, terrible inundations of the sea, and vast earthquakes and volcanic eruptions. Hesiod's entire *Theogony*, it could be argued, is one long account of a cosmic catastrophe. These events, and their impact upon Greek history and culture, are examined at greater length in the Appendix to the present volume. Suffice for the moment to note that several great Deluges, the most important of which were those of Deucalion and Ogyges, were recalled in Greek tradition, whilst almost every story from the Heroic Age has, as a central part of the plot, immensely violent and thoroughly unusual events of nature.

The Greeks, we have noted, began their history with the establishment of the Olympic Games, a festival linked to the demigod Heracles, the club-wielding giant who held the heavens on his shoulders, fired deadly arrows at the sun, and pushed apart the great rock pillars at the entrance to the Mediterranean. Heracles' Twelve Labors were very evidently related to the signs of the zodiac and the months of the year, and the hero was indeed reckoned to have inaugurated a new calendar.

It is highly likely that the catastrophic event which terminated Early Helladic culture is the event commemorated in the Olympiads, the athletic festival inaugurated by Heracles himself. The first Olympiad is traditionally believed to have been celebrated early in the eighth century BC (though all archaic Greek dates must be treated with the greatest caution). Nevertheless, if, as we say, the Late Helladic or Mycenaean epoch began around 730 or 740 BC — shortly before the Trojan War — this would mark the terminal point of the Middle Helladic Age and it is likely that this epoch began no more than a century or so earlier (the entire Late Helladic Age, which left very many remains and deep strata only lasted about one century). Thus we would regard the Middle Helladic Age, which, we remember, was closely related to and contemporary with the Protogeometric and Early Geometric periods, as having begun around 850 BC. And this is the date of the catastrophe which terminated the Early Helladic times.

Elsewhere I have shown in great detail how the biblical Exodus, an event also marked by a catastrophic upheaval of nature, can only have occurred around 850 BC.[1] The Exodus, it should be noted, was followed by the period of the Judges, an epoch which displays remarkable parallels with the

---

[1] In the *Genesis of Israel and Egypt*.

Greek Heroic Age. As in the Mycenaean Age, chariots play a big part in the warfare of the Judges, whilst various characters, but most especially Moses himself and Samson, display striking similarities to Heracles, as indeed they do to other Heroic Age personalities, such as Perseus and Theseus. Without going into details, we should note that the births of Moses and Perseus are exactly alike (both were retrieved from a basket cast into the waters), whilst Heracles and Moses were both enemies of the serpent: Thus Moses' staff devours the two serpents of the pharaoh's magicians, whilst Heracles strangles the two serpents sent by Hera to destroy him in his cradle. Just as Heracles pushes apart the two rock pillars at Gibraltar, Moses "pushes apart" the waters at the Sea of Passage; and even as Heracles does not really die but ascends Mount Oeta, there to join his father Zeus, Moses too has a mysterious end, ascending Mount Horeb, to meet Yahweh. It is interesting too that Moses' God, whose name can be reconstructed in English as "Jehovah," sounds suspiciously like one of the names given to Heracles' father Zeus — Jove.

In Chapter 3 we noted that the entire myth of Cadmus is inextricably related to the events of the Israelite Exodus, with some characters, such as Phineus/Phinehas, keeping the same name in both Greek and Hellenic tradition. This, together with many other considerations, make us believe that the Heroic Age of Greece, which began with the catastrophic ending of the Early Helladic world, was precisely contemporary with the Israelite period of Wandering in the desert and Judges, an epoch which began with the catastrophic event of the Exodus.

GREEKS AND PELASGIANS

Using the catastrophe of c.850 BC as a datum-edge, it might be possible to reconstruct the political and social history of the Aegean with an accuracy that would not otherwise have been possible. If we date the rise of the Middle Helladic and Middle Minoan cultures to the years after 850 BC, then we may perchance understand these epochs in a new way.

We have seen that the culture generally known as Middle Helladic was apparently contemporary with the earliest truly Greek culture, commonly known as Proto- or Early Geometric. These two cultures shared many features in common, and appeared to belong to two different races or ethnic groups, perhaps related to each, which shared the land of Greece. The Protogeometric culture is indubitably that of the earliest Greeks; but what of Middle Helladic?

Early Greek writers, beginning with Homer, had much to say about another race which had, at one time, occupied almost all of Hellas, but which had, gradually, been supplanted by the Hellenes. These were the mysterious Pelasgians.

It is customary nowadays to downplay or even dismiss the role of a race of "pre-Greeks," yet earlier generations of scholars — and still several today — were not so dismissive. Robert Graves, for example, wrote a great deal about the "Pelasgians" and their impact upon Greek culture. To him, their influence was immense. He saw them as a matriarchal folk who worshipped a "Great Mother" and who bequeathed much of what we now call civilization to the Achaean and Ionian tribes who first came into contact with them. A perhaps more balanced view is given by A. R. Burn:

> About the Pelasgoi the air was already so thick with theories in ancient times that it is very difficult to make any statement about them that is not open to question. Originally they seem to have been a pre-Hellenic tribe (if Herodotus is right in his account of their language as spoken in his day) whose home was in the northern regions of Greece. Here was the only "Pelasgian Land," Pelasgiotis, known to history; here was the Pelasgian Argos; and not so very far away was the sacred place of the "Pelasgian Zeus" of Dodona to whom Achilles prayed. In these regions they must have been neighbours of the first Achaians, who, by the time when the Catalogue of Ships in Iliad II was drawn up, appear to have taken complete possession both of lands, town and shrine. Nothing of the Pelasgoi remains in Homer's Greece except their name, so far as our information goes; the Pelasgoi themselves seem to have been pushed by gradual encroachments into the sea. But they were not extinct; they had taken to the sea under pressure of necessity, as any vigorous and virile race will, and Homer speaks of colonies of them in Crete and (apparently) in the Troad, in the latter of which regions they take their opportunity of striking a blow for King Priam against their old enemies the Achaioi. Fifth century historians knew of them also near Kyzikos, in Lemnos, Imbros, and Samothrace, in the peninsula of Chalkidike, and between the Strymon and the Axios rivers ...
>
> There are also stories of Pelasgoi in Attica and in Boiotia, the former of which is told with much circumstance by Herodotus and was believed by Thucydides; but it contains some suspicious features and may be a myth. It should be remembered that both these writers are deeply influenced by the "Pelasgian Theory" which can be traced back as far as the Hesiodic poets, and which equated Pelasgoi with "pre-Hellenic people" in general. Accordingly Hesiod or a poet of his school makes their eponym Pelasgos a hero of the aboriginal people of primitive Arcadia. It was a very natural theory to adopt with reference to a people who had anticipated the Greeks in so many regions; but it was a most fruitful source of misconceptions.[1]

Be that as it may, there is much evidence of a linguistic nature to suggest a non-Hellenic and perhaps non-Indo-European substratum in the ethnic make-up of early Greece. Certainly words and names associated with the Pelasgians throughout Greece are not Greek, and their origin remains mysteri

---

1 Burn, loc. cit. pp. 58-9.

ous. An enormous literature has grown up relating to these "pre-Greek" folk, and the general consensus is that their presence in the Aegean is marked by place names incorporating the sounds –nth– and –ss–. According to A. R. Burn these are "two sounds which reappear in a very large number of old Aegean place names," and he provides as examples Knossos, Larissa, Parnassos, Ilissos (in –ss–) as well as Corinth, Tiryns (or Tiyntha), Mount Kynthos, etc. (in –nth–).[1] The same types of names, he notes, appear too in Asia Minor. And in the English language "we have upwards of a dozen of these old Aegean words, taken over by us in our turn from Greek. Hyacinth, narcissus, acanthus, cypress; colossus, plinth, labyrinth; mint, absinthe, turpentine (via Latin, from terebinthos); hymn, paean, dithyramb; abyss (which in Greek originally meant depths of the sea); these and a few more remain to bear witness of our debt, through the Greeks, to the old Aegean civilization."[2]

Place names with these pre-Hellenic elements are found throughout the country, often, as we have seen, in areas specifically identified with the Pelasgians. One of the areas was the Peloponnese, home to the most powerful kingdoms of Mycenaean times. The Pelasgians of this region, it was said, were also known as Danaans (Danaoi) after Danaus, their eponymous ancestor, who is said to have settled at Argos after fleeing from Egypt. He built a citadel at Argos and his daughters brought the Mysteries of Demeter, called Thesmophoria, from Egypt, and taught these to the Pelasgian women.[3] But if the Danaans were Pelasgians, this implies that most Greeks were also, at least partly, Pelasgians: for by the time of Homer the word Danaoi implied something close to our term "Greek" and is apparently used interchangeably with the words Achaioi (Achaeans) and Hellenoi (Hellenes).

It would appear then that the Greeks of historical times were in some degree descendants of a non-Greek race or races who shared the Aegean region with the early Hellenes. The classical Hellenes derived many of their religious ideas and beliefs from these peoples. They were a folk that seemed to take delight in the beauties of the natural world, and if there is any merit at all in the great quantities of evidence brought forward by Robert Graves, then their culture was matriarchal: They worshipped a "Great Goddess" and traced their descent through the mother rather than the father.

It is of course impossible to speak with certainty on these matters; yet it is a distinct possibility that the culture known as Middle Helladic was

---

1 Ibid., p. 71
2 Ibid., pp. 71-2.
3 Pausanias, ii, 38, 4 and 19, 3; Strabo, viii, 6, 9; Herodotus, ii, 171.

that of the Pelasgians. It is notable in this regard that those areas with a strongly Middle Helladic culture, such as Argolis, tended to have little in the way of Protogeometric or Early Geometric pottery or artifacts; whilst those areas heavily "Geometric," such as Attica, had very little in the way of Middle Helladic material. The general consensus among historians is that Protogeometric appeared first in Attica, but was then copied in other areas of Greece, where the "decaying" Mycenaean culture was abandoned.[1] Yet this concept of a "spreading" Protogeometric culture is necessitated by the belief that Geometric civilization somehow evolved out of Mycenaean. Since this did not happen, we may look with suspicion on the idea of dissemination from Athens and Attica. Nevertheless, it does seem that the earliest and greatest quantity of Protogeometric and Early Geometric material did come from the latter region; and it is not impossible that Protogeometric was simply an Attic variant of Middle Helladic, which became popular and was imitated elsewhere. Certainly the parallels between Protogeometric and Middle Helladic are striking. If this is the case, then we do not need to speak of "pre-Hellenes" or "Pelasgians" in this context.

Against this, there is firm proof that, in some areas at least, Middle Helladic was the cultural expression of a non-Hellenic people. It occurs, for example, in many areas of Anatolia. And we have already seen, in Chapter 2, that Middle Helladic Grey Minyan ware occurred at Troy from the earliest phase of Troy IV and, astonishingly enough, survived there as late as Troy VIII — the first evidently Greek settlement at the site, a city normally dated to circa 700 BC (though probably arising around 650 BC). In the preceding city, that of Troy VII — commonly regarded as the settlement sacked by Agamemnon — was found an inscribed seal bearing the names of a man and wife, the only writing found from the pre-Greek period. The writing on the seal was Luwian, the language common to large areas of Anatolia.[2] Luwian was Indo-European, but retained a great many non-Indo-European or pre-Indo-European features.[3]

The discovery of this seal then would imply that Luwian, or something closely related to Luwian, was the language of at least some of the Middle Helladic folk, a language which at one time was spoken throughout Anatolia

---

1 "The theory that, in other parts of Greece where this pottery [Protogeometric] appears, such appearance is due to direct or indirect influence from Athens is that which at present holds the field." V. R. D'A. Desborough "The End of Mycenaean Civilization and the Dark Age: (a) The Archaeological Background," in *CAH*, Vol. 2 part 2 (3rd ed) p. 671.

2 J. David Hawkins and Donald F. Easton, "A Hieroglyphic Seal from Troy," *Studia Troica* 6 (1996), pp. 111-18.

3 Many traditions existed linking the Trojans to the so-called Tyrrhenians, who were often identified as Pelasgians.

and the Greek Peninsula. It may be that Cretan was also Luwian, though this is by no means clear.

So, the evidence suggests that in the years after 850 BC the land we know as Greece was settled by two or even more quite distinct peoples, each introducing its own distinct culture. Some areas, such as the Peloponnese, seem to have had a predominantly Middle Helladic/Pelasgian (Luwian) culture; others, such as Attica and Boeotia, a predominantly Geometric/Greek one. As time passed, the Greek element gained the upper hand; and certainly by the year 800 BC the great majority of the Greek mainland, even in those areas with a majority pre-Greek population, was being ruled by Achaean and Ionian warrior aristocrats. In time, the language of the "Pelasgians" passed away, though not without leaving many words and terminologies in Greek.

THE RISE OF CRETE

The evidence of art, we have seen, shows that yet another people or race inhabited the Aegean during the Bronze Age: these were the so-called "Minoans" of Crete. This latter people, unlike the Middle Hellads, possessed a material culture very different to that of the Greeks; and it was these "Minoans" (as well as the apparently related Cycladic islanders) who inspired – and probably actually produced – the stunning "Mycenaean" artwork discovered by Schliemann at Mycenae and the other ancient settlements of the Argolid. Cretan and Cycladic craftsmen, we have argued, were introduced into the region by the powerful Achaean warlords of the latter eighth century to decorate their palaces and religious centers. The culture these immigrants produced is widely understood to be little more than the mainland branch of the Minoan, though their pottery, jewelry and metalwork did evolve to suit the tastes of their Achaean masters.[1]

That these Cretans were not Greek-speaking is confirmed by very many words as well as place names and inscriptions, all described by the ancients as "Eteocretan" or "true Cretan." Indeed, these "true Cretans" survived in the west of the island into Hellenic and even Hellenistic times, during which period they preserved not only their ancient autochthonous language, but their own (supposedly extinct for six or seven hundred years) Minoan/Mycenaean art.[2] Significantly, among the provably Minoan names to survive is

---

1 Burn, loc. cit., p. 105. "The civilization and social life of Mykenai, Tiryns, Orchomenos and the other mainland settlements, was Minoan — but Minoan with certain differences; differences due in part to adaptation to the conditions of mainland life ..."

2 Ibid., p. 97. "The 'True-Cretans' of Praisos, who, as inscriptions show, still in Hellenic times spoke their pre-Hellenic language ..." For the survival of Minoan/Mycenaean art among these people, see Ernst Langlotz, *The Art of Magna Graecia* (1965) p. 15 "... even if surviving finds [of Mycenaean-type pottery in Italy] do not go back to the second millennium BC,

that of a goddess, Britomartis, which we actually know means "sweet maid"; and it is agreed that several of the Olympian deities (such as Athena, Artemis and Hephaestus), as well as very many of the heroes and demigods of Greek legend, have names which cannot be explained in Greek and may well be Cretan.

Many of the words and place names listed above and linked to the Pelasgians may equally be associated with the Minoans; and it seems reasonable to suppose that the speech of the Cretans and Cycladic islanders was similar to, if not identical with, that of the Pelasgians. Of these words, labyrinth is of particular interest, for it apparently comes from the Cretan *labrys*, meaning an axe, and so implies something like "house of the axe." Just such a Double Axe was found everywhere painted on the walls of the "Palace" at Knossos unearthed by Evans. And we become aware of how far-reaching and profound the impact of this culture was on the Greeks when we note the existence of a priestly corporation at Delphi named the Labyades, who, according to Burn, "look as if they were originally Labryades, servants of the Double Axe." Furthermore, "A name reminiscent of the sacred 'labrys' occurs also across the gulf, at Patrai and Messene, where in Roman times they worshipped a goddess Laphria, identified with Artemis, and kept a festival called the Laphria in honor of her. The name was expressly said to be derived from the region around Delphoi; where votive double axes of bronze have in fact been found."[1]

Evans' description of the native Cretan culture as "Minoan" has long been controversial, since the *Iliad* implies that Minos, the legendary king of the island, was an Achaean Greek: His grandson Idomeneus is mentioned as leading a contingent to Troy. Yet there is much evidence that Minos, or at least the epoch denoted by the term, was not a Greek. His name is certainly not Greek, and his rule, recorded in the legends, seems to reflect the very real power and prosperity of Crete during the Middle and Late Minoan epoch. Historians generally associate the Age of Minos with the period known as Late Minoan (contemporary with the "Mycenaean" Age). Both epochs, as we noted, were contemporary with the Egyptian Eighteenth Dynasty. Since the latter is dated to the fifteenth and fourteenth centuries BC — i.e., well before the Trojan War (supposedly circa 1180 BC) — this seems to place the Late Minoan Age in the time of Minos, who is said to have lived before the

they may well be genuine Cretan products of the seventh or sixth century BC, made by Cretans in their characteristic latest Minoan style."
1 Burn, loc. cit., p. 78

Trojan War (estimates vary between two and five generations before). Yet according to the chronology proposed in these pages, the Trojan War did not follow but preceded the Eighteenth Dynasty, and preceded too the Late Minoan/Late Helladic epoch. Actually, it is placed right at the end of the Middle Helladic Age. This means, essentially, that the Age of Minos, or the period of the so-called Minoan Thalassocracy, or sea empire, must also be equated with the first Cretan palace culture, that of the Middle Minoan Age.

Events may then be reconstructed as follows: After the catastrophic destruction of the Early Minoan culture, the inhabitants of Crete quickly recovered and soon produced a wealthy and powerful maritime civilization. This "Middle Minoan" epoch saw the erection of the first palaces and the production in Crete and the Cyclades of the wonderful Kamares pottery and art, a style which achieved a level of refinement and beauty never again equaled.[1] The high point of this culture, Middle Minoan II, must have been reached in the years following 800 BC. From that date till about 740 BC we may fairly reasonably place the "epoch" of Minos. Then it was that Crete levied a human tribute from Athens and the other Greek states and "... controlled the greater part of what are now Greek waters, and ruled over the Cyclades.... And he drove out the Karians and installed his sons as governors." According to A. R. Burn, the limits of this Minoan Empire may be defined, following both archaeology as well as the method of Diodorus (who called attention to the wide distribution in the islands and on the Asiatic coast of the Aegean of the significant place names "Minoa" and "Cretan Harbour"), as "... the Cyclades and southern Sporades, while its fleets terrorized and held tribute some sections of the mainland coastal regions by their raids."[2]

Burn notes that there is a perhaps significant absence of Minos-legends in the neighborhood of Mycenae and the powerful fortresses of the Argolis. The absence is indeed significant, as we shall see.

This epoch of Minoan imperialism is recalled very clearly in Greek tradition. We are told that when some Athenians murdered his son Androgeus, Minos sailed around the Aegean collecting ships and armed levies in preparation for a war against Athens. Some islanders, it was said, agreed to help him, others refused. He made an alliance with the people of Anaphe, but

---

1 According to Burn, "many lovers of Minoan art consider 'M. M. II' as its greatest age, as showing a purity of taste that is not always found in the 'great palace period' of Late Minoan times." Ibid., p. 74.

2 Burn, loc. cit., p. 92

was rebuffed by King Aeacus of Aegina, who in fact allied himself with the Athenians.[1] In the meantime, the Cretan king was harrying the Isthmus of Corinth, where he besieged the town of Nisa, later known as Megara. After some time, the defenders were betrayed by Scylla, daughter of the reigning king Nisus, and the city fell into Minos' hands.[2]

The war dragged on until Minos, finding he could not subdue Athens, prayed Zeus to avenge Androgeus' death; and the whole of Greece was consequently afflicted by earthquakes and famine. In an effort to make the earthquakes cease, the Athenians sacrificed the four daughters of Hyacinthus on the grave of the Cyclops Geraestus. When this too failed they were instructed by the Delphic Oracle to give Minos whatever satisfaction he might ask. Thus was inaugurated the terrible custom of delivering to Crete every nine years seven youths and seven maidens for sacrifice to the bull-headed Minotaur, which lurked in the depths of the Labyrinth.[3]

It should be noted here that it is widely accepted that the Minotaur is nothing more than a fabulous description of the sacred Cretan Bull (Minotaur means simply "bull of Minos") which figured in the bull-vaulting ceremony displayed so wonderfully on much Cretan art, and it is possible, even probable, that the fourteen victims of Athenian legend would have been required to take part in this often deadly game.

However we view it, it is clear that at this time the mainland Greeks were militarily inferior to the Cretans, and must deliver human victims to the king in Knossos at regular intervals. Yet, the balance of power in the Aegean was shifting, and a tradition among the "True-Cretans" of Praisos explains how the House of Minos fell. The story goes that Minos was treacherously slain in Sicily after he had sailed there in pursuit of the artificer Daedalus. After this, the Cretans were apparently powerful enough to send another fleet to the west in pursuit of the king's killers. Yet this expedition was no more successful than the first, and, in the absence of the island's best troops, disaster struck.[4] According to the Atthidographers, a group of fourth century collectors and systemizers of Athenian and Attic legend, it was then that the Greeks, led by none other than Theseus of Athens, attacked the island and sacked Knossos. We should see in this perhaps the truth behind the story

---

1 Ovid, *Metamorphoses*, vii, 480 –viii, 6.
2 Scylla was said to have cut off her father's purple hair as he slept, thereby depriving him of his strength. The obvious parallels between this and the story of Samson and Delilah need no emphasis, but illustrate once more the correlation between the Greek Heroic Age and the Hebrew epoch of the Conquest and Judges.
3 Diodorus Siculus, iv, 61.
4 Herodotus, vii, 169-171; Diodorus Siculus, iv, 77-79.

which had Theseus rescuing the victims sent into the Labyrinth as food for the Bull-Man.

One thing is certain: by the middle of the eighth century BC, the power of the Minoan Cretans was broken, and the island had a dynasty of Achaean rulers. This is reflected in the fact that two generations or so later the country could send a contingent to support Agamemnon at Troy, and in the appearance at Knossos of tablets in Linear B, the language of the Greeks.

Mycenae before Agamemnon

By the time of the Trojan War, therefore, around 720 BC, the dynasty which ruled the Argolid was the greatest power in Greece. If there is any truth in Homer's report, it would appear that the ruler of Mycenae, known as the "King of Men," could command the allegiance of just about every other state in Greece — as far north as Thessaly and as far south as Crete. It is evident then that the story of Mycenae, Tiryns and Argos must be central in any attempted reconstruction of the political history of the country.

According to legend, Mycenae was founded, or at least first fortified by Perseus,[1] an evidently mythical character whose decapitation of the dragon-monster Medusa makes him an obvious alter-ego of the demigod Heracles. Certainly Perseus, whose name seems to derive from *pterseus*, "the destroyer," was much worshipped in the Argolid.[2] Pausanias mentions a shrine to him that stood on the left-hand side of the road from Mycenae to Argos, and also a sacred fountain at Mycenae called the *Persea*. Located outside the walls, this was perhaps the spring that filled the citadel's underground cistern. As well as being linked to Heracles, Perseus was also associated with Phoenicia/Palestine, where at Joppa (Jaffa) he slew Phineus after exposing the Gorgon' head to him. As we saw in Chapter 3, Phineus is identical to the Hebrew Phinehas, grandson of Moses' brother Aaron. Furthermore, Perseus' birth and infancy (rescued from a basket in the waters) brings to mind that of Moses, and his mother's name Danaë connects him to the Hebrew tribe of Dan (and the heroine Dinah). All these names and associations, we have seen, were almost certainly introduced into the Aegean world in the wake of the catastrophe recorded in biblical tradition as the Exodus.

The cult of Danaë was important enough in early Greece to make her "the archetype and eponymous ancestor of all the Danaans,"[3] and in Homer

---

1 Pausanias, ii, 15, 4 and ii, 16, 3-6.
2 See e.g., Robert Graves, *The Greek Myths* Vol. 1 (1955) p. 245.
3 "Perseus" in Wikipedia. http://en.wikipedia.org/wiki/Perseus.

"Danaoi" was a name interchangeable with Achaeans, applied basically to all Greeks. Perseus and his wife Andromeda had seven sons, Perses, Alcaeus, Heleus, Mestor, Sthenelus, Electryon and Cynurus, through whom they became ancestors to some of the most renowned characters of Greek legend. The first of these, Perses, was said to have been left in Ethiopia, and to have become ancestor of the Great Kings of Persia, whilst Electryon and his son Eurystheus ruled in Mycenae, after which the city was ruled by Atreus, son of Pelops. Through Alcaeus, Perseus became the ancestor of Heracles, who founded a line which eventually reclaimed the thrones of the Peloponnese from the Pelopids.

It is evident then that (notwithstanding the Phoenician/Hebrew mythic influences) the "Perseid" dynasty was a native, or autochthonous, line of kings who reigned in the Peloponnese in the wake of the catastrophe which terminated the Early Helladic Age. Tradition held that it was "Perseus" who first fortified Mycenae with enormous "cyclopean" masonry, though it has to be admitted that in the Middle Helladic epoch, which we regard as corresponding to the beginning of the so-called Heroic Age, there was little fortification carried out in the Greek settlements. Thus it may be that the "Perseus" fortifications are a memory of the fortress-building carried out in the Peloponnese during the Early Helladic Age.[1]

Yet the Middle Helladic (or Protogeometric/Early Geometric) epoch was indeed a warlike one. There was much innovation in weaponry, including the appearance, for the first time, of the great "Aegean" rapier, or stabbing-sword, which was apparently of Cretan origin, but which was adopted on the mainland by Middle Helladic II, a period beginning, as we would estimate, around 800 BC. Indeed, as we shall now see, it was the Middle Helladic epoch, specifically Middle Helladic II, that saw the adoption in Greece of all the panoply typical of the "Heroic Age" warrior. The item of equipment most characteristic of this was the chariot: And it should be noted that the first concrete evidence of the horse in Greece comes at this time.[2] This, by itself, should put to rest all question as to the archaeological context of the Pelops story, which, as we saw in the previous chapter, records the arrival in Greece of the horse and chariot. We found that Pelops, whose charioteer was named Myrtilus — a typically Hittite name — must have (as his legend in any case

---

1 As the Gorgon or Dragon destroyer, Perseus may be linked to an earlier catastrophe than that which destroyed the cities of Early Helladic II. See me *Genesis of Israel and Egypt*, (2ⁿᵈ ed. 2008).

2 John L. Caskey, "Greece and the Aegean Islands in the Middle Bronze Age," in *CAH*, Vol. 2 part 1 p. 125

insists) arrived in Greece from Anatolia, whence he came as a refugee from the advance through that region of Sargon I (the "Old Assyrian" king), who utilized, for the first time, the horse-drawn, two-wheeled chariot.[1]

The dynasty of Pelops soon became the most powerful in Greece, and some of the greatest rulers of the Heroic Age were of his line. The twenty-four children attributed to him and his wife Hippodameia are a reflection, thought Robert Graves, "of the strength of the confederation presided over by the Pelopid dynasty — all their names are associated with the Peloponnese and the Isthmus."[2] Evidently the arrival in Greece of the chariot altered the balance of power in a fundamental way. The incomers, whether through a system of alliances, through physical force, or through a clever combination of both, contrived within a short time make themselves the dominant power in Greece, and it is surely to this epoch that we must date the sudden and remarkable appearance of Mycenae as a power to be reckoned with — a power expressed in the novel and profligate opulence of the Shaft Graves. We date the advent of Pelops, and the appearance of Heroic Age-style military technology, to sometime between 780 and 770 BC, which, in terms of archaeology, must be identified with the earliest of the Mycenaean Shaft Graves, those of Grave Circle B. These, it is true, from Middle Helladic II, contained burials much more modest than those of Grave Circle A (the burials probably of Atreus, Agamemnon, Orestes, etc), yet they were clearly those of a feudal elite, one newly arrived, which would soon transform the whole country.

The rise to power of the Pelopids began with the acquisition of new weaponry, but it was also influenced by an intensification of commerce, command of the maritime trading routes and, above all, by the destruction of the power of Crete and the usurpation of her hitherto dominant position in the Aegean. These developments almost certainly took place not in the time of Pelops, but in that of his sons Atreus and Thyestes.

The Greeks of later times had much to say of Atreus and Thyestes, the savage brothers whose terrible feud was a favorite subject of poetry and drama. As well as unusual cosmic phenomena,[3] tradition suggests much earthquake activity, as well as attendant famine, during this period. It is probable that the seismic activity of Atreus' time is identical to that uncovered by archaeol-

---

1 See e.g., Graves, *The Greek Myths*, Vol. 2 pp. 37-9. Graves notes too that four of Pelops' sons and daughters bear horse names. Ibid., p. 43.

2 Ibid., p. 43.

3 In one version of the myth the sun-god was said to have turned his face away in disgust at the terrible meal (a stew made of his own sons) served up to Thyestes by Atreus.

ogy at the close of the Middle Minoan epoch.[1] Indeed, the earthquakes which apparently afflicted Greece during the time of Minos must also be linked to these events, and it is widely believed that the downfall of Minos' line was precipitated by natural catastrophe.

Yet it was not natural disasters which granted mastery of the Aegean to the Pelopids so much as seamanship. The earlier Greeks, it seems, had been poor seamen, and conceded control of that element to the Cretans and Cycladic Islanders. Yet by the time Agamemnon launched his thousand-ship fleet, the situation had changed dramatically: The Greeks now ruled the waves. And it is evident from the description of events both before and during the Trojan Campaign that their control of the waterways was complete. Had the Trojans possessed a fleet of any strength, they could have carried the war to the Achaeans, harrying their undefended homes and homelands on the other side of the Aegean. As it was, they were powerless to stop the Greeks plundering and looting coastal settlements up and down the coast of Asia Minor.

What was it changed the Greeks from land-lubbers into pirates and freebooters? Perhaps we shall never know. Living so close to the sea, it is probably inevitable that they would, in time, have become accomplished fishermen and have been drawn to the sea, whether they willed it or not. And, being as they were such close neighbors of the Cretans and Cycladic Islanders, they could not fail to have picked up many of the skills of seamanship from them. One way or another, by the middle of the eighth century, the Achaeans were on a par with the Cretans, and ready to assume mastery of the sea lanes themselves.

It would appear that these developments occurred in the time of Atreus. As we shall see, the one serious challenge to Atreus' line came from a family of "Perseid" origin named the "Heracleidae," who were expelled from the Peloponnese at the start of Atreus' reign. These took up residence in the city of Thebes, but were decisively defeated by Atreus at a great battle near the Isthmus, a battle said to have occurred ten years before the Trojan War. From this point on, the House of Pelops was unchallenged, and it is surely from this time that Homer's epithet for Mycenae, *polychrusos*, or "rich in gold" dated. So wealthy and powerful was Atreus that a great tholos tomb outside

---

1 Sir Arthur Evans, *The Palace of Minos at Knossos* (1921-35), III, 14. According to Evans a "great catastrophe" took place toward the close of Middle Minoan II. Also, "A great destruction befell Knossos on the northern shore of the island and Phaestos on its southern shore." Ibid. II, 287.

the walls of Mycenae was reputed to have been his Treasury; and is so named to this day.

Was it then the Mycenaeans who invaded Crete and destroyed the "Minoan Empire"? Tradition allocates responsibility to the Ionians of Attica. Whether or not this was the case, it was Mycenae and the Peloponnesians who benefited. They and they alone were powerful enough to implant their own authority on the island and assume the mantle of "Sea Kings." It was then, during the time of Atreus, probably around 740 or 730 BC, that the Peloponnesians began to import luxury items and craftsmen from Crete in large numbers. So great was this enforced migration that within a generation or so the Peloponnese had been transformed, resembling in many ways a cultural colony of Crete. Thus was born the civilization we now know as "Mycenaean." Yet away from the palaces and great houses, the Achaean villagers and peasants carried on with their own lives almost undisturbed; producing their own Middle Helladic/Early Geometric pottery and artifacts, artifacts regularly found in Mycenae and the other great fortresses on the same level or even underneath the Mycenaean material.

As regards Crete itself, the invading Greeks intermarried with the Minoan royal family, and there is little reason to doubt that Idomeneus, who accompanied Agamemnon to Troy, really was a grandson of Minos. But he was a grandson through one of Minos' daughters, not one of his sons. And although the occupying Greek armies may originally have come mainly from Attica, they quickly became subject to the rising might of Atreus at Mycenae, whose overlordship now extended throughout the entire Peloponnese and well beyond.

THE STORY OF THEBES

The city of Thebes was believed to have occupied an important position in Greek history prior to the time of the Trojan War. As we saw earlier, the Heroic Age settlement was said to have been established by Cadmus, an immigrant from Phoenicia, who brought with him the valuable gift of alphabetic writing. We saw too that virtually all the characters associated with Cadmus provide a strong link with the biblical Exodus. As noted above, I have elsewhere shown in detail that the Exodus, which was marked by a world-wide upheaval of nature, must have occurred sometime near the middle of the ninth century BC.[1] This accords remarkably well with testimony of Greek tradition: For all the evidence, we have seen, points to a Trojan War around 720 BC, whilst the genealogy of Cadmus outlined by Herodotus would have him arriving in Greece around six generations (roughly 140 years) before that: In short, around 860 BC. — a very striking correlation between Hebrew and Hellenic sources.

The catastrophe which initiated the Age of Heroes, as we saw, has left its mark in the archaeological record with the massive destruction of the Early Helladic sites throughout the Aegean and Anatolia. This can be observed too at Thebes. Tradition told of a pre-Cadmean city ruled first by a character named Calydnus, a son of Uranus and Gaia, and later by Ogyges, son of Poseidon. Ogyges had two sons, one of whom was Eleusis, eponymous founder of the Attic city of the same name; a city famous for its mystery cult.[2] The association with Ogyges, from whom the famous flood received its name, is of the greatest interest: this character evidently stands as a symbol for the catastrophic destruction of the Early Helladic world. Yet the occurrence of Ogyges provides another link also with Phoenicia and the Near East: For he appears to be identical to Agog, the Amalekite king who attacked the Israelites in the days following the flight from Egypt. That at least was the opinion of Immanuel Velikovsky (*Ages in Chaos*, 1952), a conclusion based on the obvious similarity of the two names as well as on the fact that Julius Africanus had specifically identified Ogyges with the Exodus.[3] It should be noted too that the scholiast of Lycophron held that it was the Egyptian Thebes rather than the Greek city which was Ogyges' capital.

It would appear that Phoenician and perhaps Hebrew immigrants, settling on the ruins of Early Helladic Thebes, brought this mythic association with them; and there is little doubt that in the chaos following the natural catastrophe described in the Book of Exodus, whole populations were set in motion. We know, even from the Old Testament, that not only the Hebrews, but also the Amalekites of Arabia and the Philistines of Caphtor (probably Cyprus), were uprooted and propelled into new lands. The peoples of Phoenicia seemed to have been affected in a similar way; and it is generally agreed that the wholesale Phoenician colonization of the western Mediterranean

---

1 In my *Genesis of Israel and Egypt* (1997, 2008) and *Pyramid Age* (1999, 2007). The chronology of the Old Testament, like that of Egypt and Greece, is too long by many centuries: and indeed the application of biblical dates to Egypt and then Mesopotamia (by Eusebius and others) was largely instrumental in producing the utter distortion of ancient history now encountered in the textbooks.

2 The origin of these mystery cults, which seem to have employed mind altering drugs, is a topic of the greatest interest and is linked to the whole "Atlantean" myth.

3 Julius Africanus, quoted by Eusebius, *Praeparatio Evangelica*, x, 10

began in the ninth or eighth century BC. That Greece and the islands saw a substantial Phoenician settlement is not doubted and is confirmed, as we have seen, both by the preponderance of Phoenician/Hebrew characters and deities in Greek myth and by the occurrence of various artifacts of Phoenician origin throughout Greece; and of course by the very existence of the Phoenician alphabet in Greece, an alphabet attested archaeologically since at least the mid-eighth century.

We should not, probably, think in terms of a one-off and large-scale Phoenician "colonization" of Greece, but rather the arrival, over a period of several generations, of a trickle of merchants, traders, and even farmers. Interestingly, Herodotus speaks of a branch of these people, whom he names Gephyraeans, who in his time were settled at Athens, where they worshipped strange gods: "These Gephyraeans claim to have come at first from Eretria, but my research tells me that they were among the Phoenicians who first came with Cadmus to the land now called Boeotia. After the Argives expelled the Cadmeans from Thebes, the Gephyraeans settled in the countryside in the area of Tanagra that was allotted to them. They came to Athens later, after being expelled from Tanagra by the Boeotians. The Athenians received them and allowed them to become Athenian citizens, although they prohibited them from many of their customary rites."[1]

Thebes' archaic connections with the east were strikingly confirmed by excavations carried out between 1971 and 1973 at the so-called Ampheion, a small hill near the ancient citadel, the Cadmeion. This work, under Theodoros Spyropoulos, revealed that the Ampheion had been shaped artificially into a pyramidal hill: the sides had been molded into a series of cone-shaped banks, so that the whole structure became a stepped pyramid, made of four layers. According to Spyropoulos, this reshaping of the hill may be dated to the same epoch as the building of the Giza pyramids in Egypt.[2] The interior was even more interesting: for here the excavators found a series of corridors, steps and passageways, in the midst of which was a stone-lined chamber with two depressions in the floor — evidently the remains of a real or ritual double-burial. This called to mind the story of Amphion, for whom the hill was named, and his twin brother Zethus, who were said to have been interred side-by-side. Although the tomb had been rifled in antiquity, the

---

1 Herodotus, v, 57, 1

2 As I have demonstrated in great detail in my *Pyramid Age*, the Giza pyramids were constructed roughly between 840 and 800 BC.

team did find four gold pendants shaped like lilies and topped with pyram-
oid forms, an apparently Egyptian motif.[1]

Near the burial chamber Spyropoulos found a horizontal tunnel leading
north. Further on, this tunnel meets a vertical chamber which leads to another passageway at a different (higher) level. This area remains to be properly explored and may bring further discoveries.

Greek tradition had much to say of the kings and queens who ruled at
Thebes during the Heroic Age, and produced a genealogy of rulers stretching
from Cadmus through to the destruction of the city some ten years before the
launch of the Trojan Campaign. Since Cadmus himself cannot be regarded as
a real person, we must treat with caution also his supposed descendants and
successors, persons such as Pentheus, Amphion, Labdacus and Laius, many
of whom were well-known and celebrated in classical literature. Nevertheless, it would appear that one element of real history can be gleaned from
these legends: namely that, at an early stage, Thebes found herself in conflict
with the other Achaean powers of central and southern Greece, and that as a
result of two ferocious wars the city was destroyed and not reoccupied until
after the Dorian Invasion. It was with the last of the above-mentioned rulers,
Laius, that these events, commonly known as the "Theban Cycle," were said
to have commenced. Whether or not Laius actually existed is a moot point.
He was said to have been a great-grandson of Cadmus and a contemporary
of Pelops, and would therefore, if historical, have flourished around 780 or
770 BC.

I do not intend to go into the details of the tale, for, as we shall see, much
of it has nothing to do with Greece at all. Nonetheless, it occupied an extremely important position in classical Hellenic culture, and a large propor-
tion of Greek poetry and drama from the fifth and fourth centuries BC found
their inspiration in it. Very briefly, the story runs thus: Laius, it was said, had
a son whom the seer Tiresias prophesied would kill him. In order to forestall
this, the king ordered that the child's feet be pierced and that he be exposed
on the mountains. A shepherd however came upon the child, who brought
him to Corinth, where king Polybus raised him as his own. The child had
been deformed by the piercing of his feet, in virtue of which he was known
thereafter as Oedipus, "swollen feet." Upon reaching maturity, the young
prince learned of the prophecy which decreed he would kill his own father
and, determined to avoid this, fled from Corinth. During his travels how-

---

1 See, www.philipcoppens.com/nexus07_2.html

ever he wandered in the direction of Thebes, where he came upon a group of men with whom he got into an argument. This quickly turned violent and Oedipus slew most of the company, including, unbeknown to him, his own father. Wandering on from there, he answered the question of the sphinx, thus delivering Thebes from a terrible curse, and was rewarded with the kingship of the city. Upon ascending the throne, he married the queen who, again unbeknown to him, was his mother.

Oedipus thus rules for several years in peace and has children with his mother. Eventually however a plague breaks out and, all efforts to alleviate it having failed, the king enquires of the blind seer Tiresias as to the cause. The latter reluctantly informs him that he himself is the source of the problem and all is revealed. The king is then banished and his two sons, Polyneices and Etoecles, agree to share the throne. Conflict however quickly breaks out between them, and Polyneices flees abroad, where he raises a great army, led by the famous Seven Champions, who pledge to help him regain his throne. These duly attack Thebes, but are repulsed in a bloody battle. Both Eteocles and Polyneices are slain and the throne is occupied by the aged Creon, Oedipus' uncle. When Antigone, the wife of Polyneices, tries to bury her brother's body in secret, Creon has the girl herself entombed alive. Several years later, so the legend goes, the descendants of the Seven Champions, the Epigoni, launch a renewed attack against Thebes and this time take the city almost without a battle.

As early as 1960, Immanuel Velikovsky (*Oedipus and Akhnaton*) demonstrated that the main elements of this story belong to Egypt rather than Greece, and that Oedipus is essentially an alter-ego of Akhnaton, the heretic king of Egyptian Thebes, who had a rare deformity characterized by swollen thighs and legs (Greek has but one word, *pous*, for "leg" and "foot"), who apparently spent his youth in exile, who abolished the cult of the sphinx, who hated his father and appears to have had an incestuous relationship with his mother Queen Tiy.[1] If this is correct, we need to set aside the Oedipus story in any reconstruction of Greek history. Nevertheless, there is good reason to believe that the Greek Thebes was the centre of a conflict with the Achaean states of the Peloponnese, and that another legend from the city (that of the "children of Heracles"), which speaks of a protracted war between Thebes and the Argives, became thoroughly confused with the Egyptian story. It is notable that the story of this conflict is placed precisely contemporary with

---

1 The proofs presented by Velikovsky in *Oedipus and Akhnaton* are truly compelling, so compelling indeed that he won over a number of mainstream classical scholars, amongst whom we may mention the great Cyrus Gordon.

the Oedipus story, though the protagonists in the two cycles do not interact with each other.[1]

In the chapter to follow, we shall identify the dynasty which really ruled at Thebes prior to the Trojan War and which, after being driven out by the Achaeans ten years before the start of the Trojan Campaign, returned to the Peloponnese two generations after that event and brought to an end the age of Mycenae's dominance.

[1] Having said all that, there is some evidence that elements of the "Oedipus Cycle" really do belong in Greece. The graves of the Seven Champions, for example, were shown at Eleusis, and several of the Epigoni who were children of these (such as Diomedes, son of Tydeus) actually took part in the Trojan War. The traditional burial-site of the Seven Champions have apparently been found, where at Eleusis an enclosure-wall segregates a group of Middle Helladic graves, apparently those pointed out to Pausanias as containing the bodies of the Seven. See A. M. Snodgrass, "The Balkans and the Aegean: Central Greece and Thessaly," in *CAH*, Vol. 3 part 1 (3rd ed) p. 683.

CHAPTER 7. BRIDGING THE GAP

THE DORIAN INVASION

Two generations after the end of the Trojan War a people of north-central Greece, the Dorians, invaded the Peloponnese and Crete. This invasion is better known in Greek tradition as the "Return of the Haraclids," for the Dorians were said to have been led by a dynasty named the Heracleidae, the "descendants of Heracles," an aristocratic family of Achaean origin which had been driven out of the Peloponnese during the time of king Eurystheus of Mycenae (two generations before the Trojan War) and which had subsequently become associated with the city of Thebes. When "Heracles"[1] died, his son Hyllus, apparently born at Thebes, became leader of the dynasty. After the destruction of that city, ten years before the start of the Trojan Campaign, tradition has the Heraclids moving further north, where they formed an alliance with the Dorians under Aegimius, who at that time inhabited Oeta on the borders of Boeotia and Thessaly. Following the death of Aegimius, his two sons, Pamphilus and Dymas, voluntarily submitted to Hyllus, who thus became ruler of the Dorians, the three branches of that race being named after these three heroes. Desirous of reconquering his paternal inheritance in the Peloponnese, Hyllus consulted the Delphic oracle, which told him to wait for "the third fruit," and then enter the Peloponnese by "a narrow pas-

---

1 This "Heracles" is not to be confused with the deity who upheld the heavens on his shoulders and pushed apart the rock pillars at Gibralter. He is properly named Alcides (Alkeides) by Herodotus and is identified as a son of the Achaean prince Amphitryon. His family became associated with the god Heracles/Ares because of their particular devotion to him.

sage by sea." Accordingly, after three years, Hyllus marched across the Isthmus of Corinth to attack Atreus, the successor of Eurystheus, but was slain
in single combat by Echemus, king of Tegea.

This, the second attempt of the Heraclids to take the Peloponnese, was
followed by a third under Cleodaeus and a fourth under Aristomachus, both
of which failed.

Finally, we are told that Temenus, Cresphontes and Aristodemus, the
sons of Aristomachus, complained to the oracle that its instructions had
proved fatal to those who had followed them. They received the answer that
by the "third fruit" the "third generation" was meant, and that the "narrow
passage" was not the Isthmus of Corinth, but the straits of Rhium. They accordingly built a fleet at Naupactus, but before they could set sail, Aristodemus was struck by lightning (or shot by Apollo) and the fleet destroyed;
divine punishment for the crime — committed by one of the Heracleidae
— of having slain an Acarnanian soothsayer.

The oracle, being again consulted by Temenus, bade him offer an ex-
piatory sacrifice and banish the murderer for ten years. The Heracleidae
repaired their ships, sailed from Naupactus to Antirrhium, and thence to
Rhium in Peloponnesus. A decisive battle was fought with Tisamenus, the
grandson of Agamemnon, the chief ruler in the peninsula, who was defeated
and slain. This conquest was traditionally dated two generations after the
Trojan War.

The Heracleidae, who thus became masters of the entire Peloponnese
apart from Arcadia, proceeded to distribute its territory amongst themselves
by lot. Argos fell to Temenus, Lacedaemon to Procles and Eurysthenes, the
twin sons of Aristodemus; and Messenia to Cresphontes. The fertile district
of Elis had been reserved by agreement for Oxylus, a one-eyed Aetolian who
had come to the assistance of the Heraclids. The Heracleidae ruled in Lacedaemon till 221 BC, but disappeared much earlier in the other countries.

Although Greek writers of the Classical period had much to say about
these stories, trying to sift fact from myth is very difficult. It is generally
agreed that there is a core of history in the tale, and there can be no doubt
that the Greece of historical times, from the sixth century onwards, was a
land fundamentally shaped by the division between Dorian and pre-Dorian
(Ionian and Aeolian). Whilst in the early years of the twentieth century archaeologists believed that the Dorians had been responsible for introducing
into southern Greece the "northern" or "barbaric-looking" Geometric art-
style of the ninth, eighth and seventh centuries, this notion had soon to be

abandoned, since the first and greatest flowering of Geometric culture took place in areas never settled by the Dorians at all, such as Attica.

In fact, trying to find archaeological evidence of the Dorians is a notoriously difficult and fruitless task.[1] They have, indeed, been credited with initiating the "Dark Age" which is said to have engulfed the Aegean world from the eleventh century onwards. To this statement, we might respond: Was it the Dorians too who brought total darkness and depopulation for five centuries to the whole of Anatolia? As we have seen however the "Dark Age" is a textbook artifact created by a fictitious chronology. Since it never existed, there is no need to blame the Dorians for it.

It is therefore worth repeating that the Dorians were never regarded by the Greeks as "barbarians" from the far north, but a tribe of central Greece, allied to the Heraclid dynasty of the Peloponnese. It is true that they had — in some distant epoch — come from Macedonia (or so claimed Herodotus), but when they first enter Greek tradition they are already living in a region bordering southern Thessaly.[2] In such circumstances, we might naturally expect them to possess a material culture virtually identical to that of all other Greeks and should not be too hopeful of finding any clear archaeological "traces" of them.

According to the chronology outlined in the present work, the Dorians would have entered the Peloponnese around 690 or 680 BC and would not have destroyed the "Mycenaean" palace culture they found, but merely occupied the citadels and fortresses of the fleeing Achaean oligarchs. In the historical scheme presented in my Ages in Alignment series, I have, as mentioned in Chapter 5, argued that the Eighteenth Dynasty of Egypt came to an end only in the last quarter of the seventh century — around 610 BC. Since artifacts belonging to the pharaohs of the latter Eighteenth Dynasty have been found in the Mycenaean palaces of the Peloponnese, this means that it was during the period of Dorian occupation that these centers enjoyed perhaps their greatest prosperity. And it is worth noting, at this stage, that the name "Dorian" occurs on one of the Linear B tablets unearthed at Pylos.[3] The fact that these were written in the pre-Dorian "Cypro-Arcadian" dialect is not a problem and may be explained by the proposition that the new Dorian

---

1 "The Dorians, have as yet no distinguishing feature in terms of archaeological remains." N. G. L. Hammond, "The Literary Tradition for the Migrations" in *CAH*, Vol. 2 part 2 (3rd ed) p. 706

2 Herodotus (viii, 31) places Doris, the "original home of the Dorians" between Locris, Aetolia and southern Thessaly.

3 The word occurring, on Pylos tablet Fn867, is Dorieus, "the Dorian," a man's name. It is written in the dative do-ri-je-we, *Doriewei*. http://en.wikipedia.org/wiki/Dorians.

---

rulers simply continued to employ the scribes, as well as the entire bureaucratic structure, which they found in place when they arrived.

The economic and military predominance of the Argives in the Dorian period is in fact well accepted. Thus historians both ancient and modern have much to say of the power of Agros under its Dorian king Pheidon, a man normally placed sometime in the eighth or seventh century BC.[1] And it hardly needs to be stressed that at least one of the "Mycenaean" centers of the Peloponnese, Sparta, had to wait until the Dorian period to enjoy its greatest power and prosperity. All during the seventh and sixth centuries, the Dorian dynasties of Argos and Sparta, mimicking the activities of the earlier Achaean rulers of the same cities, sought to extend their power right throughout the Peloponnese and beyond.

As we saw in Chapter 5, the most impressive monuments of Mycenae, the great beehive tholos tombs and the huge "cyclopean" walls, were in fact raised by the Dorian Argives during the seventh and sixth centuries, who maintained Mycenae as an important defensive and symbolic centre. It is likely that at least some of these structures were erected by none other than Pheidon and his successors.

The final destruction of many of the so-called "Mycenaean" palaces of the Peloponnese, which occurred near the end of the seventh century or in the first half of the sixth, was, as we shall see, not accomplished by the Dorians, but by native Peloponnesian Achaeans: These, rising against their Dorian overlords, placed in power the Tyrants.

THE AGE OF THE TYRANTS

The later seventh and sixth centuries in Greece are often described as the Age of the Tyrants. It was at this time, in various parts of the Greek world, that demagogic leaders, known as *tyrannoi*, rose to power and overthrew the hereditary monarchies. The word "tyrant" in modern English has negative connotations, but this was not the case in Greek. It is true that some of the Tyrannoi were "tyrants" in the modern sense, yet in many cases they were not. In general, they seem to have been popular and — at least to begin with — enlightened rulers who rose to power in a wave of resentment on the part of the poorer classes against the perceived injustices inflicted by the aristocrats.

---

1 The true date of Pheidon is something of a mystery. He is said by Pausanias to have officiated at the eighth Olympiad (supposedly 748 BC), yet in the list of the suitors of Agariste, daughter of Cleisthenes of Sicyon, given by Herodotus, there occurs the name of Leocedes (Lacedas), son of Pheidon of Argos. According to this, Pheidon must have flourished during the early part of the 6th century BC.

The first of the tyrants appeared in the Peloponnese, and for a very good reason: they were the leaders of popular rebellions against the alien Dorian aristocracies. This is stated very explicitly in the case of several of the earliest, for example of Theagenes of Megara and Cleisthenes of Sicyon. The latter in particular was famous, or rather infamous, for his anti-Dorian sentiments. Thus he waged war against Dorian Argos and renamed the various tribes of his territory in a way highly prejudicial to the Dorians. His own, non-Dorian clan he renamed "rulers of the people," whilst the three Doric tribes were called after various animals.[1] For this reason, it is widely agreed that the tyrannies represent, initially and first and foremost, a popular reaction to the Dorian Invasion. Yet here we encounter again the problem of chronology. The tyrannies rose in the seventh and sixth centuries BC. The first of them, that of Cypselus of Corinth, is reckoned to have arisen around 657 BC; whilst Cleisthenes took control of Sicyon around 600 BC. This is denied by no one. Yet the Dorian Invasion occurred two generations after the end of the Trojan War, therefore around 1150 or 1100 BC, according to most estimates. If the rise of the tyrants represents a native reaction to the presence of foreign oppressors, why did the reaction take five centuries to materialize?

It should be noted also that the life-stories of many of these tyrants, whom everyone agrees were historical, display numerous typically mythic or "Heroic Age" motifs. Thus according to Herodotus, the early life of Cypselus contained all the elements of a Heroic Age character, including prophecy and miraculous divine intervention. Thus we hear that the Bacchiadae, the Doric rulers of Corinth, had been informed by the Delphic Oracle that the son of Eëtion (Cypselus' father) would overthrow their dynasty, and they consequently plotted to kill the baby once it was born. However, the newborn infant smiled at the two assassins sent by the Bacchiadae, and neither could go through with the plan. An etiological myth-element to account for the name Cypselus (*cypsele*, "chest") recounted how Labda, Cypselus' mother, then hid the baby in a chest, and when the men had composed themselves and returned to carry out the deed, they could not find him.[2] This story has rightly been compared to that of the infancy of Perseus; though its parallels with other Heroic Age characters such as Jason and Oedipus hardly need to be stressed.

Interestingly, a "chest of Cypselus," richly adorned, was seen by Pausanias at Olympia in the second century AD, and he described it in detail.[3]

---

1 Herodotus, v, 67, 68.
2 Ibid.
3 Pausanias, v, 18, 7.

The general reaction against the Dorians in the Peloponnese is reflected in one of the greatest conflicts to engulf Greece during the Archaic Age: the Messenian Wars. These were two protracted campaigns waged by Sparta against neighboring Messenia, fought, supposedly, during the eighth and seventh centuries BC. The first of these is generally placed in the eighth century, owing to the fact that the Spartan leader, Theopompus, is listed as the eighth in line from Procles, founder of the Eurypontid dynasty.[1] Yet, as we have seen, these kings should not be regarded as representing separate generations, and there is no justification whatever in placing Theopompus eight generations after the Dorian Invasion. As such, a date in the mid-seventh century is indicated.

Although it is nowhere explicitly stated, there is strong suggestion that the Messenians, who had been conquered by the Dorians under Cresphontes, had thrown out their Dorian masters, and that this was a prime motive for the outbreak of hostilities with Dorian Sparta. Certainly the Messenians were reduced to helot bondage by the Spartans, a condition elsewhere inflicted only upon non-Dorians. The actual immediate cause of hostilities is unclear, but it was said that the murder of the Spartan king Telechus by the Messenians was the spark. The Messenians apparently fought heroically under their king Euphaes and his successor Aristodemus, but were finally subdued. So severe were the conditions imposed by the Spartans — described by the poet Tyrtaeus — that the Messenians revolted within two generations. Their leader this time was Aristomenes, who held out against the invaders for eleven years. He was finally defeated at Mount Ira, but managed to escape.

It should be noted that, although the Second Messenian War is definitely historical, and placed by everyone in the seventh century, the life of Aristomenes, like so many other characters of the time, is heavily cloaked in the elements of myth. Thus for example, after his defeat at Mount Ira, he was supposedly snatched up and rescued by the gods. The Lacedaemonians were said to have flung the Messenian leader and fifty of his companions from Mount Taygetus into a great chasm in the rock below. The fifty others were killed by the fall, but Aristomenes was saved by the gods. An eagle, the legend tells, with outspread wings, carried him unhurt to the bottom of the pit.[2] So fantastic were the deeds associated with Aristomenes that Sir Richard

---

1 Pausanias, iv, 6, 5.
2 Pausanias, iv, 18, 6.

Burton regarded his life story as the principle inspiration for the character of Sinbad of the Arabian Nights.[1]

THE AGE OF COLONIZATION

Although the Dorian Invasion has left no discernable signs in terms of archaeology, there was one migratory episode of Greek history which left a very clear mark in the archaeological record: That of the age of colonization. This epic migration out of Greece began before the Dorian Invasion, and even the Trojan War. Yet, as we shall see, it was one part of Greek life that very definitely was impacted by the Dorian Invasion.

Historians are agreed that the seventh and eighth centuries BC saw an enormous outpouring of population from Greece to all corners of the Mediterranean. The epoch is actually termed the Age of Colonization. To west and east, to the north and to the south, Greek migrants traversed the seas and planted portions of their homeland on distant shores. We are told that, "This was a period of frenetic colonization. The Greeks, pressured by growing populations around the city-states, actively went looking for unpopulated or thinly populated areas to colonize in Greece, the Aegean Sea, and elsewhere. The Greek city-state began to appear on the Italian and Sicilian shores, and set up trading posts in the Middle East and Egypt. Greek culture was spreading across the Mediterranean, and Greek commerce was rapidly making the city-states wealthy and powerful. There was no military, political, or cultural centre of the Greek world in the Archaic period. Different city-states developed separate cultures; these developments, however, spread across the Greek world. The city-state culture, then, was in many ways a national culture because of the dynamic interactions between the city states. The greatest flowering of culture occurred on the city-states of Asia Minor, and especially Miletus. Greek philosophy begins in these city-states and soon spreads around the Greek world. Corinth and later Argos became great centers of literature. But perhaps the greatest of the city-states were Athens and Sparta. Sparta in particular dominated the political scene all during the seventh century BC, and would remain a powerful force all throughout its history until the Macedonians conquered Greece in the fourth century BC."[2]

Very often, cities sent out colonies as a deliberate act of policy. Other times individuals, either aristocrats, politicians or even outlaws, led groups abroad. In a very short time, the shores of Cyprus were settled, as were parts

1 See e.g., http://en.wikipedia.org/wiki/Aristomenes.
2 "The Archaic Period," www.wsu.edu:8001/~dee/GREECE/ARCHAIC.HTM

of Cilicia and Phoenicia. Greeks arrived in Egypt and North Africa, where Cyrene became almost an extension of the homeland. Southern Italy too was heavily settled, as was Sicily. Indeed, so firmly did Greek civilization take hold in this region that the Romans named it *Magna Graecia*, "Greater Greece." Colonies were established too in southern Gaul and the Mediterranean coast of Spain, whilst at the very opposite end of the then-known world, Greek migrants established themselves along the shores of the Black Sea, as far east even as Colchis (modern Georgia), destination of Jason and his Argonauts.

Scholars are in no doubt that this epic outpouring of population occurred in the eighth and seventh centuries; tradition from Greece and the findings of archaeology confirms it in a thousand ways. Yet strangely, and incomprehensibly, the eighth and seventh century migration finds an echo in a Mycenaean Age migration supposedly of the twelfth century. This migration too is confirmed both by tradition and archaeology. Here of course we are on familiar ground. In yet one more area, Greek history has been cleaved in two and the two sections separated from each other by five or more centuries.

Many of the colonies which Greek tradition dated to the eighth and seventh centuries have yielded Mycenaean Age material, whilst many of the colonies which tradition dated to the time of the Trojan War and its immediate aftermath have yielded only Geometric and Archaic material of the late eighth and seventh centuries.

How then do scholars explain the traditions of Heroic Age characters establishing colonies? Usually they do not; and the question is passed over in a rather embarrassed silence. But it is a fact that the Trojan Campaign and all the events surrounding it were clearly regarded by the Greeks as the first great movement of colonization, a movement which, with the Dorian Invasion two generations later, became almost a tidal wave. Yet none of the colonies founded at this time, all of which preserved detailed histories of their origins, placed their beginnings earlier than the eighth century.

We have already seen how the campaign against Troy was associated with the establishment of Greek rule in adjacent regions of Asia Minor.[1] Yet it was two generations later, in the immediate aftermath of the Dorian Invasion, that the coastlands of Asia Minor became virtual extensions of Greece herself. It was then that the colonies of Aeolia and Ionia were established. Not surprisingly, all of the leading families of Aeolia, the northern region around Troy, claimed descent off Greek warriors who had fought at Troy. Most of them were of the house of Atreus. It was said, for example, that Pen-

---

1 We saw how Agamemnon was, for a time, based at Cyme, during which time he concluded a peace treaty with Midas (circa 715 BC).

thilus, a grandson of Agamemnon, led the settlement of Lesbos, having fled there after the conquest of Argolis by the Dorians.[1]

The same pattern is observed in Ionia. Strabo informs us that Androclus, the son of the Athenian king Codrus (killed during the Dorian Invasion), led the Ionian colonization and was the founder of Ephesus. He goes on to name Neleus, a man of Pylian origin, as the founder of Miletus, and names the founders of the other Ionian cities, of whom two were from Pylos and three from Athens.[2] Pausanias makes Neleus (whom he calls Neileus), the second son of Codrus, and his younger brothers, the leaders of the Ionians in their overseas migration.[3] The underlying assumption in the surviving literary testimonies is that the colonization was a single organized act issuing from Athens, where refugees from other parts of Greece, fleeing the Dorian onslaught, had collected.

Genealogies of several leading families of Ionia have survived (including that of the famous Hecataeus of Miletus), and none of them, as we shall see, would place the colonization of the region before circa 700 BC.

The colonization of regions further east, including Cilicia and Cyprus, was likewise believed to have begun in the time of the Trojan War. We have already examined the legend of Mopsus and his associates, who established the Pamphylian and Cilician colonies in the immediate aftermath of Troy's conquest. In Cyprus too, it was warriors fresh from the sack of Ilion who led the settlement. This was the case, for example, at Paphos, a city founded by the Arcadian king Agapenor after he had been driven off course by a storm and separated from the rest of the Achaean fleet.[4] The great Cypriot town of Salamis was founder by Teucer, son of Telamon and half-brother of Ajax. We are told that, having failed to avenge Ajax, Teucer was unable to return home and so sailed eastwards to Cyprus.[5] Interestingly, a long line of priest-kings of a brigand tribe in Pamphylia still, in Hellenistic and Roman times, boasted their Teucrian ancestry, "and most of the priests were called Teucer or Ajax."[6]

Other warriors from Troy, among them Praxandrus, Pheidippus, Chytrus and Golgus, founded various settlements in Cyprus, some of which became prosperous and powerful.

---

1 Burn, op. cit., p. 231.
2 Strabo, xiv, 632-3.
3 Pausanias, vii, 2-4.
4 Ibid. viii, 5, 2.
5 Aristotle, *Peplos*, No. 7.
6 Strabo, xiv, 672.

The Cypriot cities have of course revealed, to the spades of the archae-ologists, a Mycenaean-style culture. And yet, as we saw in Chapter 4, the Mycenaean pottery, jewelry, weaponry and architecture of Cyprus presents incredible difficulties for conventional dating and all of these display strik-ing similarities to Greek artifacts of the Archaic Age. Again, the Greek aris-tocrats of Cyprus possessed genealogies which linked them to their heroic ancestors, yet none of these, as elsewhere in the Greek world, could push the settlement of the island farther back than the later eighth century BC.

If we look to the west, it is the same story. As we saw, warriors on their way back from Troy founded the first colonies of *Magna Graecia*, and these were added to after the Dorian Invasion. Here however there is no question as to the age of these settlements, for many of them recorded how long they had lasted in terms of years, rather than as generations: and almost all of them were founded in the latter years of the eighth century and the early years of the seventh. And these dates are confirmed, as we saw, by the ar-chaeology, which can find no evidence of settlement before circa 700 BC. These regions, as we saw, do of course produce "Mycenaean" style artwork and architecture, but in southern Italy and Sicily the context of this material makes it very clear that it represents a "late survival" of the Mycenaean style; a late survival dating from the eighth and seventh centuries.

IRON SWORDS OF TEGEA

It is universally believed that the Iron Age in Greece began in the elev-enth century BC, and is roughly synchronized with the Dorian Invasion. True, some small iron objects were found in the Shaft Graves at Mycenae, which of course are synchronous with the late Hyksos or early Eighteenth Dynasty, but these are held to be exceptional, and prove only how rare and precious iron was at the time. In fact, although very small quantities of iron have been found in settlements even of the Early Bronze Age, scholars generally equate the beginning of what is known as the Iron Age with the start of the time during which iron first came to be widely used for tools and weapons.

It was the Greeks themselves, more specifically, to begin with, Hesiod, who gave us the terms "Iron Age" and "Bronze Age." To them, however, the expressions had religious connotations. It was held that, from an early per-fection (in the "Golden Age") men had become progressively more corrupt, and with this progression came an association with metals progressively less "pure." Thus the Golden Age was followed by an Age of Silver, which was in turn followed by an Age of Bronze. The men of the Bronze Age still had a part of the divine spark; but even this they lost. The Age of Bronze was followed by the Age of Iron, a period more corrupt and degraded than anything preceding it. However, between the Age of Bronze and the Age of Iron there was placed the Age of Heroes; an intermediate period which saw the life and deeds of Hercules, the wars against Thebes, and the campaign against Troy.

Notwithstanding modern historians' attempts to depict the Dorian Invasion as marking the advent of the Age of Iron, the Greeks themselves made no such link. But they did indeed have a very clear tradition about when iron began to be used for weapons began; for it signaled a very definite military and technological turning-point. Yet the Greeks placed this event well after the Dorian Invasion.

It was said that during the reign of the Eurypontid king Anaxandrides I (supposedly circa 675 — 645 BC), Sparta had been at war with the nearby city of Tegea for many years. The Spartans had lost repeatedly to the Tegeans and, consulting the oracle of Delphi, were informed that if they physically brought the bones of Orestes, Agamemnon's son, to their own country, they would gain the upper hand in their dealings with Tegea.[1] When the Spartans proved unable to discover the grave of Orestes, they sent another delegation to the god to "ask for the place in which Orestes lay," and were answered thus:

> There's a Tegea in Arcady on smooth ground,
>
> Where two winds make breezes under strong necessity,
>
> And blow and counterblow are, and woe on woe lies.
>
>> There life-giving earth keeps down Agamemnon's son;
>>
>> Carry him home, and you'll be Tegea's helper.

> This answer apparently proved of little help until a Spartan named Liches went to Tegea and,... for which reason we are not told, went to a smithy and beheld the beating out of iron, and was in a state of marvel on seeing what was done. The smith learned that he marvelled much, and said, on ceasing from his work, "Surely then, O Laconian stranger, if you had seen the very sight I did, you would marvel very much, inasmuch as you now thus, in fact, consider a marvel the working of the iron. For I, wishing to make a well in this court here, while I dug, happened on a coffin of seven cubits. Out of disbelief that indeed human beings were born at all taller than those now, I opened it and saw that the corpse was equal in length to the coffin. Then I measured and covered it back with earth." The one, then, spoke to the other of the very sight he had seen, and the other, having in mind what was said, concluded that that was Orestes in accordance with the message from the oracle, by concluding this way: seeing the two bellows of the smith, he found they were the winds, and the anvil and the hammer the blow and the counterblow, and the iron that was beaten out the woe that on woe lay, since he conjectured in accordance with a reasoning like this, that to do evil to a human being iron was discovered.[2]

1 Herodotus, i, 67
2 Ibid.

Commentators have of course remarked at length on this passage: for it is widely held that swords of iron had been employed throughout Greece long before the time referred to in the story. Yet belief in an Iron Age beginning in the tenth or eleventh century is closely connected to the overall times-cale of Near Eastern history established in the years just prior to Schliemann. In short, the concept of a tenth/eleventh century Iron Age derives from the grossly distorted chronology of Egypt. If the history of Greece had been re-constructed without allusion to Egypt, the start of the Iron Age would have been placed much later.

We are told that Liches subsequently returned to Tegea, befriended the smith, and brought him back with him to Sparta, "And from that time, whenever they made of trial of each other, the Lacedaemonians proved far superior in war, and to them even the greater part of the Peloponnesus was in subjection."

It is remarkable that, once again, this story, though clearly of the age nor-mally regarded as historical, contains typically mythic elements and motifs. The proper location of the story depends upon the date of Anaxandrides I. We should note, however, that even if we were to accept the conventional date, this would still place the advent of the Iron Age only in the mid-seventh century. Yet such a location, late as it is, is still too early, since it depends (like all other Spartan dates) upon treating the Lacedaemonian king-lists as generations and according well over thirty years each to these. If however we take about fifty years from that date, which we have every justification in doing, this makes Anaxandrides I reign in the first quarter of the sixth century — which then becomes the true date of the advent of the Greek Iron Age.

In another place I have examined the whole question of Bronze and Iron Ages at length. Without going into the details of the arguments presented there, it should be noted that any society which possesses the ability to smelt bronze also, by definition, can produce iron: the two technologies — dependent on the charcoal-burning furnace — are essentially identical. But iron-production, throughout most of the Bronze Age, was a laborious and extremely labor-intensive operation. Only with new iron-smelting technolo-gies, which appeared in the sixth century BC, did iron (or, more accurately, steel) begin to replace bronze as the preferred metal for weapons. And this is another point worth stressing: iron as such cannot be regarded as a suitable material for weapons. An iron sword or razor cannot take an edge as sharp as one of bronze. When we speak of the Iron Age we mean, essentially, the Steel Age.

FESTIVALS AND LEGAL CODES

We have seen that the Greeks normally began their history with the foundation of the Olympic Games, an event apparently of the eighth century. Yet we have found that the Games were associated with Heracles, a typically Heroic Age character, who was also believed to have established numerous new laws, customs and institutions. Above all, he was linked to new religious ideas, chief amongst which was the abolishment of human sacrifice.

As a matter of fact, almost all the Heroic Age characters were associated with the institution of new religious and legal codes: None more so than Theseus of Athens, the hero accredited with the federalization of Attica, whose twelve self-governing communities he united.[1] We are informed that, "Theseus was a founder-hero, like Perseus, Cadmus or Heracles, all of whom battled and overcame foes that were identified with an archaic religious and social order. As Heracles was the Dorian hero, Theseus was the Ionian founding hero, considered by Athenians as their own great reformer. His name comes from the same root as θεσμός ('thesmos'), Greek for *institution*. He was responsible for the *synoikismos* ('dwelling together')—the political unification of Attica under Athens, represented in his journey of labors. Because he was the unifying king, Theseus built and occupied a palace on the fortress of the Acropolis that may have been similar to the palace excavated in Mycenae. Pausanias reports that after the synoikismos, Theseus established a cult of Aphrodite Pandemos ('Aphrodite of all the People') and Peitho on the southern slope of the Akropolis. In *The Frogs*, Aristophanes credited him with inventing many everyday Athenian traditions."[2]

One of Theseus' most outstanding achievements was the abolition of human sacrifice, recalled most obviously in his destruction of the Minotaur, which required human victims. This aspect of his character is reflected too in the story of his encounter with Cercyon, "King at the holy site of Eleusis, who challenged passers-by to a wrestling match and, when he had beaten them, killed them. Theseus beat Cercyon at wrestling and then killed him instead. In interpretations of the story that follow the formulas of Frazer's *The Golden Bough*, Cercyon was a 'year-King,' who was required to do annual bat-

---

1 R. Graves, *The Greek Myths*, Vol. 1, p. 351. Interestingly, Graves regarded the political and social reforms attributed to Theseus as late additions to the myth and claims that his "Federalization of Attica is dated several hundred years too early." Again, Graves notes how the twelve communities of Attica are "paralleled by a similar arrangement in the Nile Delta and in Etruria [both in the seventh century], and by the distribution of conquered Canaanite territory among the twelve tribes of Israel." Ibid.

2 "Theseus" in wikipedia. http://en.wikipedia.org/wiki/Theseus.

tle for his life, for the good of his kingdom, and was succeeded by the victor. Theseus overturned this archaic religious rite by refusing to be sacrificed."[1]

It should be noted, at this point, that Eleusis was an Early Helladic (and therefore pre-catastrophe) site of great importance, associated with a famous mystery cult; and therefore with archaic religious custom — prominent amongst which was human sacrifice.

So, the Age of Heroes was an epoch characterized by new religious and legal ideas; yet strangely enough, so too was the Archaic period of Greek history, the period of the eighth, seventh and sixth centuries. Virtually every city-state had a tradition of a founder-figure or semi-mythical hero legislator who, sometime usually in the eighth or seventh century, had codified the state's laws and established a rationalized system of governance. Often too these figures, many of whom were from the Age of the Tyrants (seventh-sixth century), were credited with the introduction of new religious ideas and the reform of existing institutions. We could fill many chapters with a through enumeration of these founder-heroes, but the mention of two or three should serve to illustrate the point.

According to Spartan tradition, the great codifier of their laws and institutions was named Lycurgus. The latter is described as "the legendary lawgiver of Sparta, who established the military-oriented reformation of Spartan society in accordance with the Oracle of Apollo at Delphi. He is referred to by ancient historians Herodotus, Xenophon, Pausanias and Plutarch. However, many ancient historians believed Lycurgus was responsible for the communalistic and militaristic reforms which transformed Spartan society, the most major of which was known as The Great Rhetra."[2] According to Pausanias, Lycurgus gave the laws to the Spartans in the reign of king Agesilaus I.[3] Since the latter cannot be accurately dated, much confusion exists as to the great legislator's place in history. However, it is generally accepted that he belonged to the Archaic Age.

Tradition from Athens ascribes similar characteristics to a man named Draco.

We are told that "by the 7th century BC social unrest [in Attica] had become widespread, and the Areopagus appointed Draco to draft a strict new law-code (hence 'draconian')."[4]

1 Ibid.
2 "Lycurgus." http://en.wikipedia.org/wiki/Lycurgus_%28Sparta%29
3 Pausanias, iii, 2, 4.
4 "History of Athens." http://en.wikipedia.org/wiki/History_of_Athens

A similar tradition is attached to Pheidon, the seventh-century king of Argos. According to Aristotle, this man reformed the system of land ownership, whilst Herodotus states that he "established a system of weights and measures throughout Peloponnesus, to which Ephorus and the Parian Chronicle add that he was the first to coin silver money, and that his mint was at Aegina."[1] It is generally agreed that a system of weights and measures was already in existence in the time of Pheidon, into which he introduced certain changes. A passage in the Aristotelian *Constitution of Athens* states that the measures used before the time of Solon were called Pheidonian.

As we have seen, it was almost certainly Pheidon and his successors who constructed the massive tholos tombs at Mycenae, as well as most of the cyclopean walls of the citadel, including the famous Lion Gate. These were erected from about 650 BC through to 570 BC, and stand as the earliest monumental architecture and sculpture in the Greek world, prefiguring the well-known "Dorian" style that gradually appeared from the 590s onwards.

Some Genealogies and Chronologies

Several genealogies connecting characters of the Heroic Age with persons of the historical age, usually the fifth or fourth centuries BC, have survived. None of these, no matter how much they are stretched, would place the Age of Heroes before the ninth or eighth centuries. Some of these family trees shall now be examined, but before doing so it needs to be emphasized that irrespective of what they say, the evidence thus far examined is more than strong enough to stand on its own in placing the Trojan War near the end of the eighth century and the Dorian Invasion early in the seventh. The evidence of the genealogies can, at best, be seen as giving an extra level of support to that of the archaeology. We need to remember too that we have little way of testing the authenticity of these lists, even their later parts, and the habit all of them have of beginning with a god does not inspire much confidence in the earlier sections.

That said, it is remarkable that none of the genealogies give any support to conventional chronology, and all of them can be seen as, at the very least, not contradicting the chronology proposed in these pages.

In his *Minoans, Philistines and Greeks*, A. R. Burn mentioned five genealogies which he claimed dated the Dorian Invasion to the eleventh century — around 1050 BC. Now Burn himself was very critical of conventional chronology, and pleaded for a reduction of all Greek dates prior to 500 BC. He wrote, "it is almost certain that all the dates before 500 BC given by Greek historians

---

1 "Pheidon." http://en.wikipedia.org/wiki/Pheidon

should be reduced to ... (five-sixths) of their traditional distance from 500 BC."[1] He based his calculations on the fact that these "traditional" dates were calculated by according forty years to a generation, a figure which he said was too long. He proposed, instead, generations of, on average, thirty-three years; and the result was the modest proposal of a one-sixth reduction — a proposal that was ignored.[2]

It was therefore, in the main, by counting three generations to a century that Burn reached his date of 1050 BC for the Dorian Invasion and 1100 BC for the fall of Troy. I say "in the main" because not even three generations to a century will produce these dates, and Burn had to resort to a good deal of extra legerdemain to go back so far. In the 1970s, V. R. d'A. Desborough took a more honest view, and, echoing the sentiments of classicists at the end of the nineteenth century, wondered why the genealogies should disagree so dramatically with textbook dates. Thus he famously commented on the strange fact that only five generations separated Pythagoras (sixth century) from the Dorian Invasion: "Temenos was one of the three Heraclid leaders who with the Dorians seized the Peloponnese, according to conventional chronology at the end of the twelfth century. He had a grandson called Rhegnidas, who gained control of the little town of Phlius; this would not have been much later than the middle of the eleventh century. This event, we are told by Pausanias, resulted in the departure to Samos of the leader of the opposition party at Phlius, Hippasos; and Hippasos was the great-grandfather of 'the famous sage Pythagoras.' Pythagoras should then have been living at the end of the tenth century, and so, one might think, one has an admirable Dark Age situation: until, that is to say, one discovers that Pythagoras belonged to the middle of the sixth century, a difference of no fewer than three hundred and fifty years."[3]

Not surprisingly, Burn, who tried to save at least a vestige of conventional timescales, made no mention of Pythagoras' family tree, which must inevitably have placed the Dorian Invasion sometime between 700 and 650 BC. The genealogies Burn does examine are slightly longer than Pythagoras' but, irrespective of how much they are manipulated, they still cannot place the Dorian Invasion in the eleventh or tenth century.

---

1 Burn, op. cit., p. 55.

2 Why, we might ask, was Burn's very moderate and very much called-for chronological reduction rejected? The answer is obvious: Even bringing the Trojan War down to circa 1050 BC, as he pleaded, meant opening up an even greater gap between it and the archaeological date for the high-point of Mycenaean civilization (based of course on synchronization with Egypt) — circa 1550 –1350 BC! The "traditional" date of 1184 BC, although an absurdity, at least left a slightly less embarrassing gap.

3 V. R. d'A. Desborough, *The Greek Dark Ages* (London, 1972) p.

They are as follows:

First, that of Hecataeus of Miletus, who claimed, to the amusement of Herodotus, to be sixteenth in descent from a god.[1] Hecataeus was alive in 500 BC, so in the words of Burn, "the fifteen generations, after which human ancestry ceased, take us back to 1000 — perhaps the approximate date of the Ionian capture of Miletos from the Karians."[2]

There is a very large element of dishonesty in the above statement. If we are to accord thirty-three years to a generation, there is no question that we do get back to 1000 BC (995 BC, to be precise). Yet to suggest that this was the date of the Ionian settlement of Miletus amounts to sleight of hand. Hecataeus' fifteen generations led him back to a god; but descent from gods ended one or two (or often three or four) generations before the Trojan War, and thus about four generations before the Dorian Invasion and the colonization of Miletus. In short, Hecataeus' fifteen generations take us back before the Trojan War. To go back to the Dorian Invasion we should count only eleven generations, at maximum. Now, even if we accord thirty-three years to a generation, we are thus taken back only as far as 863 BC. This is two and a half centuries later than the date normally given for the Dorian Invasion in the textbooks.

Yet even Burn's estimate of 33 years to a generation is grossly misleading. Ancient marriages tended to happen at a much younger age that at present, a necessity in a society where the average life-span of a man may have been no more than thirty or thirty-five years. It was, as we know, not uncommon for boys to be married in their mid-teens, and girls even younger. Bearing this in mind, we would be perfectly justified in assigning twenty-five or even twenty years to an average generation. If twenty-five, then Hecataeus' genealogy points to a Dorian Invasion around 775 BC — a full 350 years shorter than the date given in the textbooks. If we allow twenty years, then we would have a Dorian Invasion around 700 BC: The latter date being very close to that (circa 680 BC) which all the evidence examined in the present volume would require.

The second genealogy mentioned by Burn is that of Miltiades, the victor of Marathon, who was said to be fifteenth in line from Ajax, son of Telamon, who fought at Troy. According twenty years to a generation would place Ajax around 800 BC. This is rather early by our calculations, though it has to be remembered that these genealogies are not sacrosanct, and the reader must bear in mind that we use them only as support for what archaeology

---

1 Herodotus, ii, 143.
2 Burn, p. 49

has already proven. Many of the characters in the genealogies (like Ajax himself perhaps) are of questionable authenticity, and we have to allow, in addition, for the possibility of errors entering the tradition. These lists were, after all, probably only committed to writing in the sixth or fifth centuries BC.

The third of Burn's genealogies is that of Pyrrhus, king of Epirus, who famously waged a losing war against the Romans. Pyrrhus was reputedly born in 319 BC and, according to Pausanias, he was twentieth in line from Achilles.[1] According twenty years to a generation, this would place Achilles and the Trojan Campaign around 720 BC — precisely the date suggested throughout the present work. Yet even if we were to accord the impossibly-long thirty-three years suggested by Burn, this would still only give us a Trojan War in 980 BC — a full two centuries later than the textbook figure.

The fourth genealogy is that of Arcesilaus IV, King of Cyrene, for whom Pindar wrote his famous Fourth Pythian Ode about the year 466 BC. Arcesilaus claimed to be twenty-third in descent from Euphemus the Minyan, a member, according to Pindar, of the crew of the Argo. Again, allowing twenty years to a generation, this would place Euphemus and the voyage of the Argo around 920 BC, and it has to be remembered that the journey of the Argonauts was believed to have taken place well before the Trojan War.

The fifth and last genealogy was that of the kings of Sparta. Here Burn emphasized most of the points already made by us in Chapter 1: namely that the list was not a genealogy but just what it claimed to be — a list of kings, many of whom were probably brothers. Burn recommended allotting each king an average reign of twenty-five years — ridiculously too long in such a barbaric age.

Before moving on, it should be noted that a list of Dorian kings of Messenia is also extant but is invariably ignored as evidence because it is deemed, in Burn's words, "disproportionately short."[2]

After the Dorian Invasion, the age of kings came to an end in many parts of Greece. Thus Codrus, the last king of Athens, who was said to have sacrificed his life to prevent Attica falling into the hands of the Heraclids, was replaced not by a king but by an archon. The archon was the chief magistrate in many Greek cities, but in Athens there was a council of archons which comprised a form of executive government. Apparently from the late eighth century there were three archons, the *archon eponymous*, the *polemarch* (replaced in 501 BC by the *strategoi*) and the *archon basileus*, the ceremonial

---

1 Pausanias, i, 11, 1. Pausanias makes Pyrrhus nineteenth in line from Achilles' son Pyrrhus-Neoptolemus.
2 Burn, op. cit., p. 51

remnant of the Athenian monarchy. To begin with, archons held the position for life; and the first of these, supposedly, was none other than Codrus' son, Medon. After Medon there are listed twelve other life archons, from which time on the post was held for ten years. We have the names of seven of these decennial archons. Later archons held the position for only one year.

It is almost impossible to derive any material of chronological value from these lists, but it should be noted that the demise of kingship in Athens signaled a movement away from the entire concept of monarchy, a movement which would eventually result in the emergence of Athenian democracy. Elsewhere in the Greek world the democratic impulse is connected, as we saw, with the rise of the Tyrants. Yet the age of the tyrannies, clearly connected with a general reaction against the Dorian invaders, is not dated before the sixth or seventh century at the earliest. Athens is therefore seen as the odd man out, with her democracy commencing a full four centuries before the others. Yet another anomaly for the defenders of conventional chronology to grapple with!

EPILOGUE

Eratosthenes and other ancient authors generally agreed that history, properly speaking, started with the foundation of the Olympic Games. Everything before that was *mythikon*, the age of myths. Yet the Olympiads, we have seen, were established long before the war against Troy and apparently before the great majority of the events normally described as "Greek Myth." It is true that events surrounding the Trojan War and the lives of many of the characters who participated in it, have a distinctly mythic quality. Yet we have seen that characters who are undoubtedly historical and belong in the eighth and seventh centuries, such as Midas, have the same mythic qualities. Thus Midas met deities and had a Golden Touch and ass's ears.

The generation which fought at Troy, as well as its immediate predecessors, belonged in the eighth century BC and was undoubtedly historical. Names of individuals known from Greek legend, including Agamemnon himself, even occur on the Boghaz-koi documents, documents we have identified as being the state archives of the Lydian kingdom.

Greek history thus begins with the cosmic event which marked the establishment of the Olympiads, an event which, for a great variety of reasons, we place in the middle of the ninth century, probably within a decade of 850 BC.

Throughout the present volume I have left untouched the question of Hellenic origins. When and how the ancestors of the people who came to be known as Greeks entered the Aegean is a topic of much interest, but beyond the scope of the present study. Scholars are in general agreement that the earliest culture which may be described as "Greek" is that of the Middle Helladic Age: a culture which appeared in the Aegean in the wake of a great natural catastrophe — a disaster marked by widespread conflagrations, earth-tremors and tidal waves. This event is placed by us around 850 BC and saw the end of the Early Bronze or Early Helladic Age. The subsequently-appearing Middle Helladic shows some signs of having been introduced by an immigrant population and displays striking affinities with what had come to be known as Early Geometric culture. As we saw in Chapter 2 Middle Helladic and Early Geometric are in fact, to all intents and purposes, culturally identical.

The culture which this Middle Helladic/Early Geometric replaced (Early Helladic) presents its own intriguing questions. Was it Greek; or did its people speak an ancestral form of the Greek language? The probability is that they did, or at least spoke a dialect related to what later became Greek. Certainly there is evidence of continuity of custom, folk-tradition and legend. Many of the most fascinating elements of Greek myth, it could be argued, have their origin in this period. In point of fact, the cataclysm which terminated the Early Helladic Age seems to be a central theme of much Greek mythology, as we shall see in the Appendix. Actually, the various flood legends (Deucalion and Ogyges being the most famous), as well as theogonies (Hesiod's *Theogony* is one enormous description of a cosmic catastrophe), and the numerous tales relating to the deeds of giants, titans and heroes, almost certainly refer *inter alia*, to these disastrous occurrences. The tales of Heracles, as we have seen, are full of earth-shattering events, and the Twelve Labors are a cosmic myth relating to a re-ordering of the calendar and the signs of the zodiac.

Much of Greek myth, in short, is about the natural events of 850 BC, and natural events which preceded them. This being the case, it seems reasonable to assume that the inhabitants of the region at the time were most probably — at least in part — ancestral Greeks. The culture of these Early Helladic folk was maritime and warlike. They raised great fortifications around many of their settlements — settlements which tended to lie along the coast. They were already familiar with tin-bronze, which speaks of trading relations with Atlantic Europe; and their links with the Balkans mean that they probably were in some sense literate: The proto-script of the Balkan Vinca culture is at least as old as that of Mesopotamia. It must have been at this time that the two Linear scripts, A and B, were first used; and it has already been demonstrated that these owe their inspiration to the Vinca folk.

Early Helladic culture (and Early Minoan) has archaeologically proven associations with North Africa and the Libyan region in general. These associations find their echoes in Greek myth, where various of the mystery cults are attributed to hero-figures from North Africa. It should be noted also, at this point, that Egyptian tradition also speaks of a western origin for the mystery cult of Osiris. Indeed, we enter here a region of the most profound interest. Various clues, many of which were almost an obsession with writers such as Robert Graves, imply the existence in the Aegean in Early Bronze times of a matriarchal culture with a strong cult of the dead. Both matriarchy and the cult of the dead are characteristic also of Atlantic Europe and western Libya. And the death cult has left intriguing signs of its existence throughout Neolithic and Bronze Age Europe. Thus the mysterious symbol of the maze, found ubiquitously in antiquity, seems to depict the journey (like that of Theseus in the Cretan Labyrinth) into the land of the dead. This labyrinth or maze-cult was always associated with the Aegean region; and even until the nineteenth century peasant children in England performed a dance along a maze pattern which was called a "Troy Dance." In Etruria a medallion was discovered, from the sixth century BC, bearing a maze symbol upon which was written — backwards — the word "Troy." We should note here of course that Troy itself, Troy 2, was a major centre during the Early Bronze Age.

When considering the source of the military threat against which the Early Hellads raised their huge coastal fortifications, we need to think of Atlantic Europe and Atlantic North Africa, where a mighty seafaring culture, contemporary with Early Bronze Age Greece, is also attested. And this of course brings us into altogether deeper water, in more ways than one. For we are reminded here of the great power from the Atlantic spoken of by the Egyptian priest to Solon which sought to subdue Greece and which was repulsed by the Greeks only after a desperate struggle. But the victory of the Greeks was a hollow one: for shortly thereafter they, like the Atlanteans, were struck by a terrible catastrophe which annihilated most of the Aegean population and all but obliterated the memory of their fight with the westerners.

Appendix

Phaeton's Fire and Heracles' Labors

We noted in Chapter 1 that the Greeks regarded the foundation of the Olympic Games as marking the beginning of their history. That event has been traditionally dated to 776 BC. Yet as Benny Peiser proved in the 1990s, the latter date cannot be regarded as properly historical and is the result of retrocalculation during the Hellenistic epoch.[1] It is nevertheless true that the Olympiads were viewed as an event of the Heroic Age and were very specifically linked to the god-hero Heracles.

I have described Heracles as a god-hero because the deeds associated with him were not that of a man but of a deity. His famous Twelve Labors, as we have mentioned, are rather obviously connected with the twelve signs of the zodiac and therefore also with the twelve months of the year. The deeds performed by him during these Labors are not those of a man. He holds the heavens on his shoulders, briefly relieving the titan Atlas of the burden. He pushes apart the two great rocks which stand guard over the entrance to the Mediterranean, Abila and Calpe, two rocks which henceforth bear his name. He sails in the golden bowl of the sun — the solar disc — across the waters of Ocean, where he despoils the mystical realm of the dead. He aids the Olympian gods in their titanic clash with the giants; and it is he and he alone who saves the gods and destroys the attackers. Everywhere, he is said

---

1 B. J. Peiser, "The Crime of Hippias. Zur Kontroverse um die Olympionikenliste," *STADION. International Journal of the History of Sport*, XVI, 1 (1990) pp. 37-65 and B. J. Peiser *Das Dunkle Zeitalter Olympias* (Peter Lang, London, 1993)

to have changed the courses of rivers, to have thrown down the walls of cities and to have rained his deadly arrows on whole countries.

What, the casual reader might ask, could all this mean?

The answer is no mystery: There existed in Greece a great body of material which told of some vast upheaval of nature, or rather series of upheavals of nature, that had struck the whole region in antiquity. Legend spoke of floods and conflagrations of truly cosmic dimensions, events which shook the earth. Indeed the Greeks told of several great Floods or Deluges which had wiped out most of humanity. Two of the best-known were those of Deucalion and Ogyges. But many other inundations were mentioned. The god Poseidon, for example, was said to have fought a great battle with Athena over possession of Attica; and when the goddess was given the territory, he sent in vengeance huge waves that covered the entire coastal plain.[1] In the same way, when king Laomedon of Troy refused to pay Apollo his due for the construction of the city walls, Poseidon flooded both the town and the entire countryside. We are told that he "directed all his seas to the shores of miserly Troy, flooding the earth till it was indistinguishable from the waters, sweeping away the farmers' possessions, and overwhelming the fields with his waves."[2] Such tidal waves are mentioned throughout the Heroic Age. Thus Jason and his Argonauts, on their voyage home to Greece, were driven by a storm towards the coast of Libya, when an enormous wave lifted the Argo above the perilous rocks which lined the coast, leaving it high and dry a mile or so inland.[3] Again, Theseus' son Hippolytus was overcome by another such wave, at the Molurian Rock, also sent by Poseidon,[4] and the latter deity, who was the god of the sea, was also known as the "Earthshaker." Why should a god of earthquakes also be regarded as the god of the sea? The answer to this question appears to be: Because the shaking of the earth seems to have regularly raised vast tsunamis. In classical times travelers to the Greek islands and coastal regions were shown marker stones at elevated levels on hillsides which identified the high-point of some of these ancient tides. Often they were hundreds of feet above sea level.

Legend also spoke of world-wide conflagrations, events which seem to give an eye-witness description of the destructions uncovered by the spades of the archaeologists. Indeed, according to the Greeks, the earth was periodically and alternately afflicted by catastrophes of fire and water. These events

---

1 Herodotus, viii, 55, and Apollodorus, iii, 14, 1.
2 Ovid, *Metamorphoses*, xi, 190-205
3 Apollonius Rhodius, iv, 1228-1460
4 Pausanias, ii, 32, 8; Euripides, *Hippolytus* 1193 ff.

were believed to have terminated each World Age. "There is a period," said the Roman writer Censorinus, "called 'the supreme year' by Aristotle, at the end of which the sun, moon, and all the planets return to their original position. This 'supreme year' has a great winter, called by the Greeks *kataklysmos*, which means deluge, and a great summer, called by the Greeks *ekpyrosis*, or combustion of the world. The world, actually, seems to be inundated and burned alternately in each of these epochs."[1] The most dramatic of these conflagration-stories is that of Phaeton, the "Blazing One." The story is so well-known that it needs no repetition here. Suffice to say that Phaeton, child of the sun-god Helios, persuaded his father to permit him to drive the solar chariot for a day. Unable however to control the wild steeds which pulled the blazing disc, the sun came careering towards the earth, which burst into flame. The most vivid account of this myth comes in Ovid's *Metamorphoses*, where we hear of how rivers evaporated, forests burned, mountains spewed fire, and deserts — such as the Sahara — were created. We read:

> The earth caught fire, starting from the highest parts. With all its moisture dried up, it split and cracked in gaping fissures. The meadows turned ashy grey; trees, leaves and all were consumed in a general blaze, and the withered crops provided fuel for their own destruction. But these were trifles to complain of, compared with the rest. Great cities perished, their walls burned to the ground, and whole nations with all their different communities were reduced to ashes. The woods on the mountains were blazing, Athos was on fire, Cilician Taurus and Timolus, Oeta and Ida, a mountain once famous for its springs, but now quite dry. Helicon, the Muses' haunt, was burning, and Haemus, later to be linked with Orpheus' name. Etna's flames were redoubled, and shot to immense heights, the twin peaks of Parnassus and Eryx and Cynthus were alight, Othrys and Rhodope, destined at last to lose its snows, Mimas and Dindyma and Mycale and Cithaeron, the natural abode of sacred rites. Scythia did not escape, in spite of its chilly clime, Caucasus was in flames and Ossa too, and Pindus; Olympus, a greater mountain than either of these, was ablaze, as were the airy Alps and cloud-capped Apennines.
>
> Then, indeed, Phaethon saw every part of the world on fire, and found the scorching heat more than he could endure ...
>
> It was then, so men believe, that the Ethiopians acquired their dark skins; for the blood rose to the surface of their bodies. It was then that Libya became a desert, when the heat dried up her waters, then the nymphs tore their hair, and lamented their vanished springs and lakes. Boeotia looked in vain for Dirce's fountain, Argos for Amymone, Ephyre for Pyrene's waters. The rivers, though they ran in more open channels, were no safer than the springs. Tanais steamed in the depths of his waters, and so did aged Peneus, Mysian Caicus and swift Ismenus. Arcadian Erymanthus suffered, and Xanthus, who was later to be consumed by fire a second time: yellow Lycormas too, and Maeander who flows in looping curves, Thracian Melas and Spartan Eurotas. Euphrates, the river of Babylon, was kindled also, Orontes and swift-running Thermodon, Ganges and Phasis and Hister; Alphaeus boiled, Spercheus' banks were all aflame, the

---

1 Censorinus, *Liber de die natali*, xviii

gold that Tagus carries in his stream was molten by the fires, and the river birds, for whose singing Maeonia's banks are famous, found no coolness in Cayster's pools. The Nile was terrified and, fleeing to the ends of the earth, hid his head, which still is hidden. His seven mouths were left dusty and empty, seven channels without a river. The same fate dried up the waters of Ismarus, the Hebrus and the Strymon, as well as the rivers of Hesperia, the Rhine and the Rhone, the Po, and even the Tiber, which had been promised sovereign power.

Everywhere the ground gaped open, and the light descended through the cracks to Tartarus, frightening the king of the underworld, and his queen beside him. The seas contracted, and an expanse of barren sand appeared where there had lately been ocean. Mountains which had been submerged beneath deep waters rose above the surface, and increased the number of the scattered Cyclades. Fish swam down into the depths of their pools, and the dolphins did not dare to leap out into the air, arching their backs over the sea, as was their usual habit. Lifeless bodies of seals floated upturned on the top of the waves. They say that Nereus himself, and Doris and her daughters, as they lurked in their caves, found them warm.[1]

It has been noted by commentators throughout the centuries that the catastrophe of Phaeton seems to refer not only to a universal fire caused by the approach of some fiery cosmic body, but also to a simultaneous and universal outbreak of volcanic and earthquake activity. This is clearly indicated by the reference to the great fissures that opened in the earth, by the retreat of the sea, and by the increased activity of the volcano Etna.

These are details of immense importance in any attempt to understand the nature of these events.

The Greeks, as well as all other ancient peoples, believed that such occurrences afflicted the earth periodically, and they were equally clear in connecting them to conflicts or wars in the heavens among the gods — *theomachia*. This is graphically illustrated by Hesiod, who, in describing the battle between Zeus and the dragon-monster Typhon, says: "The huge earth groaned. ... A great part of the huge earth was scorched by the terrible vapor and melted as tin melts when heated by man's art ... or as iron, which is hardest of all things, is softened by glowing fire in mountain glens."[2]

There was, by the classical period, a general understanding that much or even most of ancient mythology related to these cosmic catastrophes. This is stated very explicitly by Plato, when, in his *Timaeus*, he has an Egyptian priest inform Solon of the cosmogonic meaning of the Phaeton story.

... in truth the story that is told in your country as well as ours, how once upon a time. Phaethon, son of Helios, yoked his father's chariot and, because he was unable to drive it along the course taken by his father burnt up all that was upon the earth, and himself perished by a thunderbolt — that story, as it is told,

---

1 Ovid, *Metamorphoses* ii, 200-270
2 Hesiod, *Theogony*, ii, 856ff.

has the fashion of a legend, but the truth of it lies in the occurrence of a shift of the bodies in the heavens which move round the earth and a destruction of the things on the earth by fierce fire, which recurs at long intervals. At such times all they that dwell on the mountains, and in high and dry places, suffer destruction more than those who dwell near to rivers or the sea; and in our case the Nile, our savior in other ways, saves us also at such times from this calamity by rising high. And when, on the other hand, the Gods purge the earth with a flood of waters, all the herdsmen and shepherds that are in the mountains are saved, but those in the cities of your land are swept into die sea by the streams; whereas in our country neither then nor at any other time does the water pour down over our fields from above, on the contrary it all tends naturally to swell up from below.

Other writers, of later times, were equally clear as to the meaning of these tales. Thus according to Strabo the myth of Tantalus had as its origin a series of violent natural catastrophes, most especially terrible floods and earthquakes, which affected all of Lydia and Ionia. Entire villages, he said, disappeared, and Mount Sipylus was overturned. Marshes were converted into lakes, and Troy was submerged.[1] According to Pausanias, also, a city on Mount Sipylus disappeared into a chasm, which subsequently filled with water and became Lake Saloe, or Tantalis. The ruins of the city could be seen on the lake bottom until it was silted up by a mountain stream.[2] Pliny agreed that Tantalis was destroyed by an earthquake, and added the detail that three successive cities were built on its site before it was finally flooded.[3]

Whatever the precise cause of these catastrophes, it is evident that vast upheavals of nature which affected the entire planet were believed to have been brought about by unusual events in the cosmos; and it is remarkable that the record of these events, as preserved in ancient myth, has not been tied to the archaeological testimony, which speaks of vast destruction — by fire and by water — throughout the Near East during the Early Bronze Ages.[4] As already noted, archaeology has in fact identified a series of these upheavals. These begin with a cataclysm at the end of the Palaeolithic, or Old Stone Age, which created most of the enormous gaping volcanic crater at Thera. The Palaeolithic catastrophe was followed by other violent breaks at the end of the Neolithic and the first phase of the Early Bronze Age. Then came the catastrophe which terminated the Early Helladic epoch. And this catastrophe calls to mind the legend of Phaeton in a most striking way; for the

---

1 Strabo, i, 3, 17

2 Pausanias, vii, 24, 7

3 Pliny, *Natural History*, v, 31

4 The most comprehensive discussion of these catastrophes, from an archaeological perspective, is found in Claude Schaeffer's *Stratigraphie comparée et Chronologie de l'Asie occidentale, 3me et 2me millénnaires* (Oxford, 1948)

agent of destruction, it appears, was — generally speaking — fire. Thus we find that the great settlement at Lerna in the Argolid, with its magnificent House of the Tiles, was razed to the ground in some terrible conflagration. And Lerna's fate was shared by all its contemporaries. "An era was ended at Lerna with the burning of the [Early Helladic] House of the Tiles; and in the whole surrounding region there are evidences of a similar catastrophe ... it is extremely probable that the great round building at Tiryns, which has a roof of similar tiles, fell at the same time as the palace of Lerna III. There was a disaster also at nearby Asine, where one of the burnt buildings had been roofed likewise with tiles. ... A few miles further north, at Zygouries in the valley of Cleonae, houses of the same age were destroyed in a general conflagration."[1] On the other side of the Aegean the second city of Troy suffered a similar fate. The city was razed in what Schliemann described as a "fearful conflagration" that left a layer of hardened ash between five and ten feet deep across the site. So powerful was the fire that a thin "stratum of scoriae of melted lead and copper, from 0.5 to 1.5 inches thick" was left through the whole site at a depth of 28 to 29.5 feet.[2] The gold and silver jewelry of the so-called Treasure of Priam, which Schliemann discovered in the burned city, was found to have been damaged by the intense heat, with many objects welded together. So complete was the destruction, and so thick the layer of hardened ash, that it completely obscured the original layout of the city, and the walls of the subsequent settlement were planned and built in complete ignorance of the orientation of the walls and passageways below. "The more recent walls run in all directions above the more ancient ones, never standing upon them, and are frequently separated from them by a layer of calcined debris, from 6.5 to 10 feet thick."[3]

Half a century after Schliemann, an expedition from the University of Cincinnati returned to the site of Hisarlik. They made a thorough investigation of Schliemann's Burnt City, which by this time was no longer associated with the Trojan War of Homer but recognized as belonging to an earlier epoch.

> The stratum of Troy IIg had an average thickness of more than 1 meter; it consisted mainly of ashes, charred matter, and burned debris. This deposit apparently extended uniformly over the great megaron and across the entire site, eloquent evidence that the settlement perished in a vast conflagration from which no buildings escaped ruin. This is the 'Burnt City' of Schliemann ...

1 John L. Caskey, "Greece, Crete, and the Aegean Islands in the Early Bronze Age," in *CAH* Vol.1 part 2 (3rd ed.) p. 785
2 Schliemann, *Troy and its Remains* (London, 1875) pp. 16-7
3 Ibid., p. 302

> In all areas examined by the Cincinnati Expedition, it is obvious that the catastrophe struck suddenly, without warning, giving the inhabitants little or no time to collect and save their most treasured belongings before they fled. All the houses exposed were still found to contain the fire-scarred wreckage of their furnishings, equipment, and stores of supplies. Almost every building yielded scattered bits of gold ornaments and jewelry, no doubt hastily abandoned in panic flight.[1]

Flight, but flight from what? The sheer quantity of ash speaks of a natural disaster rather than enemy action. It must be remembered that this ash was calcined, i.e., compressed and hardened like stone; yet even in this state it was over three feet deep. The original depth of ash, to produce this thickness of hardened material, must have been immeasurably greater. The normal burning of a town would produce an ash layer no deeper than an inch or two, and time would compress and harden this to a stratum measured in millimeters. Evidently this fire was neither the result of enemy action nor accident; and in search of anything comparable we are drawn to Pompeii, where volcanic ash and cinders buried a large settlement to a considerable depth. As there are no active or even dormant volcanoes anywhere near Hisarlik, nor indeed near any of the contemporary sites across Anatolia and mainland Greece that shared Troy II's fate, then we must consider an event of world-wide dimensions. For the same tell-tale signs of massive destruction are found in every contemporary site throughout the Aegean and Anatolia. According to J. Mellaart, "The end of the E.B.2 period is marked in Western and Southern Anatolia by a catastrophe,"[2] and that the disappearance of human settlement in so many sites was the result of a disaster "is made clear by the burning of Troy II, Poliochni V, Beycesultan XIIIa, Kusura B, Tarsus, Ahlatlibel, Polatli I, the destruction of Demirci Hüyük and a few hundred other sites. In the Konya plain every town site of the E.B.2 period shows signs of conflagration, mostly followed by destruction .."[3]

Yet even this writer under -estimated the range and impact of the event: For this was a disaster felt far beyond the shores of the Aegean. Claude Schaeffer, one of the greatest archaeologists of his generation, came to Troy to compare the destruction there with what he himself had found at Ras Shamra, the ancient port of Ugarit on the Phoenician coast. He came to the conclusion that the earthquakes and conflagrations he had noted at Ras Shamra were synchronical with the earthquakes and conflagrations at Troy.

---

1 Blegen, *Troy and the Trojans* (London, 1963) p. 69
2 J. Mellaart, "Anatolia, c. 4000-2300 BC," in *CAH* Vol. 1, part 2 (3rd ed.) p. 406
3 Ibid., p. 407

He noted too that the same effects were observed at the same time over a vast area of the Mediterranean and Near East. "There is not the slightest doubt," he wrote, "that the conflagration at Troy II corresponds to the catastrophe that made an end to the habitations of the Old Bronze Age in Alaca Hüyük, of Alisar, of Tarsus, of Tepe Hissar [in Asia Minor], and to the catastrophe that burned ancient Ugarit (II) in Syria, the city of Byblos that flourished under the Old Kingdom of Egypt, the contemporaneous cities of Palestine, and that was among the causes which terminated the Old Kingdom of Egypt."[1]

The myth of Phaeton is therefore very definitely reflected in the archaeo-logical record, an event which seems to have occurred around 850 BC. This is a topic I have covered in detail elsewhere, and all that needs to be said here is that all these events seem to be linked, one way or another, to some form of comet or comet-activity, and that even the word disaster implies "evil star." Whether or not one follows Immanuel Velikovsky in attributing these events to actual disturbances in the planetary order, it is evident, from any honest consideration of the evidence, that a catastrophe or series of ca-tastrophes, of a magnitude far beyond the scale of anything in modern expe-rience, is indicated. According to Velikovsky, the earth had been threatened periodically during the Bronze Age by a giant comet which the ancients vari-ously referred to as a "smoking star" or "bearded star" or a star with a tail. One particularly graphic account of this body is given by the Roman writer Pliny, who had access to much scientific and philosophical literature of the ancients that is now lost. He named the comet "Typhon" and described it as "terrible" and likened it to a "ball of fire."[2] It was this comet's encounters with the earth, according to Velikovsky, which brought about the series of catastrophes recorded in all ancient myth. In his vastly controversial *Worlds in Collision*, Velikovsky argued that sometime early in the first millennium BC, this comet came into contact with another cosmic body, lost its tail — or was "decapitated" — and thereafter ceased to be a threat to mankind.[3]

According to Velikovsky, the comet, with its apparently serpentine body, was the origin of the dragon legend. To this fearsome deity hecatombs of human beings were offered in an attempt to avert further disaster. The "de-struction" or "decapitation" of the comet in the first millennium was a cause of celebration. Freed from the threat of imminent destruction, the peoples of the earth began to abandon the practice of human sacrifice. And sure enough, the great hero-deities of the time are all credited with outlawing this bar-

---

1 Schaeffer, loc. cit., p. 225
2 Pliny, *Natural History*, ii, 91.
3 See Velikovsky's *Worlds in Collision* (1950)

baric practice. Indeed, the disappearance of the comet brought about a social revolution. A whole new cosmology, mythology and philosophy developed. It could be argued that much — if not almost all — the ritual and religious custom found amongst the ancient peoples dated from this time. Along with the new mythologies and belief-systems, there arose new rituals and religious codes.

Early biblical history needs to be viewed in relation to these events — events which have now been effectively effaced from the textbooks. It can be demonstrated for example that to this epoch belongs the entire Moses *mythus.* He is the classic founder-figure; and basically all that we understand as Judaism derives from him. Whether or not there actually existed such a person as "Moses" is beside the point. What is important is that during some form of cosmic catastrophe, a new religious and legal code, presided over by a completely new god — Yahweh — appeared. In my *Pyramid Age* I examined the character of Moses in great detail and there produced manifold proofs showing him to be mythically identical to Heracles. Again, without going into the details, we should remember that Moses (the "son") has a mysterious birth, as does Heracles (whose father is the Zeus, the Roman Jove — identical apparently to Moses' Jehovah/Yahweh); Moses is the enemy of the serpent — he destroys the two serpents of the pharaohs' magicians, whilst Heracles strangles the two serpents sent by Hera to kill him in his cradle; Moses "pushes apart" the walls of water at the Sea of Passage, Heracles pushes apart the rock pillars at the entrance to the Mediterranean; Moses does not die, but ascends the sacred mountain to his father, whilst Heracles ascends to his father Zeus at the top of Mount Oeta; and so on.

Like Moses, Heracles was credited with initiating a religious revolution: He was, above all, the hero responsible for ending human sacrifice.

The Age of Moses was thus one and the same as the Age of Heracles. Now, it is true, as we noted in Chapter 3, that according to biblical chronology, Moses would have lived around the fifteenth century BC, and this might be seen as providing proof, independent of Egyptian chronology, for placing Heracles and the Heroic Age also in the fifteenth century. However, as I demonstrate in some detail in my *Pyramid Age* (following the lead provided by Professor Heinsohn), Egyptian chronology itself was based around that of the Old Testament, with Ramses II, for example, of the Nineteenth Dynasty, being placed circa 1400 BC because he was believed to have been the pharaoh of the Exodus (the Book of Exodus claims that the Israelite slaves had been forced to build a city called "Ramesses"). The fact that Heracles and the Heroic Age are thus placed, along with Moses, around the fifteenth or sixteenth centuries BC therefore demonstrates nothing other than the fact that Egyptian and by extension Heroic Age Greek chronology was constructed in order to agree with that of the Bible. In fact, as we have demonstrated in scores of ways in the present volume, the Age of Heracles, the Heroic Age, cannot be placed earlier than the ninth and eighth centuries BC, which means, in effect, that this is where the Exodus too needs to be placed. And indeed the catastrophe described so vividly in the Book of Exodus is rather obviously a Hebrew recalling of the very same events described in Greek tradition associated with Heracles. With this cataclysmic disaster a new World Age commenced.

The inauguration of the World Age was marked everywhere by new religious codes, regulations and festivities.

It has long been known that many types of sports and sporting events had their origins in ritual re-enactments of cosmic events. This is seen perhaps most obviously in the various types of Mesoamerican ball games. In these, the players were specifically identified as deities, and the game usually ended with the sacrifice, often by decapitation, of the losing team. In Maya legend, for example, the Ballgame of the Heavenly Twins against the Gods of the Underworld, recounted in the Popol Vuh, has clear catastrophic associations. We hear that, "On the way to Xibalba, the underworld, One Hunahpu and Seven Hunahpu throw a heavenly 'ball' at one another. The impact of this ball is so powerful that it results in an earthquake. This seismic event indicates that the ballgame was not an ordinary contest. The gods of the underworld, Hun Came (One Death) and Vukuh Came (Seven Death) feel provoked by the crashing bang of the impacting ball. 'What's happening on the face of the earth? They're just stamping and shouting. They should be summoned to play ball here. We'll defeat them, since we simply get no deference from them. They show no respect, nor do they have any shame. They're really determined to run right over us!... They must come. Would that they might come play ball with us here ... and they should bring their playthings, their yokes and arm guards should come, along with the rubber ball.'"[1]

Such "sporting" events were at one time prevalent all over the world; including in Greece. We moderns tend to imagine the Olympiads as an athletics festival pure and simple and view the ancient celebrations as an earlier

---

1 Benny Peiser, "Cosmic Catastrophes and the Ballgame of the Sky Gods in Mesoamerican Mythology," *Society for Interdisciplinary Studies: Chronology and Catastrophism Review: Proceedings of Braziers College Conference* (1995) p. 31

version of the modern event. Yet nothing could be further from the truth. For the Greeks, particularly for the early Greeks, the Olympiads were above all a religious festival; and its religious character becomes very obvious after even a rudimentary examination of its nature and origins. Not only were the festivities established by a deity, Heracles, but every aspect of their ritual and management was surrounded by the strictest religious protocols. And we must bear in mind that the Olympiads were merely one of many religiously-inspired sporting festivals found in almost every ancient culture that we care to examine. Even in Greece itself there were rival festivals to the Olympiads, all of which were established by deities or at least semi-divine hero-figures. There was, for example, the Isthmian Games at Corinth, founded by Sisyphus,[1] and the Pythian Games at Delphi, in honor of Apollo. Outside of Greece, the Romans celebrated the Equiria in February and these, held on the Campus Martius, the "Plain of Mars," were established by Romulus — apparently in the eighth century BC — in honor of the war god himself. The Celts held similar sacred games; and even well into the Christian epoch the Irish marked the Aonach Tailteann, the Tailton Games, held near Tara, in honor of the god Lugh (Lugos). There is some evidence too that the Britons celebrated a similar festival in the vicinity of Stonehenge, for even as late as the eighteenth century local youths held there, at regular intervals, a ball-game very similar to hockey or the Scottish shinty.[2]

There can be little doubt that these festivals, all dating either from the ninth or eighth century BC, were ritual re-enactments of a cosmic battle witnessed by the peoples of the earth, a cosmic battle apparently between a dragon-deity (comet-deity) and the hero-god who decapitated it.[3]

The establishment of the Olympiads was associated with a reform of the calendar. This is implied in the fact that they were held every four years — evidently marking the extra day, the Leap Year, added every four years, to keep the civic calendar aligned to the sidereal. Heracles' link to a new calendar is implied also in his performance of the Twelve Labors, the twelve months of the year; and along with his calendar reforms, he was linked too with a plethora of new customs, beliefs and practices. Classicist Robert Graves connected him with the introduction of a new alphabet or system of annotation. He noted too that the same character was linked to dramatic changes in religious observance, most notably to the abolition — in most

---

1 Apollodorus, iii, 4, 3, and Pausanias, ii, 1, 3.

2 See my *Arthur and Stonehenge* (2001).

3 Heracles' decapitation of the hydra, a dragon-monster, clearly identifies him with Perseus, as does his rescue of the Trojan king Laomedon's daughter from the sea monster — exactly parallel to Perseus' rescue of Andromeda.

circumstances — of human sacrifice, and he was convinced that Heracles' enmity to the goddess Hera was indicative of the rejection of an earlier more matriarchal religious system, a system described by Graves and others in great detail.

Thus the Heracles myth is widely believed to mark a veritable revolution in religious belief and practice. And other heroes of the time, from the various cities and territories, shared many of the characteristics of the son of Zeus. They too were enemies of the goddess and the dragon; they too were connected with the founding of religious and athletic festivals; and they too were looked upon as the founders of a revised calendar and writing system. Often they were also credited with introducing new systems of weights and measures, new technologies and arts, as well as, crucially, new legal codes. Such, for example, as we have seen, was the case with Theseus of Athens, Minos of Crete, and many others. All of these were regarded as contemporaries of Heracles.

The cataclysm described in the Book of Exodus (Ten Plagues and opening of the Red Sea) and in Greek myth (Flood of Ogyges and Phaeton) was the last in a series that had periodically afflicted the earth from the end of the Pleistocene (Old Stone Age) right through to the termination of the Early Bronze Age. In various publications I have argued that the whole custom of blood (and human) sacrifice owed its origins to the psychological trauma of these events. (See for example my *Pyramid Age*). Terrified and unable to fully comprehend what was happening, people fell back upon a potent expedient: Sacrificial propitiation. The gods of the sky delight in death and destruction: What if we voluntarily offer them the blood they seem to desire? Perhaps then they might leave the world in peace. Thus were constructed the first temples and shrines, where the altar, upon which were immolated the hapless victims, was invariably upon a raised platform or hilltop, all the nearer to the heavenly deities, chief amongst which was the Cosmic Serpent, the Great Dragon.[1] Thus the first pyramids were little more than very large altars for sacrifice.

Throughout the Early Bronze Age, which in Hindu cosmology is actually termed the "Age of Sacrifice," such bloody offerings continued atop the raised platforms. Yet at some point, towards the end of the Age of Sacrifice, the threat from the sky was removed: the Cosmic Serpent was slain or decapitated, and the Age of Sacrifice came to an end. The peoples of the

---

1 See for example Victor Clube and Bill Napier, *The Cosmic Serpent: A Catastrophist View of Earth History* (London, 1982).

earth celebrated; a new World Age was initiated. The heroes of the time —
characters such as Moses, Heracles, Theseus, Arthur (Artos the Bear God)
— were remembered for having put an end to human sacrifice. Stability had
been restored to the solar system and the Sword of Damocles which had
hung over the heads of humanity for so long had been lifted. Men celebrated.
They commemorated in religious and athletic festivals the destruction of the
dragon, and they raised temples in which to perform these rituals. These
temples could be built of stone, for men were now convinced they would
endure. Yet the earth was still beset by vast and frequent tremors. The new
temples, shrines and fortresses had to be built to withstand these. And so
was invented the "megalithic" style of architecture.

One of the most outstanding characteristics of the Mycenaean period
was the custom of building using enormous polygonal blocks of stone. The
walls of Mycenae itself are a prime example of the *genre*, and these were said
by Homer to have been "raised by the hand of giants for god-like kings of old."
The giants in question were the cyclops, sons of Poseidon, the "Earthshaker,"
who piled the stones on top of each other at the behest of Perseus.

Now these cyclopean or megalithic ("great stone") structures had their
counterparts all over the world. In Western Europe, at a similar time, men
began to raise great numbers of enormous tumuli, the most outstanding example of which is perhaps Stonehenge. It is recognized that Stonehenge is
roughly contemporary with Mycenae at its peak, and parallels between the
two cultures and architectural-styles have long been observed. Yet scholars
have denied any definite link between the two and have shied away even
from the idea of common inspiration.

But the custom of raising walls of giant and often interlocking stone
blocks appeared at one time over almost the entire earth. Everyone is familiar with the most spectacular examples of these: the pyramids of Egypt and
the megalithic structures of Central and South America. The case of the latter is the most interesting. Here the construction of megalithic walls began
long before the time of the Incas. No one is sure exactly when, but it is generally believed to have commenced early in the first millennium BC. The walls
of these early temples and fortresses present a truly astonishing sight, with
blocks of stone sometimes weighing over fifty tons cut into polygonal interlocking shapes — like jigsaw pieces — with an amazing degree of precision.
How such blocks could have been cut and lifted into position is itself a wonder that has never been fully explained. The Incas, the inheritors of the civilization of these ancient masons, continued to build in the style of their ances-

tors, though the stones they used were considerably smaller. Nevertheless, there is no question at all as to why both the Incas and their predecessors built in such a style: this was the only way they could ensure the structures would withstand the vast earth tremors that periodically shook the Andean Cordillera. They were built to be earthquake-proof.

The walls of Mycenae, built by the sons of the Earthshaker Poseidon, were constructed in a similar fashion for exactly the same reason.

It should be noted that Britain, now one of the least seismically-active regions of the earth, had legends of enormous earthquakes, which caused vast irruptions of the sea and drowning of landmasses. And it needs to be pointed out that the enormous lintels at Stonehenge are attached to the uprights with mortise and tenon joints. Such joints are nowadays completely redundant, as the fiercest force which nature can now throw at the building is gale-force winter winds. But in an earlier age, an age recalled by British tradition, much greater forces were at play: And it was against these that Stonehenge was secured.

TABLE 2. BRONZE AGE AND IRON AGE CONTEMPORARIES

DATE	BRONZE AGE DEFINITION	IRONAGE DEFINITION
	Early Helladic II	
850 BC	Catastrophe	
	Early Helladic III	
	Middle Helladic I	Protogeometric
	Middle Helladic II and III	Early Geometric
750	Late Helladic I (Early Mycenaean)	Middle Geometric
	Late Helladic II	
	Late Helladic III	Late Geometric
650		Archaic

TABLE 3. REVISED CHRONOLOGY OF GREECE
SHOWING MAJOR EVENTS

Date	MAJOR PERSONALITIES AND EVENTS	EPOCHS
	"Eumolpus"	"ATLANTEAN" WAR
850 BC	GREAT CATASTROPHE	
	"Perseus" and "Danaus"	
800		
	(Introduction of Alphabet)	
	Pelops (Chariot introduced to Greece)	ANATOLIANS SETTLE IN PELOPONNESE
	(Grave Circle B at Mycenae)	
750		
	Atreus and Thyestes	SACK OF THEBES
	Agamemnon (Grave Circle A at Mycenae)	TROJAN WAR
700	Orestes	
	Tisamenus	DORIAN INVASION
	Pheidon (Construction of Tholos Tombs at Mycenae)	
650		
		RISE OF THE TYRANTS
600		

TABLE 4. REVISED CHRONOLOGIES OF GREECE, EGYPT AND ISRAEL

DATE BC.	GREECE	EGYPT	ISRAEL
	Early Helladic	Third Dynasty	Egyptian Exile.
850	GREAT FIRE	INTERMEDIATE AGE	EXODUS
	Middle Helladic I	Fourth Dynasty Cheops	Age of Wandering
800	Perseid Dynasty	Chephren	
			Joshua. Conquest of Canaan
	Pelopid Dynasty	Hyksos (also Sixth) Dynasty. King Sargon I	
750		Pepi I	Epoch of the Judges
	Atreus and Thyestes	Pepi II/Apopi II (Naram-Sin)	
	Agamemnon and Trojan War	Expulsion of the Hyksos. Ahmose and rise of Eighteenth Dynasty	King Samuel and David
700		Amenhotep I	
	Dorian Invasion. Founding of Ionic colonies.	Hatshepsut	King Solomon
		Thutmose III	Division of Israel into Northern and Southern Kingdoms
650	Pheidon of Argos. Construction of great tholos tombs at Mycenae.	Amenhotep II	
	Rebellions against the Dorians. Rise of the Tyrants.	Amenhotep III	Asa, king of Judah and Baasha, king of Israel

BIBLIOGRAPHY

BOOKS

Akurgal, Ekrem, *Die Kunst Anatoliens von Homer bis Alexander* (Berlin, 1961)

Blegen, C. W., *Troy and the Trojans* (New York and London, 1963)

Blegen, C. W., and M. Rawson, *The Palace of Nestor at Pylos in western Messenia*, 6 Vols. (Princeton, 1966)

Blegen, C. W., *Korakou, a Prehistoric Settlement near Corinth* (Boston, 1921)

Blegen, C. W., John L. Caskey, and M. Rawson, *Troy*, 6 Vols. (Princeton, 1958)

Boardman, J., *The Cretan Collection in Oxford* (Oxford University Press, 1961)

Boardman, John, *Early Greek Vase Painting* (Thames and Hudson, 1998)

Borovka, G., *Scythian Art* (London, 1928)

Bowra, Maurice, *Homer and his Forerunners* (Edinburgh, 1955)

Brea, L. B., *Sicily Before the Greeks* (New York, 1966)

Burn, A. R., *Minoans, Philistines and Greeks* (London, 1930)

Carpenter, Rhys, *Discontinuity in Greek Civilization* (Cambridge University Press, 1966)

Chadwick, J., *The Decipherment of Linear B* (London, 1958)

Clube, Victor and Bill Napier, *The Cosmic Serpent: A Catastrophist View of Earth History* (London, 1982)

Cook, R. M., *Greek Painted Pottery* (London, 1997)

Curtius, E. and F. Alder, (eds.) *Olympia, Die Ergebnisse der von dem deustchen Reich veranstalteten Ausgrabungen*, 10 vols. (Berlin, 1890-7)

Desborough, V. R. D'A., *The Last Mycenaeans and their Successors* (Oxford, 1964)

Desborough, V. R. D'A., *The Greek Dark Ages* (London, 1972)

Dörpfeld, Wilhelm, *Alt-Olympia* 2 Vols. (Berlin, 1935)

169

Dörpfeld, Wilhelm, *Homers Odyssee, die Wiederherstellung des ursprünglichen Epos*, 2 Vols. (Munich, 1925)

Evans, Arthur, *The Palace of Minos at Knossos*, 7 Vols. (1921-35)

Froedin, O. and A. W. Perssons, *Asine: Results of the Swedish Excavations 1922-1930* (Stockholm, 1938)

Galinsky, G. Karl, *Aeneas, Sicily and Rome* (Princeton, 1969)

Ginzberg, L., *Legends of the Jews*, 7 Vols. (1961 ed.)

Gjerstad, E., *The Swedish Cyprus Expedition, 1927-1931* (Stockholm, 1934)

Graves, Robert, *The Greek Myths*, 2 Vols. (Penguin, 1955)

Griffo, P. and L. von Matt, *Gela: The Ancient Greeks in Sicily* (Greenwich, Connecticut, 1968)

Hall, H. R., *Aegean Archaeology* (London, 1915)

Hampe, Ronald and Erika Simon, *The Birth of Greek Art* (Thames and Hudson, 1981)

Hawkes, Jacquetta, *Dawn of the Gods* (London, 1968)

Heinsohn, Gunnar, *Die Sumerer gab es nicht* (Mantis Verlag, 1988)

Heubeck, Alfred, *Die homerische Frage* (Darmstadt, 1988)

Higgins, Reynold, *Minoan and Mycenaean Art* (3rd ed, London, 1997).

Jeffrey, L. H., *The Local Scripts of Archaic Greece* (Oxford, 1961)

Lacy, A. D., *Greek Painted Pottery in the Bronze Age* (London, 1967)

Langlotz, Ernst, *The Art of Magna Graecia* (Eng. Trans, Thames and Hudson, 1965)

Lorimer, Helen L., *Homer and the Monuments* (London, 1950):

Minns, E. H., *Scythians and Greeks* (Cambridge, 1913)

Mylonas, G., *Mycenae and the Mycenaean Age* (Princeton, 1966)

Nilsson, M. P., *Homer and Mycenae* (London, 1933)

Ogilvie, R. M., *Early Rome and the Etruscans* (Fontana Books, 1976)

Page, Denys L., *History and the Homeric Iliad* (Berkeley, California, 1959)

Peiser, B. J., *Das Dunkle Zeitalter Olympias* (Peter Lang, London, 1993)

Petrie, Flinders, *The Making of Egypt* (London, 1939)

Rice, T. T., *The Scythians* (New York, 1957)

Rostovzeff, M., *Iranians and Greeks in South Russia* (Oxford, 1922)

Schaeffer, Claude, *Stratigraphie comparée et chronologie de l'Asie occidentale; 3me et 2me millénnaires* (Oxford, 1948)

Schliemann, Heinrich, *Tiryns* (London, 1886)

Schliemann, Heinrich, *Troy and its Remains* (London, 1875)

Schweitzer, Bernhard, *Geometric Greek Art* (English trans. Phaidon Press, London, 1971)

Sweeney, Emmet, *Arthur and Stonehenge: Britain's Lost History* (Domra Publications, 2001)

Sweeney, Emmet, *The Ramessides, Medes and Persians* (2nd ed. New York, 2007)

Sweeney, Emmet, *The Genesis of Israel and Egypt* (2nd ed. New York, 2008)

Sweeney, Emmet, *The Pyramid Age* (2nd ed. New York, 2007)

Torr, Cecil, *Memphis and Mycenae* (Isis Publications, London, 1988)

Velikovsky, Immanuel, *Ages in Chaos* (New York and London, 1953)

Velikovsky, Immanuel, *Oedipus and Akhnaton* (New York and London, 1960)

Velikovsky, Immanuel, *Worlds in Collision* (New York and London, 1950)

Ventris, M. and J. Chadwick, *Documents in Mycenaean Greek* (London, 1956)

Von Vacano, O. W., *The Etruscans in the Ancient World* (trans. S. Ogilvie, Bloomington, 1965)

Webster, T. B. L., *From Mycenae to Homer* (London, 1958)

ARTICLES

Barnett, R. D., "The Sea Peoples," in *The Cambridge Ancient History* Vol.2 part 2 (3rd ed.)

Bethe, E., "Troja, Mykene, Agamemnon und sein Grosskönigtum," *Rheinisches Museum* 80 (1931)

Caskey, John L., "Greece and the Aegean Islands in the Middle Bronze Age" in *The Cambridge Ancient History* Vol. 2 part 1 (3rd ed)

Chadwick, J., "The Linear Scripts and the Tablets as Historical Documents" in *The Cambridge Ancient History* Vol. 2 part 1, (3rd ed)

Desborough, V. R. D'A., "The End of Mycenaean Civilization and the Dark Age: (a) The Archaeological Background," in *The Cambridge Ancient History* Vol. 2 part 2 (3rd ed)

Dunbabin, T. J., "Minos and Daidalos in Sicily," *Papers of the British School in Rome*, Vol. XVI. New Series, Vol. III (1948)

Edgar, C. C., "The Pottery" in *Excavations at Phylakopi in Melos* [supplementary paper no. 4] of *Journal of Hellenic Studies* (London, 1904)

Evans, A., "Mycenaean Cyprus as Illustrated in the British Museum Excavations," *Journal of the Royal Anthropological Institute*, XXX (1900)

Frickenhaus, A., "Die Hera von Tiryns," in *Tiryns*, Vol. 1 (Athens, 1912)

Gadd, C. J., "The Dynasty of Agade and the Gutian Invasion," in *The Cambridge Ancient History* Vol.1 part 2 (3rd ed.)

Götze, Albrecht, "The Sins of Madduwata," *Madduwattas* (Wissenschaftliche Buchgesellschaft, Darmstadt, 1968).

Götze, Albrecht, "The Hittites and Syria (1300-1200 BC)," in *The Cambridge Ancient History* Vol. 2 part 2 (3rd ed)

Gurney, O. R., "Anatolia, c.1600-1380 BC," in *The Cambridge Ancient History* Vol.2 part 1 (3rd ed.)

Hammond, N. G. L., "The Literary Tradition for the Migrations" in *The Cambridge Ancient History*, Vol. 2 part 2 (3rd ed)

Hawkins, J. David and Donald F. Easton, "A Hieroglyphic Seal from Troy," *Studia Troica* 6 (1996)

James, T. G. H., "Egypt: From the Expulsion of the Hyksos to Amenophis I," in *The Cambridge Ancient History* Vol.2 part 2 (3rd ed.)

Jeffery, L. H., "Greek alphabetic writing," in *The Cambridge Ancient History* Vol. 3 part 1 (3rd ed.)

John L. Caskey, "Greece, Crete, and the Aegean Islands in the Early Bronze Age," in *The Cambridge Ancient History* Vol.1 part 2 (3rd ed.)

Lorimer, H. L., "Homer and the Art of Writing: A Sketch of Opinion between 1713 and 1939," *American Journal of Archaeology* 52 (1948)

Mellaart, J., "Anatolia, c. 4000-2300 BC," in *The Cambridge Ancient History* Vol. 1, part 2 (3rd ed.)

Murray, A. S., "Excavations at Enkomi," in A. S. Murray, A. H. Smith, H. B. Walters, *Excavations in Cyprus* (London, 1900)

Oakeshott, N. R., "Horned-head Vase Handles," *Journal of Hellenic Studies*, 86 (1966)

Page, D., "The Historical Sack of Troy," *Antiquity*, Vol. XXXIII (1959)

Peiser, B. J., "The Crime of Hippias. Zur Kontroverse um die Olympionikenliste," *STADION. International Journal of the History of Sport*, XVI, 1 (1990)

Peiser, B. J., "Cosmic Catastrophes and the Ballgame of the Sky Gods in Mesoamerican Mythology," *Society for Interdisciplinary Studies: Chronology and Catastrophism Review: Proceedings of Braziers College Conference* (1995)

Peiser, B. J., "Re-Creating the Dark Ages of Greece: Fatal Flaws in the New Chronology,"

Petrie, Flinders, "Notes on the Antiquities of Mykenae," *Journal of Hellenic Studies*, XII (1891)

Pottier, E., "Observations sur la céramique mycenienne," *Revue Archéologique*, 28 (1896) pp. 19-23.

Ramsay, W. M., "A Study of Phrygian Art," *Journal of Hellenic Studies*, IX (1888)

Reinach, S., "La représentation du galop dans l'art ancient et moderne," *Revue archéologique*, 3e série, tome XXXVIII (1901)

Snodgrass, A. M., "The Balkans and the Aegean: Central Greece and Thessaly," in *The Cambridge Ancient History*, Vol. 3 part 1 (3rd ed)

Stubbings, Frank, "The Rise of Mycenaean Civilisation," in *The Cambridge Ancient History* Vol.2 part 1 (3rd ed.)

Tovar, A., "On the Position of the Linear B Dialect," in E. L. Bennet, Jr. (ed.) *Mycenaean Studies*, (University of Wisconsin Press, 1964).

Velikovsky, Immanuel, "Theses for the Reconstruction of Ancient History," monograph, *Scripta Academia* (Jerusalem, 1945)

Venedikov, Ivan, "Thracian Royal Tombs," in Ivan Marazov (ed.) *Ancient Gold: The Wealth of the Thracians* (Harry N. Abrams, Inc., 1997)

INDEX